One Man and His Dig

VALENTINE LOW

One Man and His Dig
Adventures of an Allotment Novice

POCKET
BOOKS

LONDON • SYDNEY • NEW YORK • TORONTO

First published in Great Britain in 2008 by Pocket Books
An imprint of Simon & Schuster UK Ltd
A CBS COMPANY

1 3 5 7 9 10 8 6 4 2

Simon & Schuster UK Ltd
Africa House
64–78 Kingsway
London WC2B 6AH

www.simonsays.co.uk

Simon & Schuster Australia
Sydney

A CIP catalogue record for this book is available
from the British Library.

ISBN: 978-1-84739-128-5

Typeset in Horley OS by M Rules
Printed and bound in Great Britain by
Cox & Wyman Ltd, Reading, Berks

To Eliza

Acknowledgements

I am for ever indebted to John Thompson, who sowed the seed, and Humfrey Hunter, who watered it.

I am also grateful for the assistance provided by David Beasley, Librarian, the Goldsmith's Company.

Contents

1

In the Beginning

Few things taste better than a dish of new young vegetables,
lovingly cooked. No need for meat or apologies.

Jane Grigson, *Jane Grigson's Vegetable Book*

I can remember with the utmost clarity where I was when the
penny dropped. My wife Eliza and I were having dinner with
friends in west London, a couple who live in one of those streets
that occupy the no man's land between the moderately fashionable (David Cameron is only a few streets away) and the utterly
hopeless (the local park is one of those green spaces that seem to
have been created solely for the disposal of dog faeces and hypo-
dermic syringes; oh yes, and bombs too – one of the London
21/7 attackers dumped his device there after he lost his nerve).
The assembled company included a *Guardian* columnist and

novelist, a museum director, a garden designer, someone from the fashion business and a woman with a frightfully clever-sounding job in the film industry (Mrs Low, as it happens). Then there was me, a journalist on the London *Evening Standard*, an old-fashioned news man who in his time has reported from the war in Iraq, the tsunami in Thailand and New York in the aftermath of 9/11 (those were the career highs, of course; I would not be giving the full picture if I failed to mention rather less glorious episodes such as the week I spent as a young reporter pursuing Michael Jackson round the streets of London, or the fortieth-anniversary re-enactment of the evacuation of Dunkirk which I chose to mark by passing the entire Channel crossing being sick over the side of a Thames narrowboat).

Given such company, we should perhaps – if we had been acting to type – have spent the evening talking about Damien Hirst, or the new Ken Loach movie; or, if things got really desperate, schools and house prices. But we didn't: we talked about beans. Broad beans, to be precise – how to grow them, when they are going to be ready, and how best to cook them. Not to mention radishes (is there any way to stop the flea beetle eating the leaves?), spinach (how do you prevent it bolting?), tomatoes, courgettes, garlic and potatoes.

The idea that such a collection of people could spend their evening happily talking about the whys and wherefores of vegetable gardening would have seemed extraordinary just a few years ago. Now it is different; now vegetables are cool. Most of us gathered round the dinner table that night wouldn't normally be associated with dirt under the fingernails, but we had all become part of the new urban phenomenon that has seen increasing numbers of people take on allotments or turn their back yards into kitchen gardens as they embrace the joys of growing their own vegetables. Not so long ago having an allotment was definitely a minority pastime, up there with pigeon fancying and whippet racing – something indulged in by old men who wore flat caps and smoked roll-ups. Now everyone wants to do it. The garden designer and her museum director husband used to have an allotment in London, and now have one in Bath; the *Guardian* columnist had one down by the Thames, and has since converted his back garden into a vegetable-growing utopia; and as for my wife Eliza and myself, we had just got ourselves one down the road from our house in Shepherd's Bush, and were full of the enthusiasm of the newly converted. As gardeners go, we were not completely inexperienced – we had a few shrubs and flowers growing in the garden, and over the years had managed to raise a few tomatoes in pots outside the back door – but getting our hands on an allotment had opened our eyes to an exciting new world of vegetable husbandry. No sooner had we got our plot than we discovered how many people we knew were secret allotment-holders – friends whom we had assumed to be normal, regular members of society but turned out to have a passion for growing their own veg. There was the hairdresser (a fellow mother from our children's nursery school) and her photographer husband, the book-keeper, the yoga teacher, my cousin Jane and several hacks of my acquaintance. Everywhere I looked there were people who had an allotment, were on the waiting list for an allotment, or at the very least dreamed of getting an allotment. There was no doubt about it: we were on the crest of a Zeitgeist (I don't know if you can actually be on the crest of a Zeitgeist, but if you can, we were there).

The question is: why? Is there actually any point in growing your own vegetables? Isn't it all just a fashionable bit of foolishness, a fad we will all grow out of when the next big thing comes along? Allotment gardening is a tiring, frustrating, bothersome business, where you spend the whole year working your fingers to the bone in the cold and the wet only to find that a malign confederation of slugs, pigeons, blackfly, greenfly, whitefly, caterpillars and light-fingered local vandals has got to your produce before you, and even if you do manage to salvage some of your precious crops, they are usually deformed, discoloured and full of holes. And incredibly dirty. Let's be honest: the stuff in the shops is much better. It is clean, and fresh, and usually comes in a nice plastic packet which tells you which sun-drenched paradise it has been grown in. There are no surreptitious slugs hiding inside the cabbage leaves, like some long-forgotten Japanese soldier who hasn't been told that the war is over, and if you are really lucky someone has been kind enough to trim off all the unsightly bits, so that all you have to do is throw your Kenyan beans into a pan of boiling water, wait a couple of minutes and then eat and enjoy. What could be simpler?

And please don't tell me that you are saving money by growing your own vegetables. Have you seen the price of carrots in your local supermarket? Or potatoes? They practically give the things away. Yes, you might have to fork out a few bob if you want sugar snap peas from Guatemala in the middle of February, but then you wouldn't be eating them at all if it were not for the wonders of air freight. And when you consider the expenses you incur when growing your own veg – the seeds, the tools, the fertilisers (the prices some people charge for manure are a national outrage – at that rate it's a wonder the horses don't cut out the middle man and start selling it themselves) – there is no doubt in my mind that if you manage to save any money at all, it is a pitiably small amount. Then when one takes into account all the work that is involved – well, the whole thing makes no sense at all. It is madness, pure and simple, and I am going to give it up just as soon as I have got the onions in. And the broad beans, of course: it wouldn't do to miss out on the broad beans. And perhaps it would be fun to have some sugar snap peas again, so lovely and sweet that you have usually eaten the lot before you get home. Then there is the purple sprouting broccoli to consider, and the sweetcorn, not to mention the two varieties of squash I am hoping to try out this year. No, perhaps I won't give it all up quite yet. I'll give it another year.

Wind the clock back a couple of years. It is a cold, dark Sunday evening in November, and my wife Eliza and I have just got back from staying with her parents in the country. As usual, there's no food in the house: it is the end of the weekend, after all. But it shouldn't matter, because we live in west London, and if there is anything to be said for living in this multicultural urban jungle, it is the proliferation of ethnic food shops and convenience stores near us. Within about two minutes of our house there is Michael K Vegfruit, and the Continental Stores who own the place now that Michael K (or is it Mr Vegfruit?) has gone back to his native Cyprus. The Co-op is a couple of doors down, and if none of those will do there is always Damas Gate a couple of hundred yards in the other direction, and the Supreme Food & Wine directly opposite. No one needs to starve in Shepherd's Bush, they really don't.

But this was Sunday evening. Outside most of these shops there were long vegetable displays, rack after rack of salad and spuds and carrots and aubergines and what have you, and perhaps if you were driving past in a bit of a hurry, or rather on the short-sighted side, or perhaps just not paying very much attention – well, in those circumstances you might just about imagine making the mistake of thinking that you could rustle up some kind of supper from what was on offer. Iceberg lettuces that had long since seen better days. Carrots wrinkled with neglect. Mushrooms grown old and black and disappointed. All we wanted was to make a nice soup, but it simply wasn't on the cards. In the end we gave up, and bought one of those soups that come in squat Tetra Pak cartons, the ones which like to give the impression they are homemade but aren't like any homemade soup I have ever had. The good varieties had all gone, naturally, and all that was left were the ridiculous fancy ones, the ones dreamed up by marketing executives with too much time on their hands: parsnip, sweetcorn and coriander, perhaps, or courgette and swede surprise. I cannot remember what we went for in the end – some memories are best wiped clear from the system – but it was definitely something that set new standards in culinary horror. And I remember thinking this: that if we grew our own vegetables, we wouldn't have to put up with this kind of thing.

For most of us, vegetables are something we get in neat, shrink-wrapped packages from the supermarket. But it wasn't always like that. We are one of the first generations where people do not grow their own veg as a matter of course, and many people of my age have a memory of their parents or grandparents growing their own produce. It might have been just a little patch in the back garden where they had a few runner beans and perhaps the odd lettuce; perhaps it was a full-blown kitchen garden, with row after row of carrots and turnips, cabbages and cauliflowers, and sacks full of spuds to keep the family going through the winter. My own personal memory is of going to stay with my grandparents in Wiltshire as a small boy: on summer's days I would wander out the back door, through the orchard, past the old water trough – taking care not to let my bare legs brush against the stinging nettles – and then through a small gap in the trees (hazel? beech?) and into my grandfather's vegetable garden. I cannot remember much of what went on there, except that there were several beds, with grassy paths in between, and plants which I now reckon must have been runner beans growing up some kind of beanpole. And there was my grandfather – well, stepgrandfather actually, but he felt like the real thing to me – who in my mind's eye was always digging, or forking, or picking, or doing something grown-up and important. At mealtimes he would bring in the produce of the day for my granny to cook: and what I will never forget is how she would always save the water that the beans had been boiled in, and pour it into a teacup for him to drink with his lunch. It was green.

It is memories such as these which tend to give one a rather idealised, romantic view of the theory and practice of growing vegetables. For those without their own Proustian memories of the cabbage patches of their childhood, there is always Beatrix Potter to help them out. I am sure I am not the only person whose view of the idealised kitchen garden has been heavily influenced by that most seminal of works, *The Tale of Peter Rabbit*. As I write this I have borrowed my children's copy of the book to remind myself of exactly how it was depicted by Miss Potter: there were lettuces and French beans and radishes for a hungry rabbit to eat; a row of carrots, nice and straight and tapered, next to an old fork handle stuck in the ground on top of which a robin is perched; tomatoes growing in pots; a cold frame;

a bed full of young cabbages (untouched, I note, by any cabbage white caterpillars); a gooseberry cage, whose netting was nearly to prove so fatal for poor old Peter; a sieve, or riddle, which also nearly did for Peter; one of those nice old-fashioned metal watering cans, which provided an effective if damp hiding place for a rabbit on the run; and, finally, a tool shed and a scarecrow. We should not, of course, forget the central character, a charming and naughty rabbit with brown leather slippers and a blue waistcoat with brass buttons. Those who grow vegetables in the country, however, know that rabbits are not delightful little rascals who get put to bed with camomile tea, they are rapacious bastards who eat everything they can find and should be shot on sight. These days I have a lot more sympathy with Mr McGregor than I ever did as a child; he was, after all, only trying to feed his family.

Even in my most hopelessly romantic daydreams, though, I knew that if I did succeed in finding somewhere to grow vegetables, it would not be in some Beatrix Potter-inspired rural idyll. It would not be surrounded by fields and woods, there would be no lanes for rabbits to run down, or old fir trees where they could make their home; instead it would be in London, with all its noise and dirt and traffic, and I would just have to get used to it. Charming it may not be, but the soil in London would surely be just as fertile as anything that Mr McGregor had to contend with; and sun is sun, and rain is rain, and beans probably do not give a fig for charm.

Recently, however, I discovered something that rather cheered me up. Like most people I have always associated Beatrix Potter with the Lake District, but in fact she was brought up in Bolton Gardens, in Earls Court; and the original Peter Rabbit was a pet rabbit called Peter Piper which was bought for the young Beatrix from a pet shop in Uxbridge Road, Shepherd's Bush. It was probably only a couple of hundred yards from where we live, although it certainly is not a pet shop any more: a halal butcher, more like – poor Peter! – or possibly one of those wretched convenience stores that litter Uxbridge Road.

The moment I knew there was no turning back happened one Saturday at a birthday lunch thrown by friends. They have a reasonably large garden by London standards, about 100 feet or so, and the bottom third was given over to a vegetable patch. I stood and stared at it for a bit, then insisted that my hostess give me a guided tour, demanding a detailed commentary about each and every crop they had growing there. At the end, rather pointlessly and probably just because I could think of nothing else to say, I said that I wished we had an allotment. 'Well,' she said, as if it were the simplest thing in the world, 'you should get one.' It turned out that there was a site just around the corner, and if I dropped a letter to the secretary there was really no reason why Eliza and I should not get one.

Something dramatic must have happened to me that day, because by Monday afternoon I had tracked down the allotment secretary via Google, written her a suitably fawning letter and generally worked myself up into such a state of excitement that I was practically planning my crop rotation already.

The excitement lasted about a week. Having worked out the crop rotation we were on to our seed selection – dwarf French beans or climbing ones? Cherry tomatoes or beefsteak? – when we got The Letter. Anyone who has ever applied for an allotment knows what it is like to get The Letter: it is the one where the allotment secretary says, 'Thank you very much for your interest, but I am afraid that we are totally full at the moment, and there is in fact a waiting list with 400 names on it, or at least there would be were it not for the fact that several of the potential applicants have been waiting for so long that they have probably died of old age long before getting their hands on a plot, and so if you are really so naive as to believe you might get an allotment you had better think again.' Our particular letter went on to make a number of distinctly pointed remarks, to the effect that the people who really need and deserve allotments are elderly, do not have gardens of their own and are, not to put too fine a point on it, generally members of the deserving working classes, who would probably starve to death if they did not get some land on which to grow their potatoes. You, on the other hand, it implied, are quite obviously one of those *Guardian*-reading middle-class types who buy up all the houses round here, you probably work in the media and if I had it my way you would not be getting your allotment until sometime in late 2035.

The letter was not entirely negative, however: it added in a casual aside that there were some other allotments in the area, run by the Acton Gardening Association, and perhaps we ought to try them. I was immediately suspicious of this, naturally: what was wrong with the Acton Gardening Association? Did they have less stringent entry criteria? Had they indeed been taken over by the *Guardian*-reading classes? Or was there something wrong with their land? Perhaps it was riddled with industrial pollution, and had not produced a successful crop since around the abdication of Edward VIII.

But by then it was too late to back off: we were hooked. Having started trying to get ourselves an allotment there was simply no way we were going to give up, and so we composed a second letter, possibly even more fawning than the first, which was sent to the Acton Gardening Association. I cannot remember how long it took them to get back to us, but the answer was along similar lines to the first one: no vacancies at the moment, long waiting list, blah blah blah. It was a touch more positive than the first letter, though, and did not actually tell us to go away and stop bothering them. In fact it might even be said to have held out a whisper of a hint of a suggestion that if we played our cards right we might, one day, get ourselves an allotment.

Now, if I was to draw up a list of my strongest attributes, qualities like determination and perseverance would not necessarily be top of the list. Giving up at the first obstacle is not only a perfectly decent strategy for dealing with life's vicissitudes, but it is also the best way of avoiding wasting time on lost causes, and indeed is probably the only thing that has kept me sane all these years. My wife, on the other hand, is an entirely different kettle of fish. When things look hopeless she carries on fighting until the battle is absolutely, completely and irrevocably lost; then she carries on fighting a bit more, just in case. Given, therefore, the slim possibility that the Acton Gardening Association might actually give us a plot one day, Eliza embarked on a campaign of harassment to wear down their resistance. She wrote letters. She made phone calls. She made more phone calls. When she got tired of making phone calls, she roped me in to make some more. Gradually the Acton Gardening Association, in the form of its secretary, Michael Wale, began to weaken. By the time he got in contact with us to ask what, if they gave us a plot, we would be able to bring to the Association in terms of skills, we knew the battle was all but won. We had no idea what he was talking about, of course: was he enquiring about our pruning expertise? Our ability, using my journalistic experience, to produce an allotment newsletter? Or was he asking whether we would be able to do a turn at the allotment Christmas party?

Somehow, however, we managed to compose a letter that was not completely meaningless twaddle, and hoped for the best.

At last, around the end of October, we got the phone call. It was Michael Wale: somehow we were being offered a plot on the Bromyard site of the Acton Gardening Association, and this no more than six months after we first started looking. It was the most fantastic, brilliant, surprising news, little short of a minor miracle and quite the best thing that had happened to us since our children were born. Accordingly, on hearing the glad tidings we did what any sensible person would do in the circumstances: we started having second thoughts. Did we really want an allotment? What's wrong with shop veg? Would we really keep it up? And even if we did want an allotment, were the Acton plots really the best we could do? Shouldn't we hold out for the garden fascists down the road? And what about the Dukes Meadow allotments? Dukes Meadow is a large green open space on the banks of the Thames in Chiswick, with lots of playing fields and a large allotment enclosure that is probably the nearest thing that the west London vegetable grower will ever get to a rural paradise. Wouldn't it be nice to have an allotment there?

Well, yes, it probably would be. It would also be nice to have a large country estate with some Capability Brown-designed parkland, a spacious walled kitchen garden and a gamekeeper on hand to shoot the rabbits, but it wasn't going to happen. And anyway, Chiswick was just a little too far away, so that even if we did get a plot there we would probably never go. Then we would be just another one of those sad couples who take on an allotment only to find that after three months it has disappeared under a forest of weeds, so that they are forced shamefacedly to hand it back again. I could almost hear the tut-tutting of disapproving committee members as they whispered to each other:

'Aye, I knew they were no good from the moment I clapped eyes on them. *Guardian* readers, if I'm not mistaken.' So Bromyard it was.

Before we could get our hands on a plot, though, we had to go and meet our plot representative. His name was John Roberts, and we arranged to meet him one fresh autumn morning. Bromyard turned out to be a funny little afterthought of an allotment site, three minutes down the road from the main site, known as Perryn. Situated a couple of hundred yards off the Uxbridge Road, the main road leading from Shepherd's Bush to Acton, it is sandwiched between the entrance and exit roadways of the Virgin Active sports club. The perimeter is a green wire-mesh fence, the gate – which is on Bromyard Avenue, opposite a Stalinist-looking block that used to house social security offices and is now being turned into flats – a fearsome affair with sharp metal spikes at the top, secured by a hefty padlock. It was not quite clear whether all this was to prevent intruders getting in, or the vegetables getting out, but two things were apparent. One was that security was An Issue; the other was that the charms of the Bromyard allotments would take a little time to reveal themselves to the casual acquaintance.

With John Roberts, we were pleased to discover, it was quite the opposite. A West Indian in late middle age, he was wearing a cloth cap and a big, friendly smile when we first met him, and I do not think it is an exaggeration to say that in all the time I have known him since I have never seen him without either of those two things. In theory it should not have taken him long to show us round the site; there are, after all, only fifteen plots on Bromyard – five across, three deep – and conducting a tour of inspection should really have been a matter of minutes.

But John was a man with much to say. There was the state of

the soil, for a start (very good, apparently), the extent of the weeds, the life and times of the previous occupant of our plot, the iniquities of the Park Club, a sports and leisure club for well-heeled locals (rather more upmarket than our own immediate neighbour, the Virgin Active) and a subject about which I would soon find myself learning considerably more, the virtues of blue potatoes and, perhaps most important of all, the joy of sheds. In particular, of course, the joy of John's shed, which, like so many on the allotment, was entirely homemade. Old doors, discarded pallets, builders' offcuts: it would take an allotment archaeologist to identify with any kind of precision exactly where all the pieces originally came from, but two things were moderately certain. One is that John did not pay any more than he had to for his shed; the other is that he built it all himself – none of your B&Q rubbish for him. Inside, while not being exactly luxurious, it had everything one could reasonably hope for from a shed. As well as the usual shelves, and places for tools, there was a radio for listening to the test match, a kettle and a comfy chair. One got the impression that were it not for the need to take the occasional bath, and perhaps to reacquaint himself with his wife, John would be quite happy moving into his shed on a permanent basis.

Our tour of the site ended with an important decision. John told us that we did not have to take the whole plot if we did not want to: if we preferred we could just have half, and the other half could be let to someone else. It was a very tempting prospect, for looking at the plot in the cold light of day, it did seem awfully big. Officially it was five rods in area, or about 150 square yards – in practice a little smaller – although to our eyes it looked more like one of the larger US states: we were just a couple of people hoping to grow a few vegetables for our supper, not Midwestern

14

grain farmers driving our tractors across the Great Plains. Indeed, we even had a friend – Jeanette – who had expressed an interest in sharing a plot with us, should we ever get our hands on an allotment. It made perfect sense, really. Here, then, in cold print, is my formal apology to Jeanette for being selfish and greedy; after all that time waiting for a plot of our own, I was damned if I was going to give up half of it to someone else, however nice they were, or deserving. Ever the cold-eyed rationalist, I told myself that if we found that we could not manage a whole one, we could always sub-let half later; but if we gave half away right at the very start, and later wanted more space because it wasn't big enough, we would be stuck. So, sorry Jeanette.

Before we left the allotment, John decided that we should not walk away empty-handed. He went to his shed, got out an old plastic bag, found some parsnips hiding in a box and filled the bag with them. In case that wasn't enough, he dug up some of his blue potatoes, gave them a bit of a rinse in the rainwater tank next to our plot – did I say our plot? – and put them in the bag too. To the outsider, it was just some slightly grubby root vegetables in a dirty old bag, but to us it was a highly symbolic moment. Not only did we have our very first homegrown vegetables from land which we could almost call our own, but we had joined the ranks of allotment folk. We were one of them now, and no one could take that away from us.

2

Spade Work

Growing vegetables is easy. All you need is earth and seeds.

Hugh Fearnley-Whittingstall, *The River
Cottage Cookbook*

Digging. We didn't know much, but the one thing we did know
was that we were going to have to start with some digging. And
digging involved a spade: we knew that, too. We had got one of
those from B&Q, along with a fork, because something at the
back of our mind told us that digging might also involve the use

of a fork and, well, you could never be too careful. Very nice tools they were, too, with lovely smooth wooden handles and shiny metal bits, all gleaming and new, quite the smartest things you had ever seen; and very, very embarrassing. It was quite obvious from the moment that we first saw the allotment that people there did not really do new, or shiny, or smart. They did old, and shabby, and worn; spades that looked as if they had owned them all their lives, possibly even been used by their fathers and grandfathers before them, not bought a couple of hours before in the local DIY superstore along with all the other weekend gardeners. Turning up with a spade so gleaming that you could have used it as a mirror to shave in was, we felt, not really the done thing. We would be rumbled as know-nothings before we had even started.

I decided to make up for this woeful but unavoidable faux pas by making sure that I had the digging thing completely sorted in my mind before I even set foot on the allotment. Books were consulted: and while I secretly suspected that our fellow allotment-holders were the sort of people who had never read a gardening book in their lives, at least I could do my research work in the privacy of our own home. No one need ever know that I was such a neophyte that I had to learn how to dig over my soil by looking it up in a book. I read: I learned: I inwardly digested, and by the end of it I could have gone on *Mastermind* to answer questions on the subject of digging if I had wanted. The techniques. The posture. The difference between single digging and double digging. The way you use the soil from one trench to fill in the trench you have just dug, thus turning over the soil in an orderly and effective manner. Digging? I was the man.

What no one really tells you, of course – and even if they did you wouldn't believe them – is that all that digging is really hard work. You dig one trench, eighteen inches wide and one spade deep, and you feel OK, that was quite interesting, I'm just getting warmed up. So you dig another. And that's OK, so you dig another, and yes, that's proper work, isn't it? And you dig another, and another, and phew, perhaps it's time for a break. And you dig a few more, and then you stop for lunch, because actually you're getting a bit tired. Then you decide to have another go after lunch, and you discover you can't move any more. Your back has seized up. Your legs have turned to jelly. Your arms are simply no longer interested in obeying orders. Your body is, in effect, making a general announcement along the lines of 'I do not know what the hell you think you were doing before lunch, Mr So-Called Gardener, but I am not doing that ever again. Forget it. We are downing tools. Now, where's a good place for a nap?' But you soldier on, because you have to; and because the ground has to be dug; and because if you don't you know that you will feel like the most pathetic fraud that ever put on a pair of wellies.

It was at about that stage that I met Michael. I had dug an area about twelve feet square when this Irish fellow appeared. He seemed quite old, seventy if he was a day, and wore a dirty old jacket and a flat cap: I was beginning to think that somewhere along the line all the old boys who had plots on our site had read that allotment gardeners always wore flat caps, and had decided they ought to fit in. I was even beginning to think I ought to get one myself. Anyway, this character did not really introduce himself, but just walked up to our plot to have a look at what I was doing, looked rather amused at something, and then said: 'Are ye building a swimming pool, then?'

Blimey, I thought, what on earth is this man on about? Quite clearly I am single-digging according to the prescribed method, one spit deep, well perhaps a bit deeper on account of my enthusiasm, and turning the soil over just like it says in my Reader's Digest *Gardening Year*. 'Er, no,' I replied, stupidly.

'Are ye digging your way to Australia?' he said. I laughed, somewhat sheepishly: now he came to mention it, the trench was quite deep; perhaps I had got a bit carried away. No wonder I was so knackered. And maybe that hard stuff I had encountered deep down in the soil wasn't a bit of old brick, maybe it was the outskirts of Perth . . .

It was with quite a measure of relief, therefore, that I listened as Michael explained that there was really no need to dig that deep, that in fact the soil was in reasonably good condition because the previous occupant of the plot had looked after it quite well, for a Kerryman. Michael, like most Irishmen, did not have a frightfully high opinion of Kerrymen; according to him, all Paddy O'Casey ever grew was potatoes, without ever bothering to move them round the plot from year to year, which for those of us who know all about crop rotation (it's on page 432 of *The Gardening Year*) is a bad thing. 'You grew your potatoes there last year,' Michael would tell him. 'No I didn't!' Paddy would say.

Two stubborn old Irishmen, arguing about their spuds: it is what I got an allotment for, really.

Funnily enough, all this talk about Paddy was curiously humbling. It wasn't so much the thought that, for all his potato-centric obstinacy, Paddy had probably forgotten more about vegetable gardening than I will ever know, Reader's Digest or no Reader's Digest; it was the realisation that this allotment which we had just acquired, and which we would no doubt one day regard with such pride (assuming, that is, that we ever managed to grow anything on it), was not really ours at all. We were just tenants, looking after it until the day when we got too old, or tired, or ill to manage it any more. That is what had happened to Paddy: he was in a home in Hounslow, apparently, and while it took me about a year to get a straight answer from anyone as to what had happened to him (over the next year I would come to learn that if it's evasive, confusing or outright incomprehensible answers that you are after, allotments are the place to go), it was clear that his gardening days were over. In fact they had been over for at least a year before Eliza and I appeared on the scene, but allotments are, for the most part, rather caring and cooperative places. When Paddy became too frail to do any gardening, his friends on the allotment took over the cultivation of his plot, digging it, looking after the vegetables and making sure it was properly tended until it was clear that he would not be coming back.

It is not just our allotment where this happens, either: it is everywhere. Some time later I had reason to visit some allotments in east London, and one of the old boys happened to mention in passing how one of his fellow plot-holders had dug his patch while he had been in hospital. He wasn't making a big deal of it; he certainly did not seem to think it was anything special. It was just one of those acts of everyday kindness that cement a community together; you help each other out, in the knowledge that when you are in need someone will help you out, too. A couple of hundred yards away, in the bustling, traffic-clogged madness that is the Uxbridge Road, there is city life, impersonal, alienating, unfeeling; but on the allotment there is something much more akin to village life, with a nurturing sense of togetherness that you probably do not even get that often in the countryside these days.

It also explains one of the curiosities of allotments – namely, why do they often seem both oversubscribed and neglected? We are always being told how hard it is to get an allotment, how they are always heavily in demand and how long the waiting lists are. You can wait ten years for a plot in Highgate, north London. Yet walk round any allotment site and there is always a handful of plots that seemingly have not been looked after for years; sad, forgotten, thick with weeds, they look as if they are in desperate need of love and attention. So why don't they get given to people who are going to look after them? My theory is that these neglected patches belong to the old, the sick and the frail, long-standing plot-holders who have been there for years and who have found themselves unable for whatever reason to keep up with the work on their patch. The allotment committee have probably known them for ever, grown old with them, and are not about to issue an eviction notice just because they got behind with the weeding last summer. So the plot gets overgrown; possibly someone with time on their hands does their best to keep it in shape. Only when they know that old Jim really isn't coming back does the plot get taken back and given to some newcomer.

One of the old hands – I think it was John Roberts – had been looking after Paddy's allotment while he was ill, and you could see that a certain amount of cultivation had been going on. There were some old cabbages around, a few unidentified members of the onion family, and the odd potato lurking underground: and, yes, there were some weeds. There was grass, and dandelions, and thistles, and weeds with nasty pernicious roots that seemed to go deep, deep underground, probably coming to an end somewhere around the outskirts of Melbourne. No doubt about it: we were good for weeds. Before tackling the weeds we had faced what was to become merely the first in a series of allotment dilemmas, namely: Rotavator or fork? (A couple of years down the line, I have come to the conclusion that such dilemmas are the privilege of the newbie gardener, the dilettante who comes along without ever having had the pleasure of getting earth under his fingernails. If you have been growing vegetables all your life, if you learned everything you know about potatoes from your mum or dad, who in turn learned everything they knew from their parents, then to your mind there is only one way of doing things. It may not be the right way, it may not be the way that is recommended in the books, but it works for you, and that is a pretty unassailable argument. Michael, for instance, cuts his seed potatoes into quarters before planting them, thereby ensuring that he gets four times the crop. It is not a technique I have ever seen recommended in any book, but then neither have I ever seen Michael go short of potatoes. It probably helps to be Irish.)

So: Rotavator or fork? I don't think I had really heard of a Rotavator before I got an allotment, but apparently they are the bee's knees for cultivating land. They chop as they turn as they dig as they plough, or something like that, turning your weed-infested rainforest into nicely churned topsoil, all in a matter of minutes – and without the terrible backache you get from digging. I knew I could get one from my local tool hire shop, and I must admit it was terribly tempting. However, something inside of me, something instinctual told me that the likes of Michael and John weren't really Rotavator people, and perhaps I shouldn't be either. It wasn't just that Rotavators weren't very allotment (old men in flat caps have been cultivating their land with spade and fork for centuries, so who was I to cop out and go and enlist the help of some mechanical tool?); it turned out that there was a good practical argument against them as well. It's all that chopping: those perennial weeds with their nasty long root systems like nothing better than being chopped up into tiny little pieces by the blades of a Rotavator. Instead of there being one weed, suddenly there are a hundred tiny pieces of root, each one of which will grow into a new weed. Perennial weeds are bent on world domination, and any gardener who uses a Rotavator when they are around is simply playing into their hands.

So, fork it was, and thus one chilly Saturday morning Mrs Low and I embarked on the slow and arduous task of forking over the whole allotment, painstakingly sifting out all the weeds from every forkful of soil we lifted. We knew we had to be particularly careful, because John had come over just as we were starting and said: 'You'll find some little white roots while you are forking it over. You'll want to get all of that out.' The way he said it was rather serious, portentous even, and there was no doubt in our minds that we ought to heed his words. John did not actually say what these white roots were called, but we soon found out. Bindweed, it was: a charming little fellow, with whom we were to become quite familiar over the coming year.

Excuse me for a moment while I go and kick the furniture. Bastard bastard bastard bindweed. Evil, pernicious, unkillable bindweed, greedy, grasping, creeping, life-sucking, horrible . . . *weed*. Bindweed is the Freddy Krueger of the allotment, a resourceful bit of nastiness that, whenever you think you have finally got rid of it for ever, comes back again even stronger and more evil than before. The rational thing to do would be to deal with it once and for all with a good dose of Roundup, the Agent Orange of modern weedkillers. Roundup is the stuff you turn to when all else fails, the stuff that brings hope when all around is despair. The trouble is, it is not exactly organic. And, like so many new allotment gardeners, when we got our plot there was an unspoken assumption by Eliza and myself that we were going to do it organically.

Why bother growing your own if you are not going to be organic? There are perfectly good vegetables available in your local supermarket, fresh (more or less), clean (so they tell us) and inexpensive (or are they?). But pesticides and fungicides have been used to produce those perfect specimens that look so tempting in the shop. The concern is not just the question of chemical residues on your vegetables, or the effect of long-term exposure to such chemicals on the health of farm workers, it is also the effect that such chemicals have on the environment. Pesticides kill beneficial insects as well as the ones they are targeting, and have over the years been responsible for a catastrophic decline in insect populations as well as a corresponding fall in bird populations.

Equally damaging is the use of modern fertilisers. For generations man has used muck – whether it is from horses, cows, chickens or, in the case of some less fastidious societies, humans – and other natural products such as seaweed to return the goodness taken out of the ground by his crops. As it rots down it provides the soil with the nutrients it requires, gradually and slowly, as well as improving the structure of the soil. Modern fertilisers are brilliant at providing the soil with all the nutrients a plant could possibly want, or at least the major ones, but not so good at looking after its long-term interests. Being water-soluble they get washed out by the rain, so that our rivers and groundwater become polluted with excessive levels of nitrates and phosphates. And that's bad news for fish, for shellfish, and for anyone who wants to drink the water at some point down the line. At the time of writing 55 per cent of the UK has been officially designated as 'nitrate vulnerable zones'. The situation seems unlikely to improve in the near future; the Environment Agency reckons that with the current regulations, it will be impossible to reverse the long-term trend of increasing nitrate levels in groundwater. The other bad news is that as organic material is not being replaced, the structure of the soil gradually breaks down so that it becomes vulnerable to soil and water erosion. In southern Spain, where much of the landscape is now covered in plastic, the telltale scar tissue of modern intensive agriculture, diggers have to be brought in to replace the soil when it becomes saturated with chemicals or exhausted by the demands of three harvests a year.

We were, therefore, committed to the organic way: not so committed that we were going to stick to the rules even if it killed us, but sufficiently serious not to reach for the Roundup as soon as we saw our first weed. Mind you, there was an awful lot of bindweed . . .

Digging, quite obviously, is man's work. It is physically demanding, requiring strength, stamina and endurance; it is also rather boring and repetitive, and therefore just the sort of dull-but-hard activity that men are used to. So quite why Eliza is such a satisfactory digger is something of a mystery to me, albeit a welcome one. The best thing that I can say about her technique is that she gets on with it: she starts at one end of a patch, and keeps digging – and picking out the weeds, which is the really boring part – and carries on until she has got to the other end. This has a number of advantages, apart from the obvious one of getting the job done in half the time. It means that often I have company while I am digging, which given the soul-destroying tedium of the job (on a bad day, that is; on a good day a bit of mindless digging can be quite therapeutic) is

26

a welcome distraction; and perhaps more importantly, it is an incentive to me to keep up. I am the sort of person who is easily distracted ('Oh look, there's a robin, ooh, I think it's looking for worms, yes, look it's got one . . .') and if there is one thing guaranteed to make me keep up my work rate it is the thought of avoiding the indignity of having my wife dig more than me. These things are important, you know.

The result, therefore, of this digging frenzy is that by the end of the second day we had dug about a third of the allotment. It does not sound much, I know, and indeed it does not even sound much to me but we felt like we had done something marvellous and heroic, akin to building the Great Wall of China single-handed. 'Great,' said Eliza. 'Let's plant something.'

This was shocking. I wasn't really emotionally ready to plant anything: we hadn't finished digging the allotment, nowhere near, and anyway it was November. What on earth could you plant in November?

'Let's plant some onions,' she said. Oh OK, let's plant some onions. Whatever that involves. My wife was ahead of me here: it turned out that John had a bag of onion sets in his shed which he had bought from the allotment shop and which were surplus to his requirements. They were ours for £1 or whatever it was that they cost him in the shop. Now, until that moment I do not think that I had the faintest idea of how people grew onions, or what onion sets were. I suppose that if anyone had asked me I would have said that you bought onion seeds, and planted them in the ground, and, er, grew them. And, yes, you can do that. But it helps if you have a greenhouse if you want to grow them from seed so that you can get them going early in order to harvest them in decent time. The alternative is to grow them from sets, which is essentially just a smart name for baby onions. The technique is as follows: you get your baby onion – sorry, onion set – you put it in the ground, you wait about eight months or so until it has grown into a full-sized onion, and then you pull it out of the ground. Isn't nature marvellous? If allotment gardening was going to be all like that, I thought to myself, even I might be able to get the hang of it.

In went five rows of onions and then, because we were on a bit of a roll, in went four rows of garlic. The technique for garlic is pretty much the same as it is for onions, except that you plant a clove of garlic and wait for it to turn into a whole head. The other difference is that the garlic was free, or at least free in the sense of us not having to shell out any more money for it. We happened to have a load of garlic at home, Rose du Tarn, which we had bought from the sort of fancy west London grocer where they stick labels on the garlic to tell you what variety it is.

Now onions are all very well, an essential part of any self-respecting allotment and a crucial ingredient in the kitchen, but they are not exactly very exciting. Broad beans are something else, however. Those lovely pale green beans, smooth and plump, all tucked up nice and comfy inside those fur-lined pods: when they are young and tender they are possibly the most delicious thing on earth. I can get quite excited about broad beans, and the prospect of growing them myself, so that I can pick them as young and as tender as I like, was one of the main reasons why I wanted to have an allotment in the first place. There is another reason why broad beans are good chaps: it is because they are incredibly hardy, which means that with many varieties you can plant them in November and then just forget about them. The weather can do what it likes – frost, sleet, snow, the lot – and the beans will just happily carry on growing regardless. You've got to admire that in a bean, haven't you?

As luck would have it, one of the few things we had to our name during those first few weeks of allotment ownership were some broad beans. They were one of a small number of seed packets we had acquired over the previous year from Sarah Raven, the gardening-writer-cum-cut-flower-guru who runs a mail order business in Sussex. She is very much one of the new generation of garden people, espousing ideas about varieties, design and even lifestyle that a lot of twenty-first-century gardeners find very appealing; but when it comes to our allotment, she has a lot to answer for.

It was all my fault, really. During the time we were looking for an allotment, I gave Eliza for her birthday a place on a two-day vegetable-growing course at Sarah Raven's garden school at Perch Hill. What better way of giving us an instant grounding in the basics, I thought to myself, as well as some more interesting modern ideas that could help us create an allotment a little out of the ordinary? And, of course, it would be a very charming way for Eliza to spend a couple of days, learning how to grow lots of lovely vegetables and then, *Blue Peter*-style, eating the ones they had prepared earlier – a whole lot earlier – for lunch.

What I had not really catered for, however, was that she would come back from the course with Ideas. Ideas Of Her Own. Ideas which ran counter to my own ideas, which were of course the ideas of decent, right-thinking vegetable growers everywhere, proper common-sense ideas whose merits could be seen by anyone who gave them the slightest thought. Take companion planting, for instance: Sarah Raven is very big on companion planting. This is the theory that states that some plants perform better when planted next to another. For example, you might want to plant your carrots alongside your spring onions, because carrot flies find carrots to lay their eggs on by means of smell, so that if there are some onions in close proximity the smell is going to confuse them. Perhaps it works: perhaps carrot flies really are that stupid. But haven't they got eyes in their heads? Can't they see some nice juicy carrot fronds lurking behind the onion stalks? It all sounds a bit dubious to me. My main objection, though, is aesthetic. I like rows. Nice neat rows of onions here, carrots there, cabbages over there, the sort of thing that Peter Rabbit would recognise as a proper vegetable garden. With companion planting, however, it all gets to be a bit free-form. There is some summer savory among the broad beans, and look, here's one row of carrots mixed with spring onions, and just for a change another row all jumbled up with cornflowers. Maybe it works, maybe it doesn't, but to my mind it just doesn't look right.

Companion planting is one thing; the real trouble with Sarah Raven is the way she awoke in Eliza a desire to experiment with different vegetable varieties. New, exotic, radical varieties. Now, I do not think I am being too presumptuous when I say that in a long life devoted to the growing of vegetables, I do not suppose that Mr McGregor ever once felt the need to grow a purple Brussels sprout, or black tomatoes; come to that, I don't reckon that Mrs McGregor ever started chipping in with her opinions at sowing time, suggesting that it would be rather interesting if this year the McGregors tried growing this fancy new variety of turnip she had heard about. No, she stuck to the things she knew about, like making tasty rabbit pies, and everyone was happy.

Unfortunately that sort of attitude does not really cut it these days. Our allotment is a collaborative enterprise, with my wife and I putting in an equal amount of work, and taking an equal responsibility for the important decisions. We are, as it were, equal shareholders, each with 50 per cent of the voting stock, and, well, if I am a paid-up member of the Flat Cap Tendency with a natural affinity to all things old and traditional, and if she subscribes instead to the Pink Trug Collective (I am not suggesting for one second, of course, that she actually owns a pink trug: not even Eliza would go that far), then perhaps it is a good thing, ensuring that our vegetable-growing activities are never dull but characterised instead by a spirit of free debate and always open to the possibility of innovation and change. And if Eliza ever oversteps the mark, then I can always remind her about the black flowers. Of which more later.

Anyway, in the interests of reconciliation, I have to confess that Ms Raven does quite often get it right. Unlike other seed suppliers, which offer you a long list of different varieties, each sounding equally delicious and easy to grow, she does the groundwork for you and offers up instead a short – very short – list of varieties which she has found to be the best. That is how, back on that grey November morning, we found ourselves with a packet of Super Aquadulce broad beans which we proceeded to plant in a double row along one end of what was to be our bean bed. In they went, one every nine inches, two inches deep – I am not sure if Eliza, who happened to be doing the sowing while I did something rugged, like digging, actually used a ruler to check the planting depth, but such was our desire back then to do things by the book that I would not have put it past her – and with a piece of string stretched between two old sticks to mark each row. Then we stood back, and felt incredibly pleased with ourselves. The onions were in, the garlic was in, and now the broad beans were in. Were these things actually going to grow? It seemed scarcely believable, but apparently that was what was meant to happen. So we went home, had a cup of tea to celebrate, and dreamed of eating baby broad beans.

3

Safi's Paradise

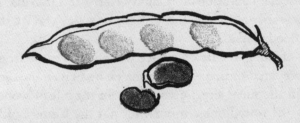

On a fine March morning, the old woman sat up in bed, sniffed the sweet spring air and said, 'It's time for us to sow the vegetables!'

Aleksei Tolstoy and Niamh Sharkey, *The Gigantic Turnip*

It was round about the time we were planting the onion sets that we began to understand the first rule of allotment life: namely, that the best things in life are free, and that you should never, ever pay for anything when there is a possibility that you can get it for nothing. It is a rather fitting philosophy, seeing as how in a sense the whole practice of allotment gardening is about getting vegetables for free, or at least as free as you can manage. Free seeds, free sheds, free manure, free anything you can get your hands on; but the greatest of these is, without doubt, free advice.

33

On the allotment the one thing that is never in short supply is free advice. No matter who you are, no matter what you are doing, there is always someone who has got a good idea on how you could be doing it better. Indeed on occasion they are right: I certainly was not so foolish as to believe that *The Gardening Which? Guide to Growing Your Own Vegetables* was the fount of all vegetable knowledge. And then sometimes, well let us just say that perhaps some pieces of gardening lore really only pertain to the particular conditions in County Kerry, or Grenada, and do not necessarily translate that well to the soggy clay of the East Acton flood plains.

One of the first bits of advice we received came from John as we prepared to plant the onions he had given us. Go up to the main allotment site, he said, look for the pile of wood chippings – the rotted ones, mind you, not the fresh – and bring back a few wheelbarrow loads to spread over the ground where you have planted your onions. I wasn't quite sure why we were meant to be doing this, but it sounded very convincing, and John seemed to know what he was talking about; and, of course, the composted wood chippings were free. So I found a wheelbarrow (free, of course: there were so many old wheelbarrows hanging around the allotment in various states of disrepair that it was quite clear that I did not have to waste any money on buying a new one for myself) and walked the two hundred yards up the road to the main allotment site where there were assorted piles of stuff in varying states of decomposition. Yup, there were the wood chips (dark and crumbly and rotting down nicely, as far as I could see), and so into the barrow they went, down the road and on to the onions. I might not have known what on earth I was doing, but it certainly looked professional.

A few days later Michael – he of the amusing observations about swimming pools and Australia – happened to be passing. As seemed to be his habit, he wandered over to have a look at what we were up to, presumably on the grounds that when you have been growing vegetables all your life, and have got used to just about everything that the vegetable gods care to throw at you, then one of the few sources of unpredictability and amusement left open to you is to discover what new foolishness the latest allotment arrivals have managed to come up with. He looked up and down our onion rows, which I happened to think were looking good and straight and generally tickety-boo, shook his head sadly and said: 'Oh, I don't know why you've covered them with that. Oh no, I wouldn't do that. Not yet. No, I'd wait until the spring before I did that.' And off he went, still shaking his head and happy in the knowledge that he had done a good morning's work.

If my allotment neighbours were not going to be able to agree on their advice (and little though I realised it at the time, I would later learn that Michael and John would sooner pour paraquat on their King Edwards than actually agree on anything), I thought that perhaps the advice on offer in books would be a little more reliable and consistent. So off I went, determined that with hard work, meticulous research and a clear head I would soon find the book that would answer all my vegetable needs. Or perhaps a couple of books, just to cover myself. For a few delirious weeks I spent just about every moment of my free time scouring local bookshops for gardening books, and any time I wasn't actually in, near or about to travel to a bookshop, I was sitting at my computer as I ordered the more obscure volumes from Amazon. By the time the buying spree was over I was the owner of the following:

*The Gardening Which? Guide to Growing Your Own Veget-
ables* – Liz Dobbs
The New Kitchen Garden – Anna Pavord
The Vegetable & Herb Expert – Dr D. G. Hessayon
The Royal Horticultural Society's *Fruit & Vegetable
Gardening* – Michael Pollock
The Organic Salad Garden – Joy Larkcom
Planning the Organic Vegetable Garden – Dick Kitto
These would later be joined by:

The Great Vegetable Plot – Sarah Raven.

Yes, that Sarah Raven. That was actually bought for Eliza, an
example of the spirit of generosity and mutual tolerance with
which we approach the growing of vegetables. Sometimes.

Quite why I needed to buy all those books is not immediately
obvious, apart from the fact that I am a man, and it is a well-
known fact that for most men one of the chief attractions of
having an interest is the opportunity it affords you to buy stuff,
like books, gadgets, tools, specialist clothing and all the other
paraphernalia associated with your hobby. But ALL of them?

The *Gardening Which?* book was just an obvious starting
point. Our friend Claire, who has an allotment on the site that
turned us down, a subject on which I am simply not bitter, not
at all, it is all water under the bridge now, and if they think their
allotments over there are so great, well . . . What? Oh, yes, sorry.
Anyway, Claire swore by the *Which?* book, said it was a good
basic all-rounder, told you everything you needed to know. So I
had to get that. And of course no one should ever indulge in a
hobby without owning a book by the great Dr Hessayon, the
experts' expert. Apparently he was the second-most successful

author of the 1990s, after Catherine Cookson, and has sold some 40 million books worldwide: *The House Plant Expert* alone sold 11 million. He is also wonderfully old-fashioned – the growing of garlic gets a tiny footnote in the book, as though it were a strange and exotic practice, indulged in by foreigners and other suspicious types. As vegetable-growing is in itself rather old-fashioned, that seems rather suitable. So he was in.

Anna Pavord: she is just rather wonderful. She writes elegantly, and sensibly, and is strong on design. She also has the wonderful knack of making you feel that things will somehow turn out all right, and there is no need to get too hung up on rules and the right way of doing things. Her section on the rustic mixed hedge – it's not all cabbages and beetroot, you know – starts with the words 'For taking away the backs of your knees, there is nothing like a slug of sloe gin.' She would, I felt, be an invaluable antidote to the post-war austerity of the good Dr Hessayon.

Another wonderful woman is Joy Larkcom, who is really the patron saint of organic salad-growing. Back in the 1970s she embarked on a kind of vegetable pilgrimage, travelling round Europe with her young family and seeking out the sort of salad plants such as rocket and mizuna which are now supermarket commonplaces but were then so exotic as to be virtually unheard of. She wrote the book, both literally and metaphorically, and has been writing it ever since. Having an allotment library without Joy Larkcom is a bit like having a cookery library without Elizabeth David. I could have chosen just about any of her books, but I went for her salad book from 2001; fairly similar to all the others, I expect, but with prettier pictures.

If I had to nominate my desert island book, it would probably be the RHS one. It's not charming, and it's not cheap, but it is supremely reliable, and has everything in it, from instructions on how to build a tunnel cloche to the list of problems faced by komatsuna – better known as mustard spinach. Want to know what those problems are? This is the full list: birds, bolting, boron deficiency, caterpillars, clubroot, cutworm, damping off, downy mildew, frost damage, leaf spot, leatherjackets, mealy cabbage aphid, molybdenum deficiency, white blister and whitefly. Perhaps I won't grow any komatsuna.

Then there is Dick Kitto. Most readers will not have heard of him – I certainly hadn't before I came across a copy of his 1986 volume in Kensington Library. It is a gardening book totally unlike any other I have ever seen; uncompromising, serious and deeply eccentric, the work of a man who, according to the blurb on the jacket, had been gardening organically for thirty-five years, and it shows. Reading the book you realise that he knows just about everything there is to know about organic gardening, not because he has swotted it up but because he has done it all himself. It is not necessarily a book for beginners – there are perhaps a few too many diagrams for that – but on the other hand one cannot help but warm to a man who calls himself 'an insatiably curious peerer over hedges and through cracks in fences'. Someone else described him as 'shabby in apparently indestructible tweeds', which sounds to me like a good look for an unsung hero of the organic movement. Kitto also wrote an entire book about compost, which was regarded as the first book on the subject to make sense. His general advice is 'Take it easy; learn by stages; do what seems sensible; work with nature and nature will work with you.' I will try to bear that in mind the next time the slugs run riot through my lettuces.

Armed with my Kitto and my Pavord, I felt I was ready for anything the allotment had to throw at me. But did I really need to own any of these books, let alone all of them? Does John go running to *Gardening Which?* whenever he runs into a problem? Does Michael owe everything he knows about potatoes to Sarah Raven? Possibly not. Books are really only there to help ignoramuses like myself, people who cannot tell their salsify from their scorzonera, and – as I said before – most people who grow their own vegetables probably just rely on doing what their parents did before them. That option wasn't available to people like me, though; we live in a different world now, and there is no point pretending that I could have gone to my mother – when she was alive – and asked her when it was safe to start sowing carrots, and how you knew it was time to start digging up your potatoes. She just would have thought I was being peculiar. On the other hand, perhaps you do not have to go and spend a week's wages on a pile of books that you will probably look at once a year, if you're lucky.

Hugh Fearnley-Whittingstall has got some sound advice on this point: he calls it seed-packet gardening. It goes like this. You buy a packet of seeds; you follow the instructions on the back of the packet; and, er, that's it. When to sow, how deep, how far apart, when to thin, when to harvest – is there much more that anyone needs to know? Well, perhaps there is: pests, for a start, and soil problems (that old devil, molybdenum deficiency . . .), and advanced stuff like seed saving. But much of that you can pick up as you go along, and there is always the likes of John and Michael to help you out. Still, I had made my choice, I had bought the books, and frankly with all that assembled knowledge there was nothing I would not be able to find out about the finer points of carrot cultivation, or how to produce perfect runner beans. I was unbeatable.

Before I explain exactly how wrong I was (and believe me, I was going to take the whole concept of 'wrongness', not to mention 'foolish pride' and 'knuckleheaded obstinacy', to hitherto unexplored heights), there was one question that Eliza and I had not yet resolved: the whole issue of what we were going to grow. We had by then – and this was sometime in early February – more or less finished digging over the plot and removing the worst of the weeds, although I have to confess that as we worked our way down to the other end of the plot, and spring grew ever closer, the dedication with which I removed every single weed from every single spadeful of soil had begun to lessen somewhat.

Deciding what to grow is a slightly trickier question than it might first appear. You have to ask yourself: what on earth are you growing vegetables for in the first place? Is it to get stuff that you cannot find in the shops? Is it because you think that home-grown produce is going to taste better than anything you can find in the supermarket? Or is it because by growing them yourself you know exactly what has gone into your vegetables, and you know that there is at least one patch of land that has not been poisoned by artificial fertilisers, pesticides, fungicides and all the other chemical weapons that are used to bring you your chlorine-washed bag of supermarket salad?

Getting stuff you cannot find in the shops is, I think, a bit of a red herring. If you live anywhere near a decent-sized town, you will find you can get pretty much anything you want. Cavolo nero, pak choi, butternut squash – all the things that were considered exotic and rarefied a few years ago are now everyday staples, and you would have to be trying fairly hard to be growing things that were really unavailable elsewhere. On the other hand it is true that there are some crops where freshness really makes a difference, and that by growing your own you can enjoy them in a way that will never happen if you get them from the shops. Sweetcorn, for instance; the moment you pick it the sugars in the corn start turning to starch, which you don't need a biochemist to tell you is probably a bad thing. So the quicker you can cook your sweetcorn after harvesting it, the sweeter it will taste. Michael Rand, in his book *Close to the Veg*, reckons that he holds the record by getting his corn from plant to barbecue in two and a half seconds. Slacker. If I start training this summer, I can see no reason why I can't take back the record for the Acton Gardening Association.

Siren voices will tell you that there is no point in growing your own onions, because you can get them easily in the shops, where they are really cheap, and anyway they are not exactly interesting, are they? And the same goes for potatoes. And cabbages, which everyone knows are really difficult to grow, and don't the ones you can buy look really good? Leeks, too – they take for ever to grow, taking up valuable space for about nine months of the year, so there is no point in growing them either.

All this seductive talk is missing the point. I just want to grow my own veg. I don't care if I can get it elsewhere, I don't even care if I am not saving much money. It's not about the money, it's about the pride and the pleasure of it all, the knowledge when that steaming pile of buttered Savoy cabbage is placed on the table that I grew it myself. A lot of the time it tastes better, I would argue, but even when it doesn't – and even I have to confess that sometimes a baked potato is just a baked potato, wherever it came from – I don't care. Those vegetables – we sowed them, we grew them, we nurtured them, we picked them: they are ours.

So: what to grow? The basics, for a start – carrots, beans (French and runner, as well as the broad beans we had already planted), potatoes, cabbage, broccoli, tomatoes, cucumbers, courgettes, all the things that make up the core of just about every vegetable garden you have ever seen; vegetables that might get a nod of approval from Mr McGregor (although he might draw the line at courgettes, wondering what we thought we were doing picking our marrows so small). With the basics sorted, we could start branching out. Rainbow chard, which is like Swiss chard except that the stalks come in red, yellow and orange instead of just the regular white: greens for the easily amused. Like me. Red Russian kale. (It's kale. It's red. And, presumably, it's Russian, whatever that involves.) Kohlrabi – crazy name, crazy veg: round, and pale green in colour, there is something of the alien life form about kohlrabi, but Sarah Raven reckons they are fantastic, and says that when you are bored with cooking them you can always ring the changes by grating them into salads, so who am I to argue? When we first bought the seeds, I don't think I had ever tasted kohlrabi; come to think of it, at the time of writing, I still don't think I have ever tasted it, so you can judge from that what a resounding success it was.

Most daring of all, we bought some globe artichoke seeds, only instead of the usual variety, which appears to be good enough for the French, Eliza managed to persuade me that it would be much more interesting to grow *Violetta di Chioggia*, which according to the seed catalogue is not only red in colour (by now I was beginning to lose the battle with my wife over the fancy coloured varieties) but smaller than traditional artichokes and even more delicious. (Quick aside: you don't have to spend much time with the seed catalogues to realise that a lot of the interesting Italian vegetable varieties have '*di Chioggia*' in their name. I don't know where Chioggia is, but I feel it has to be a rather special place.)

Salad, of course. My wife is very big on salad. We eat salad several times a week, almost every day during the summer, and I sometimes think that my wife won't ever really be happy until

42

we are having salad with every meal. One of these days I think I might investigate Eliza's family tree, just to make sure that there isn't a rabbit in there somewhere, a few generations back. That, or a tortoise. To accommodate Eliza's salad habit we invested in quite a few packets of salad seeds: lettuce, of course (Lobjoits, a type of Cos, Green Oak Leaf, Merveille de Quatre Saisons, Cocarde, Little Gem), but also red giant mustard, mizuna, corn salad and rocket. And if that little lot didn't keep us going in leaves, then nothing would.

There was one more thing: beetroot. I would never wish to claim that I am a perfect husband, and I have indeed been known to behave thoughtlessly on occasion. Sometimes I forget to take the rubbish out; and it has to be admitted that it took rather more reminders than it should have done before I got round to mending the garden fence. I go out regularly to play poker with my friends, and once or twice have drunk more than is strictly advisable, or admirable. But all these failings are more than wiped out by the selfless gesture I made in agreeing to grow beetroot on the allotment. Our allotment.

Beetroot: what is the point of beetroot? No one in their right mind could possibly like beetroot. It is a disgusting, rank, horrible vegetable, wet and clammy and . . . *purple*. The colour by itself should be enough to warn people: don't eat this stuff! It's poisonous! Or at least really not very nice! I have vivid childhood memories of being served pickled beetroot in salads: in terms of gratuitously unpleasant experiences, it is up there with the Russian salad they used to force us to eat at school, and banana custard. But did I let any of this colour my judgement? No I didn't. I said, 'Eliza, if you want to have beetroot on the allotment, then beetroot you shall have. It is, after all, our allotment.' I then made a mental note of it, under Favours To Be Cashed In

At A Later Date.

Having made our crop selection, the next step was actually to start growing something. I do not propose to recount in too much detail exactly what happened when we first tried sowing seeds, but suffice it to say that there are a number of mistakes that are often made by the novice gardener; and carefully, methodically, and with meticulous attention to detail, we made them all. Sowing our first batch at home, with a view to getting an early start so we could plant out the seedlings on the allotment as soon as it warmed up, we would forget to water them, so that the poor little mites shrivelled up and died. Keen to ensure we didn't make the same mistake again, we then proceeded to water the next lot rather too much, which meant that they got damping off disease, and keeled over and died. Then we thought the seedlings would get enough light if we kept them by the window. They didn't, and in their desperate attempts to get a bit of sunshine on their leaves, they grew all leggy. Good on a supermodel, not so good on a cabbage seedling. Out they went, too.

Slowly, and with no small amount of grief, we managed to get the hang of things. A mini pop-up greenhouse was purchased and set up in the back garden at home, so that our seedlings could be brought up properly. We learnt how to water young plants without killing them. Bit by bit the mini-greenhouse began to fill up with seed trays and small pots, each one containing the nascent beginnings of what would one day be dinner. It seemed scarcely credible.

The one thing that we never thought to question was that the end result, the whole point of the exercise, was food on the plate. We had the allotment because we wanted to eat our own vegetables, and if we had some fun along the way with the growing of them, then that was a welcome by-product – nothing more. Then we met Safi, and we realised that we had not even begun to understand the allotment life. Safi had the plot by the gate of the Bromyard site, and it is no exaggeration to say that it was a plot totally unlike any other I had ever seen. For a start, it was totally enclosed, with fencing all round the perimeter, and a gate of its own which was secured with a padlock. Inside there was a shed, only it wasn't really a shed at all, but a shack, an improvised home with a roof, and chairs, and somewhere for Safi to have an afternoon snooze (which he often did). A handwritten notice in marker pen announced the name of this abode to be Kabul House, Safi being an Afghan, and to this day I still don't know if it was written by some mischievous allotmenteer, or by Safi himself in a fit of nationalistic pride. Across the path from his front door there was a pile of plastic bags, and assorted piles of rubbish collected from the skips of west London: old doors, and pipes, and various lengths of wood, all of which was no doubt earmarked for the second phase of the Kabul House development programme. Safi – a tall, bearded man in his seventies, with a booming voice and a ready smile – was one of life's scavengers, a man who could not pass a skip without reckoning that it must contain something that would come in use at a later date. What that use was, or when that date was, were things that were not always clear, at least not to the outsider. So the pile of material outside Safi's plot steadily grew.

The most significant thing about Safi's plot was not the construction, however, or the shanty town architectural style: it was the fact that there was not a single vegetable in sight. Not a bean, not a lettuce, not even a lowly sprig of parsley. Instead there was a profusion of flowers – daffodils, dahlias of every colour, several rose bushes and more roses clambering up the sides. He did not even cut the flowers to take home: instead the allotment was where he chose to spend his days, pottering about, doing nothing in particular except enjoying his flowers. He had a flat somewhere, which judging from what he said was not up to much: he was separated from his wife. In the absence of a home worth the name, the allotment was where he took his pleasure. 'This is my paradise,' he would announce happily. You could see his point.

It was also a remarkably well-appointed paradise. One day we were on the allotment with the children when he informed us, in his slightly fractured English, that he had a couple of toilets on his plot which we were welcome to use at any time. I think we smiled in that polite, slightly panicky way that people do when they don't want to offend, but are convinced that the person they are talking to has finally revealed himself to be certifiably mad. Toilets? Yes, he said, pointing through the wall of roses at some sort of construction which we could see housed a white, porcelain lavatory bowl. We thanked him kindly, and changed the subject: it was never mentioned again.

4

Kitty Gets the Spuds In

Our vegetable garden is coming along well, with radishes and beans up, and we are less worried about revolution than we used to be.

E. B. White

It was shortly before she won her Oscar as Best Actress for her performance in *The Queen* that I had to reassess my image of Dame Helen Mirren. We all know about Helen Mirren, don't we? Bit of a toughie – I don't know about the criminals, but her DCI Jane Tennison in *Prime Suspect* would have got me to confess to anything she liked, from the Great Train Robbery onwards – quite a sharp sense of humour, not a woman to keep her clothes on for a role unnecessarily, not unless the part really demanded it. Then, in some interview or other, she says this: 'I don't think people have grasped how much I love horse manure . . . for all the things it can do, and the smell of it.' Helen, Helen, why didn't you say? It turns out that you're my kind of woman after all. A quick bit of research revealed that Her Royal Dameship has been a keen gardener – and manure obsessive – for quite some time now. Talking about her enthusiasm in an interview with Roddy Llewellyn back in 1997, she said: 'I have got very involved with vegetables and I have learned to love manure in a big way.' Once she was asked by a magazine for a photograph of her favourite thing, and sent them one of some horse manure. 'I sent them a little message saying, "You wouldn't believe it but my favourite thing in life is bullshit."'

Every gardening book I have ever read has emphasised the importance of dosing your vegetable patch with regular helpings of manure. The way they talked about it, it seemed to be some kind of magical ingredient, the horticultural equivalent of the potion in the Asterix books. It improved your soil structure (regardless of whether you gardened on clay or sand, which was the really clever bit), it added valuable nutrients and, most crucial of all, it was an inseparable part of allotment culture. But where was I going to get some from? Shepherd's Bush, despite the images of rural tranquillity conjured up by its name, is quite some way from the nearest farm. As with almost all of life's difficulties, the W12 manure shortage could probably be solved by throwing money at the problem – the question was, how much money? A company called Fenland Organic Composts, which boasts that it 'feeds life to London soil nature's way', sells rotted manure for £5.50 a bag. A bag will cover two square metres thickly, or three square metres thinly, according to the company's website. As our allotment is about 110 sq. m, that would mean buying between 36 and 55 bags, or spending between £200 and £300. Every year.

It did not take me long to rule out that option; fortunately, it did not take me long to discover Ealing Riding Stables, either. The riding school has a sign outside that, when I first drove past, filled my heart with the purest joy. 'Gardeners!' it declares. 'Free manure! Just bring a bag and a shovel.' Which is exactly what we did. After a preparatory phone call to ensure that they really were going to give away all that wonderful black gold (well, black once it is rotted down), and a brief stop at our nearest B&Q to pick up thirty strong plastic rubble bags, the Lows set off to Ealing on what we hoped would be the first of many annual family manure trips. On arriving there, we found the set-up to be even better than we had hoped for. A friendly chap in the office-cum-café said it was perfectly all right to drive the car in, and explained that there were two manure piles to choose from – fully rotted over there in the corner, and the fresh stuff by the stables. We did not feel quite brave enough for the fresh stuff, but the rotted was perfect, a great big slag heap of lovely, dark brown, crumbly manure, just what our vegetables had been dreaming of. Helen Mirren would have been very happy. She wasn't the only one: the children were in seventh heaven, too. When you are that age – Kitty and Orlando were, respectively, seven and five at the time – and there is an enormous great pile of horse poo the size of a small house to clamber up and down on, and you have even come equipped with your own spade and fork to help bag it up, what's not to like? While the children mucked around on top of the muck – 'helping', as they liked to call it – sometimes I would shovel and Eliza would hold open the bright blue bag, and sometimes Eliza would shovel and I would hold the bag; and as we stood there, silhouetted against the Ealing skyline, all clad in our wellies and gloves and doing our best to ignore the fact that it had started raining, I suppose we must have seemed a marginally eccentric little group. Afterwards, though, everyone agreed that it had been an excellent day out: perhaps other families have their own ways of having fun.

We learnt a few interesting lessons that day. Fully rotted horse manure does not smell. A VW Passat estate with the back seat down will take about thirty bags of manure. And, disappointingly, thirty bags of manure, if you are spreading it thickly, does not actually go that far. Once we had got it back to Bromyard Avenue and emptied out the bags, it covered somewhere between a quarter and a third of the allotment. A couple of days later I had to make a return trip to Ealing, without the assistance of Mrs Low, or even the little Lows, to get some more. The most important lesson of all, however, was this: that with a bit of ingenuity and hard work you don't have to spend money if you don't want to – you can, as it were, get shit for free.

By now things were beginning to proceed apace. The ground had all been dug, or forked over, although I was not entirely convinced that we had got rid of all the bindweed; a good dose of manure had been applied to most of the ground, carefully avoiding the carrot bed, because as any fool knows if you put manure there you will get forked carrots, and what we were after were nice straight Bugs Bunny carrots, not the sort of strange misshapen creatures that people used to send off to Esther Rantzen; and I had tools. Oh boy, did I have tools. A few weeks earlier it had been my forty-sixth birthday, and when I returned from work there had been a big pile of presents waiting for me in the kitchen, all wrapped up so I could not guess what they were, although perhaps it would not have taken a genius to work it out. Unwrapped, they revealed themselves to be a hoe (a push hoe, to be precise, which you use in a stabbing motion, as opposed to a Dutch, or pull, hoe), a fork (yes, I know that we already had one gardening fork, but frankly you can never have too many forks) and an onion hoe, which is like a Dutch hoe, only hand-sized, for hoeing between onion rows where a bit of finesse is required if you don't want to decapitate all your onions. There was more, too: something magazine-shaped which even I had guessed was probably not the latest issue of the *New Statesman*. It turned out to be *Kitchen Garden* magazine, the first copy of a twelve-month subscription Eliza had bought me. It is hard to give sufficient justice to the thrill I felt on opening the magazine, which might not have had the sophistication of the *New Yorker*, the erudition of the *Literary Review* or the naked girls of *FHM*, but had more articles on parsnip propagation than those publications could ever dream of. There were pieces on red cabbages, and how to grow onions, and ten fascinating facts about artichokes, and at the back of the magazine a gardener's guide to weeds (February's weed of the month was nipplewort, which I will be sure to look out for). All in all, I don't think I had ever received such an excellent haul of presents, not since I was seven and my parents gave me a James Bond suitcase for Christmas.

So, we had the tools. We had the seeds. We had the land, obviously, and we had the manure to make it all lovely and nutritious. Wasn't it time actually to start putting a few more plants into the ground? So, one Saturday morning in the middle of February, we planted our first seeds of the year in a small corner of one of the beds: radishes, of course. Everyone grows radishes: they are quick, they are easy, they are remarkably good-tempered – it takes incompetence of a very special kind to get one's radish crop to fail – and, perhaps most important of all, and the factor which makes them so attractive to children, you can eat them straight out of the ground. In went the radishes, then: French Breakfast, one of the more popular varieties but one which poses a question I have never heard answered satisfactorily – has anyone ever seen a Frenchman eating radishes for breakfast? Croissant, yes; baguette, yes; a small black coffee, a glass of brandy and half a packet of Gitanes, yes – but radishes? It does strain the old credulity somewhat.

We also put in a line of carrots (Early Nantes), right next to the onions, which, by some wonderful miracle of nature, had been doing the decent thing and steadily growing all winter, just like they are meant to, so that by this time they had smart little green shoots sticking up out of the ground.

As February turned to March, as the days got longer and the soil got warmer, we started to sow more and more. We became unstoppable. We sowed mizuna. We sowed lamb's lettuce. We sowed red giant mustard. Half a line of spinach went in, and a line of mixed lettuce and wild rocket: before long, it was quite clear, we would be enjoying the best and most exciting salads in west London. Two days later we put in some more carrots, next to a band of spring onions (the faith we had in companion planting was touching, really). It was a veritable orgy of seed sowing. The first flowers went in, too: some salvia, and a small patch of marigolds, which were backed up a few days later by the arrival of a rose bush (Tinwald), which my parents-in-law had bought for their garden in Wiltshire and had turned out to be surplus to requirements. Now, it might seem a little odd to be growing flowers on an allotment when, Safi aside, everyone knows that allotments are meant to be about vegetables. Flower production, however, was a crucial part of our plan: not only would it make my wife happy, which is of course a worthy aim in itself, but it would also save us a small fortune. Eliza likes to have flowers around the house, but they don't come cheap, and there are times when I feel that our weekly flower bill could usefully refloat the economy of a small Third World country. But even at my most curmudgeonly I would have to admit that flowers in the house are, generally speaking, a good thing, and growing them ourselves would be a huge improvement on buying them from the dodgy stall down the road or, worse, one of those fashionable flower shops in the smarter parts of town which seem designed for the sole purpose of discovering just how much you can charge for half a dozen tulips and a sprig of euphorbia (the answer, of course, is: as much as you like).

Naturally we were going to have to grow some potatoes. People on allotments always seem to grow spuds: it is just one of those things. Our predecessor, of course, appeared to grow little else, and Michael was obviously pretty keen on his potatoes too. We had ordered a couple of varieties over the Internet (Charlotte, an early potato and good in salads, and Symfonia, a Hungarian maincrop that, for reasons that escape me now, I was convinced would be a good all-round spud for later in the season).

For the past few weeks they had been chitting in the spare bedroom – and no, until I bought my first seed potatoes I did not know what chitting was either. Or seed potatoes, for that matter. Seed potatoes are basically little potatoes: you put them into the ground and each one becomes a new plant, which produces lots of potatoes of its own. Clever stuff, really. Before you do any of that, though, you are meant to chit your potatoes by placing them in something like an egg tray and leaving them in a light, cool but frost-free room for a few weeks so they can start growing their chits, or shoots. It is all pretty simple, really, except for the bit about finding a light, cool but frost-free room. For those of us who live in seventeen-bedroom mansions with extensive outbuildings, it is probably a bit of a cinch, the only difficulty being deciding on whether to chit your spuds in the pantry, the conservatory or the scullery maid's room. For those of us who tend to use all the rooms in our house, and in the chill depths of late winter prefer them to be not just frost-free but actually warm, it is a little harder. We are lucky enough to have a spare bedroom: the catch is, however, that it gets used regularly, most notably by my parents-in-law on their frequent (and can I say for the record, entirely welcome) trips to London. Eliza and I managed to reach an uneasy compromise over this, which consisted of her turning on the radiators whenever her parents came to stay, and my turning them back off again the moment the in-laws had left the house. Somehow we managed to avoid the twin catastrophes of hypothermia in the in-laws, and hyperthermia in the potatoes, but it was a close-run thing.

The planting of the potatoes came on a glorious spring morning in the second half of March. Eliza and young Orlando were otherwise engaged, and so Kitty and I repaired to the allotment with our egg trays full of potatoes and set about preparing the trenches. We soon reached an amicable agreement about the division of labour: I would do all the digging and the ground preparation, while Kitty would do the potato selection and the writing of the labels: the measuring of the gaps between potatoes and between rows was a joint effort. Astonishingly enough, it all worked very smoothly: there is nothing quite like the enthusiasm of a 7-year-old girl who wants to help her dad, and who feels she has an important role to play in the task in hand. We were, in short, a team; and while I have had many enjoyable days on the allotment – those rare occasions when Eliza and I are there together instead of our usual habit of making separate trips are always a treat – I don't think I have enjoyed myself quite so much as I did that day. It helped that we spent the morning working in bright sunshine, and in fact it was so warm that I even took off my shirt for an hour or so. By the time we had the last potato planted I was sunburnt, my shoulders and back a rather vivid pink.

I do, however, have one regret about that idyllic Saturday morning: it is that the Education Secretary Alan Johnson wasn't there to see us. He would have been ever so proud. Mr Johnson was not in the job at the time, but exactly two years later he launched the government's new parenting strategy in which he said that parents should be encouraged to bond with their children by working together on an allotment. He also mentioned something about visiting sports grounds, playing music and taking photographs as possible alternatives, but I think that my eyes glazed over at that point. 'The involvement of fathers is crucial,' Mr Johnson said. '[It] is associated with children's better educational outcomes, school attendance, behaviour, higher educational expectations and better social and emotional outcomes.' I like to think that in forty years' time or so, when Kitty goes to collect her Nobel Prize for medicine, or possibly nuclear physics – I don't think she has decided yet – she will tell the world that she owes it all to the day she went to plant the potatoes with her dad.

The seed-sowing frenzy continued into April. We put in a line of chard, and some 'Red Russian' kale which is meant to be very good in salads when young. We also planted some chervil, and four more different types of lettuce – Lobjoits, Green Oak Leaf, Freckles and Merveille de Quatre Saisons. I also planted some horseradish, on the grounds that I am rather partial to horse-radish sauce, and quite fancied the idea of making it myself from homegrown roots. It comes in the form of pieces of root that – in a technique that even I was beginning to pick up on – you just put in the ground and wait to grow. Eliza mentioned something about how it was incredibly invasive, and that once people have horseradish in their garden it is impossible to get rid of. Determined not to be put off, I bought a large, cheap plastic bowl which I cut the bottom out of and then buried in the ground: by planting the horseradish inside this bottomless basin, I reasoned, it could go down as far as it liked but would not be able to spread laterally. 'Don't worry,' I told Eliza, 'everything will be perfectly all right.'

5

Death by Washing-Up

On every stem, on every leaf, and at the root of everything that grew, was a professional specialist in the shape of grub, caterpillar, aphis, or other expert, whose business it was to devour that particular part.

Oliver Wendell Holmes, *The Poet at the Breakfast-Table*

There are various rites of passage in becoming a dedicated allotmenteer – sowing your first seed, eating your first crop, realising for the first time exactly how much you hate pigeons – but in terms of emotional significance there is nothing quite like the time you raid your first skip. Before you take that great step, it does not matter how many carrots you have grown, how straight your leeks are or how round and bonny your onions: you're just another vegetable gardener. But the moment you peer into your first skip, wondering what there is in that big pile of discarded tat that could possibly be turned to good use on the plot: that is the moment you become a true allotment-holder.

It is all to do with the allotment gardening world's first commandment: never pay good money for anything when you could possibly get it for free. Out in Virginia Water gardeners might take pride in shelling out a small fortune on the latest model of lawnmower, or a rather luxurious greenhouse; on the allotment such behaviour would be regarded with curiosity, if not downright suspicion. It is not a question of whether or not you can afford something: there have been plenty of occasions when we could easily have splashed out on a new compost bin, or bought a frightfully rural-looking handwoven willow wigwam for growing our runner beans – but we didn't, because it would not have felt right. The world of the allotment is not sleek, or shiny, or even necessarily well kempt; it is second-hand and makeshift, a place where fences are built out of old central heating pipes and discarded nylon string, and wheelbarrows made from ancient prams whose charges have long since grown up. It has a strange beauty of its own, one which owes its appeal to the knowledge that someone used their considerable ingenuity to create that cold frame out of an old semi-glazed door and did not just buy it from Harrod Horticultural ('superior products for every gardener').

The allotment approach to things did pose a bit of a challenge to me, however. Some people might be able to build their own wheelbarrows, or turn a few lengths of wood and some corrugated plastic into a convincing polytunnel, but I am not one of them. I am to the world of DIY what Ronnie Corbett is to all-in wrestling: not really a contender. I think I put up a shelf once, but it took me three goes and the whole experience was so unnerving that I vowed never to do it again, at least not without a team of builders on hand to patch up my mistakes and a therapist to provide on-site counselling.

Then one morning I saw Michael at work. It was a lovely spring morning, the sun was shining, and Michael – who is not a young man: he has, one might say, seen a few potato harvests – decided it was a good day to move his shed. For some reason, Michael has two allotments (one to our immediate west, next to the fence that backs on to the Virgin Active, and one to the south of our plot, next to the other fence), and wanted to move the smaller of his two sheds to a new position up against the Virgin Active fence. In the space of about an hour Michael dismantled the shed – made, as far as I could tell, out of old doors and scrap wood – moved it across the allotment and erected it again, as good as new. For a DIY klutz such as myself, it was a highly impressive performance and made me feel – well, useless. From that moment on, though, I resolved not to be quite so useless in future, and while I would not be entering myself for Amateur Shedbuilder of the Year I would embrace the allotment culture with enthusiasm.

It wasn't hard, to be honest. Once you have seen everyone else around you cobble together their compost bins out of a couple of discarded estate agents' signs and a dismantled pallet, you want to do the same: which explains, more or less, why I found myself scrambling around on the skip next to the Allied Carpets shop one wet Saturday night picking out bits of old carpet. We had spotted the skip a couple of hours earlier as we drove home from our local park, and I had been scarcely able to contain my excitement. 'Look, darling,' I said, 'a skip full of bits of old carpet!' Or words to that effect: and yes, I must admit that now I look back on the occasion it must have sounded pretty odd. The casual observer could have been forgiven for thinking that

I was finally beginning to lose contact with reality. However, we had a compost heap to look after, and one of the few things I knew about compost heaps is that it is quite a good idea to keep them warm, to help all those microbes get on with the job of rotting down that plant matter and turn it into compost. And here was a free supply of old carpet, just waiting to be cut up into suitable-sized pieces for putting on allotment compost heaps. When I returned two hours later, with my Stanley knife and rigger gloves, I was confident that I was doing nothing wrong: the carpet offcuts were definitely not wanted any more, and in a sense I was doing the world a favour by putting them to good use. All the same, I was quite glad that it was dark by this time, so that no one could see what I was up to, and that even if they did, they probably would not recognise me in the dark. Even when you are in the right, there are some things which remain stubbornly hard to explain: and nicking crappy bits of old carpet from outside shops is probably one of them.

The Allied Carpets raid was just the start of it. Once I had diverted one piece of useful allotment kit from what would otherwise have been an inevitable trip to the landfill site, I then set my mind to working out what else I could find. My walk home from work one afternoon turned up an old wire basket, the sort of thing that might have been someone's in-tray in the days when people still had in-trays: ideal for keeping the pigeons off my seedbed of cabbage seedlings. Perhaps the best find, though, was literally right on my doorstep: a block of flats was being built next door to us, and amongst the rubbish they threw out were several lengths of blue plastic piping, the sort that plumbers use. As it happens, they are not the only people who use it: as soon as I saw it I recognised it as the stuff that several of my allotment neighbours used to construct small cages to protect cabbages and other plants vulnerable to attack: you bend it into a semicircle, jam each end into the ground, repeat every metre or so, and you have a frame over which you can drape some netting to make the perfect anti-pigeon protection, or anti-cabbage white protection, or whatever it is you are trying to defend yourself against. A quick word with the site foreman, and several lengths of piping were mine.

The more I took, the more brazen I got. For several months the one thing I craved more than anything else was a few lengths of metal piping, such as you might get from an old central heating system. It is the construction material de rigueur on our allotment: you see it used to make fences, to form a sturdy support for the wall of a manure heap, to make a runner bean frame – it was everywhere, and I wanted some. Unfortunately, I couldn't find any. Every time I passed a skip I would stop to see if there was any of the precious piping, but the search proved maddeningly frustrating. Driving around Shepherd's Bush I took to varying the route to and from our house, nipping down unexplored side streets to see if I could catch some invading yuppie in the act of ripping out the radiators in his newly purchased house: nothing doing. New homeowners seemed to have put an unofficial moratorium on large-scale home improvements: either that, or the more switched-on members of the Acton Gardening Association were so assiduous in their pipe-harvesting techniques that they did their trawl of the local skips before breakfast, just to make sure they got there first.

In the end the answer proved yet again to be right on my doorstep: my work doorstep. The offices of the newspaper where I work were having some renovation work done, and as I went out for lunch one day I noticed that tucked away behind some hoarding was a pile of old piping. Oh joy! Or rather, joy tempered with the faintly worrying thought: how on earth was I going to take my find home without being spotted by any of my colleagues? Because if there was anything likely to raise eyebrows, it was walking down Kensington High Street in a suit and tie with some bits of old piping under one's arm. The first step was embarrassing enough in itself: asking one of the men in hard hats whether the pile of stuff that was quite obviously rubbish was, in fact, rubbish (one has to go through the formalities, you know), and would they mind if one took some? The answer is always along the same lines ('What? Er, yeah, help yourself mate', or possibly the same, only in Polish): the tricky bit is resisting the temptation to explain why you want it ('It's not for me, it's for my runner beans'), which is a wretchedly pointless waste of time, because: (i) they could not care less about your runner beans, and (ii) they have already made up their mind that you are mad, and nothing you say could possibly make any difference now. Negotiations complete, I left the office that afternoon, took a deep breath, looked left and right, and marched out on to the High Street with my scrap metal booty . . . and walked straight into my colleague and friend Patrick. 'Hello Patrick,' I said, in the sort of voice that implied that walking to the bus with an armful of cental heating pipes was the sort of thing that people did all the time. 'Hello Val,' he said, giving me the sort of look that implied that no, it jolly well wasn't. Still, at least I had my pipes.

I am getting a little bit ahead of myself there, however; the Great Pipe Hunt did not happen until a little while later, when I had become rather more architecturally ambitious on the plot than I was at the beginning. Fortunately I have a pretty good idea of what we did and when, because one of the few smart decisions we took when we first started cultivating the allotment was to keep a diary. That way we were able to keep a record of what we planted and when, as well as any other useful information such as which varieties we chose and when we made our feeble attempts at pest control. There was one more sort of information which the diary was used to record, possibly the most important information of all: harvest time. As I sit here writing, I have the diary entry right there in front of me: '24 April. We ate 2 radishes from Kitty's plot = THE FIRST CROP!'

Yes, we were pretty excited. I can understand that to the out-sider, two radishes may not sound an awful lot – an *amuse-gueule* for the easily satisfied, a canapé fit for a supermodel on a par-ticularly strict diet. In terms of feeding the family, it was not really much of a start: but it was an undeniably thrilling moment. Now, it may not have escaped the attention of the more perceptive reader that the radishes came from Kitty's plot. Which was fine: I am not a petty-minded man. I can be gener-ous in my praise, give credit where credit is due, and if my 7-year-old daughter wants to prove some point by growing radishes faster and better than I can on the grown-ups' plot, even though we bought the seed and dug the ground and generally did all the work, and even though she probably has not read a single book on radish cultivation whereas I am, though I say it myself, something of an expert on the radish and its ways, that is perfectly OK by me, I am not going to be bitter and resentful. Not in the slightest. On the other hand, if she thinks I am not going to eat her radishes the moment they are ready, she had better think again.

A few days later we had another harvest: this time some mizuna and red giant mustard that we had been growing as salad leaves under a tunnel cloche. 'Marvellous,' we thought, 'we are going to be having one of those sophisticated salads we see in the magazines, all interesting leaves of different shapes and sizes and textures. Restaurants charge a fortune for this kind of thing, you know.' Then we looked at our leaves a little more closely, and considered that on reflection perhaps the salads in the illustrations do not normally come with all those holes in them. Neat, round little holes, scattered liberally throughout our mizuna and mustard, making it look as though someone had peppered it with a shotgun. We were a little disappointed to say the least. The whole point of growing our own vegetables was to produce crops that were perfect and lovely, all dew-fresh and hand-picked and gorgeous, not things that looked like they had fallen victim to the kitchen garden equivalent of the clothes moth. Suddenly I knew how Adam and Eve felt – there was an interloper in our Garden of Eden, and he/she/it was about to spoil everything. It wasn't too difficult to find out the identity of the serpent in our vegetable paradise: it was a little chap called the flea beetle, a well-known nibbler of all things cabbage-related. I had by this time acquired a volume called *The Pest & Weed Expert*, by my old friend Dr D. G. Hessayon, so I looked up the flea beetle, and the entry informed me that the flea beetle was a serious pest during warm and dry spells in April and May. 'The tiny beetles jump when disturbed,' it added. I bet they do – they had certainly better jump if I ever caught up with them, I thought to myself. The flea beetle had just earned itself the title of the inaugural Public Enemy Number One on the Low family allotment, and I hope it felt proud. That salad dinner was going to cost it dear.

The arrival of the flea beetle was a harbinger of ill fortune. Until that moment things had been going very well – the broad beans were growing nicely, the onions were looking good, and who could forget our radish feast? – but after the appearance of

Mr Mini Cabbage Muncher things began to go sharply down-hill. Beds where we had carefully sown lines of lettuce became festooned with weeds almost overnight, which was a bit of a problem, particularly when we had adopted the fashionable practice of band sowing. The traditional way of sowing seeds is to make a drill in the ground, water if necessary, sow the seeds thinly and then cover them with soil: this makes for proper lines of vegetables, all neat and straight – just the sort of thing that Mr McGregor would have indulged in. However, there is a school of thought which says that sometimes it is a good idea to mark out a band in the soil four to six inches wide instead of a narrow drill, and sow your seeds by scattering them along that. It is particularly suitable if you want to grow baby leaves which you cut before they get too big.

There is, however, a slight flaw in the theory. Weeds. Now, I don't know about any of these clever gardening writers, but down on Plot Number 8 we get weeds. We get weeds in the beds: we get weeds on the paths. We sow a line of seeds: we get weeds. We dig over a piece of ground: we get weeds. We nip round the corner to the local greasy spoon for a cup of coffee, and by the time we get back we have got weeds. What they like above all else is when you have prepared a piece of ground for sowing, dug it all over thoroughly, added some compost perhaps, watered it, raked it to what they call in the books a fine tilth and basically got it into tip-top condition for the crop of your choice. 'Hooray,' say the weeds – yes, really, I could swear I have heard them – 'there's a fine tilth. It must be for us.' The result, when you have done your band sowing of your mixed salad leaves, is that you have simply no idea what is going on. Your carefully prepared band is full of tiny little seedlings, but as seedlings do not tend to come with identity papers and as you are at this stage still a gardening ignoramus, you have simply no idea what they are. 'If I cut that lot,' you say to yourself, 'will I be enjoying a tasty but tender mixture of purslane, salad burnet, Chinese leaves and rocket, or will it be a dandelion and bindweed surprise?' The answer, I came to learn quite quickly, was usually the latter.

Weeds were not the only unwelcome arrivals on the plot. The broad beans, which until that moment had been looking perky and healthy and generally a bit of a success story, had suddenly become covered in blackfly, creating a nasty, sticky black mess all over the growing tips of the plants. Not good news at all, since broad beans are probably my favourite vegetable, and I had been looking forward to them ever since we sowed them the previous autumn. The fact that the blackfly obviously had the same taste in vegetables as I had did not in any way endear them to me. No, what I thought was something more along the lines of 'Greedy thieving bastards, they are going to die.' Fortunately for us (and unfortunately for the blackfly) there is a relatively straightforward way of dealing with this type of aphid invader: I like to call it 'death by washing-up'. The one thing that really does for aphids is detergent, and so a good way of killing them is make up a solution of washing-up liquid in some water, and then either spray it on your bean plants or, if you are feeling particularly assiduous that day, apply it with an old cloth and actually wash the blackfly off. Either way the result is the same: a bunch of dead blackfly, and some really, really clean broad bean plants. Eliza, I am pleased to say, is one of the more painstaking people I know (I, in contrast, have spent my life striving to find new meaning to the word 'slapdash'), and so no sooner had we spotted the infestation than she was out with her J-cloth and her bottle of Ecover (come on, you didn't think it was going to be Fairy Liquid, did you?), and before we knew it, the horrid old blackfly were just a memory. And you know the best thing about it? She did all the washing-up, and I didn't even have to dry.

Other problems were less easily dealt with. There was the mystery of the disappearing beetroot, for instance. One day we had a line of beetroot seedlings, all looking rather delectable with their pretty red-veined leaves: the next day we didn't. I don't know who got them – whether it was slugs, pigeons, sparrows, or something else I had not even thought of – but they were most definitely gone, and there wasn't anything that was going to bring them back (not that I was overly concerned on a personal level, what with my feelings on the question of beetroot, but I felt for Eliza's loss and, on a more general level, it was just extremely annoying: we did not go round sowing beetroot just for unidentified intruders to come in and snaffle them before they were out of short trousers, as it were).

The disappearance of the beetroot was bad enough; the carrot seedlings did not even bother to appear. We had gone through the whole business of sowing them with some spring onions as an exercise in companion planting; unfortunately, while the spring onions fulfilled their part of the bargain, the carrots did not seem to get the whole 'companion' part of the deal, and simply failed to show up at all. So we sowed another row, this time taking the precaution of covering the row with some fleece, just in case it had been a little too chilly for the little darlings. We waited. We checked under the fleece. We waited a little more. We checked under the fleece again. Nothing doing. So, in that stoical way with which I like to think we dealt with adversity, plus a dash of ill-tempered frustration, we sowed another line.

Fleece. Wait. Check. Wait more. Check again. Get really cross. What is it with these wretched carrots? Do we not tend them? Do we not love them? Are they not being offered a lovely home, where they will be cared for and watered and looked after, as if they were our own flesh and blood? WHAT IS THEIR PROBLEM? Don't they want to grow? And what have they been saying to the parsnips? Because the parsnips weren't much better, to be honest. We had sowed our parsnips ever so carefully as it happens, because we had heard that parsnips had a bit of an attitude problem. They don't like it too cold. They don't like it too windy. They don't like it when the soil is too claggy, or there are too many stones, or if there is anything else going on that could upset their sensitive natures. Well, I am not quite sure which aspect it was of our allotment which the parsnips took exception to, or whether it was simply that they decided to withdraw their cooperation in sympathy with the carrots, in a sort of root vegetable secondary action, but whatever it was they had obviously decided that they were not going to show up either.

On and on it went. We sowed some corn salad – you might also know it as lamb's lettuce, or if you are feeling a bit Continental, mâche – but it simply refused to germinate, not under any of its many aliases. We tried wild rocket, which one might have thought – what with being wild and that – would be of a rampant rather than retiring disposition. Not a chance: the rocket stayed firmly unrocketed. We sowed some more carrots, just for a laugh; nothing. We tried some kohlrabi; not interested. Nothing was growing: it was a total disaster, we were never going to grow anything, the whole allotment enterprise was a complete waste of time and we might as well give back the keys there and then because we were never going to get a single vegetable off this benighted plot.

Then, on Saturday 28 May (I know, it's in the diary) we picked our first broad beans. They were quite small, but as we were about to go away for a week with my brother-in-law Piers and his family we decided we could not wait any longer; and anyway, small is beautiful when it comes to picking broad beans. It was a lovely sunny morning – it is always nice weather when one picks broad beans: somehow the mere fact of gathering the world's greatest vegetable makes the sun come out – and after we had filled the swill bucket with beans we took them home and I podded them while Eliza went down the road to one of the local Arab shops to get the other ingredients. Lunch was very lightly boiled broad beans – tiny ones, sweet and tender – dressed with olive oil and fresh mint and served with feta cheese crumbled into it. It was, beyond a scintilla of a doubt, the most delicious thing I had ever eaten. Perhaps we would keep the allotment after all.

6

A Fine Crop

We have descended into the garden and caught three hundred slugs. How I love the mixture of the beautiful and the squalid in gardening. It makes it so lifelike.

Evelyn Underhill, *Letters*

On paper, going away for a week was a wonderful idea. We had rented a friend's house in Normandy, which we had never seen before but turned out to be completely charming, the weather was lovely, and Piers and his family were, as always, excellent holiday companions (if a little exhausting: in a good way, though). The only trouble was that we were not on the allotment. Who knew what was going on behind our backs? We certainly didn't, but that did not stop our imaginations running riot. Would the broad beans be completely overgrown by the time we returned, all big and mealy and everything that broad beans shouldn't be? Would the plot be smothered with weeds? Would the combined pest battalions of Shepherd's Bush and Acton have laid waste to all our lovingly nurtured vegetables?

We got our answer the day we returned. We arrived back in London early on the following Sunday, and naturally went straight to the allotment to see what was going on. The good news was that the broad beans were fine: it was definitely time to pick another batch, but they were still satisfyingly small and we ate some later that day with onions and pancetta, a recipe we got from my favourite Italian cookery writer, Marcella Hazan. But, oh dear, the weeds . . .

In the time we had been away, the whole plot had been over-taken by this rather pretty weed with leaves of dark green and red. Before we had gone to France they had been tiny, tiny seedlings, so small you would hardly notice them; by the time we got back they were up and running, thousands and thousands of them, if not tens of thousands, covering every square inch of the plot and generally doing a very good impression of a weed bent on world domination. It was such a depressing sight that for a couple of days I did not really know what to do. The weeds were so ubiquitous, so closely interspersed with all our salad seedlings that digging them up seemed an insurmountable task, and the more I stared at them, dull-eyed and listless, the more my will to live ebbed away.

It was while I was hanging around the plot one day, wonder-ing when on earth I was going to get round to dealing with the weed invasion, when Monty came over to have a chat. Monty is one of the older residents on the Bromyard site, a bearded West

Indian chap of advanced years who, like a few of the more senior plot holders, does not get to visit his allotment as often as he would like because of his various health problems. I know he has had trouble with his health, because Monty is a man who clearly believes in the therapeutic powers of problem-sharing, and many is the time that he has graced me with a full and detailed description of his symptoms, his diagnosis, his various dealings with assorted members of the medical profession and – most special of all – his surgical operations. At least I think that is what he has been doing: there are times when I have found his accent a little hard to follow, which has perhaps been something of a saving grace whenever he has got on to the more gory bits. Anyway, he is a friendly soul, and I am sorry that he has not been well: I am always happy to pass the time of day with him. It was during one of his medical monologues that, in a desperate attempt to change the subject, I gestured towards my weed-choked acres and said something about my plot being in a bit of a state. 'Oh yes,' said Monty, 'you've got yourself a fine crop of callaloo there.'

I stared at him, with what I fear was a rather stupid expression. 'Callaloo?'

'Yes,' said Monty, 'a fine crop.'

'What,' I asked him, 'is callaloo?' I cannot remember his exact reply, but the essence of the answer was that you cook it like spinach. More experienced gardeners than myself – and indeed more experienced cooks – will recognise this as one of the standard responses of the vegetable world: when faced with a strange new vegetable, there is a 95 per cent probability that those familiar with it will tell you that it is very simple, you just cook it like spinach. A couple of hours later, John was passing and I decided to get a second opinion from him. His verdict – and I summarise the essence of what was in reality a half-hour conversation – was as follows: 1. It was a fine crop of callaloo. 2. You cook it like spinach. 3. Don't eat it raw, on account of the fact that it is poisonous uncooked. 4. It is very nice with garlic and chilli.

At that point Lucy wandered over (our plot is almost slap bang in the middle of the site, so that almost everyone is either next to us, or has to walk past us to get to their own plot), and stopped to see what all the chat was about: she likes a chat, does Lucy. 'Ooh,' she said. 'Callaloo! Can I have some?' Which would be all very well, if Lucy were a member of the West Indian fraternity which forms such a significant proportion of the Acton Gardening Association (they are outnumbered only by the Venerable Society of Irish Working Men of Advanced Years, of whom Michael on our plot, and his friend Joe up the road, are members): Lucy, however, is Polish, and as far as I can establish callaloo is not one of the staple crops back home in the Carpathian lowlands, or wherever it is that Lucy comes from. I was beginning to feel as if I had stumbled on some secret cult of dedicated callaloo growers, determined to turn the allotments of west London into one big callaloo production facility.

Still, they were at least telling the truth: I soon managed to establish that callaloo is the name of both a Caribbean dish popular in Trinidad and Tobago, Guyana and Jamaica, and the leaf vegetable that is its principal ingredient (how on earth did gardeners manage before the Internet, I wonder?). Friends who had been on holiday in the Caribbean confirmed that they had eaten it – at this point I was beginning to feel just a little unworldly – and I even spotted it for sale in Shepherd's Bush Market, in bags specially imported from the West Indies. So, yes, callaloo was real, and not some elaborate practical joke at our expense: perhaps we ought to try it. We weren't quite up to cooking the dish itself – we were a little put off by the fact that there are about 300 variations, which may or may not include coconut milk, crab, lobster, meat and chilli – but Eliza, being the culinarily adventurous sort, did take home a plastic bagful and yes, cooked it like spinach. Then she sautéed it for a few minutes in garlic and chilli and, I have to admit, it was really pretty good.

The next day we took the hoe and weeded out every last scrap of callaloo on the allotment.

As the weather warmed up, it brought out not just more callaloo but also an assortment of plot-holders of whom we had not seen much evidence over the winter months. Gardeners are a bit like plants, I suppose: some are frost hardy, and don't really care how cold it gets, while some are tender, and should be kept indoors while there is any chance of severe weather. Lucy – a slim, blonde woman who looks as if she might be quite young but in fact has a grown-up son – is definitely one of the tender varieties, which is probably why she chooses to live in England, not Poland. The warmer it got, the more frequent became Lucy's appearance until the height of the summer, when she was there almost every day, wheeling her bicycle down the path past our plot to settle herself down for whatever remained of the day. She would listen to the radio; she would bring a friend, and chat away in animated fashion in Polish; sometimes a bottle of wine would be produced. Somewhere along the line a bit of work must have got done, because she always kept her plot looking well tended, but it is fair to say that Lucy was not one to slave away unnecessarily, not while there was warm sunshine to be enjoyed.

Some of the other plot-holders remained rather more shadowy figures. Gladstone had the plot next to us, between us and the gate: one of the aged West Indians, he was a man who moved incredibly slowly and, while remaining perfectly civil and friendly, did not waste time engaging in unnecessary conversation. He had his onions, and his potatoes, and his weeds, and as the months passed the latter would advance at the expense of the former. I do not think that the Committee – they who make sure the place is kept up to scratch, and in theory turf off anyone who isn't looking after their plot – was particularly pleased with him, but he somehow managed to do just enough to keep them at bay.

Next to him was the Mysterious Bean Woman. I do not know who she is, or what part of the world she originally came from, but she definitely liked broad beans, which made her OK in my book. Her plot was divided into a patchwork of beds of varying size, with assorted bits of wood marking the boundaries between beds: around a third of it was given over to broad bean production. There were some other crops, too, that I was unable to identify: once I tried asking her, but English wasn't really her first language, and I was never quite sure what the answer was. The only thing I could establish was that her children did not seem to be terribly keen on vegetables, which seemed a bit of a shame.

The biggest puzzle of all was the plot immediately to the north of ours, which did not have a single vegetable, anywhere. It had flowers, lots of them; it had a trellis, a serious-looking construction supported by massive posts so thick they looked as if they had been hewn from giant redwoods; and it had a pond, just a small one but strictly against the rules from what I could gather. What it did not have was anyone to look after it. For month after month the plot-holder simply failed to turn up, and gradually what had been a rather beautiful flower garden became more and more overgrown, until it eventually became a sad tangle of weeds. Yet for some reason no one ever did anything about it. We all knew that there was a waiting list for allotments, and that there were people desperate to get their hands on a plot; and here was one going totally neglected. It was a mystery, and curiously depressing.

An assumption often made by outsiders is that people – and when they say people, what they really mean is men – take on allotments in an effort to get away from their family. If that is what they are doing, then they are not succeeding particularly well, because it is blindingly obvious to anyone hanging round our allotment for more than a day that all they are doing is replacing one family with another. There was a complex web of relationships between the dozen or so people who occupied the site, with feelings that ranged from the warmest mutual regard to outright enmity, seasoned with regular doses of petty annoyance, but however much they bickered – and boy did they bicker – they could not actually do without each other. Take Michael and John, for instance: anyone could see that they were simply the Acton Gardening Association's version of the Odd Couple. I am not sure which was which, although if pushed I would have to nominate John for Jack Lemmon and Michael for Walther Matthau, on the grounds that John was constantly fighting a losing battle to keep the paths between plots neat and tidy, while Michael was rather more on the mischievous side, not to say tricky; John is also a committed Christian, who occasionally shares his opinions about the power of the Lord, and while I do not remember the Jack Lemmon character in the movie being particularly godly, it kind of rules John out for Walter Matthau.

The fundamental point was the same, anyway – that here were two sharply divergent characters, who spent half their time arguing with each other, and the other half complaining about the other behind their back, and yet one could not help believing that deep down they were really very fond of each other. I lost count of the number of times that John would vent his fury to us about some minor outrage committed by Michael – I could not always make out exactly what the alleged crime was, although it often seemed to be nothing more serious than digging a trench a little too close to the path – while in turn Michael would amuse himself by making jokes about John's Christianity. Michael and I were talking about the expected yield from some crop or other – I think he had just told me that a particular variety of potato I had just planted would never grow on our allotment, that no one ever had any luck with it in these parts – when, just as he was walking away, a thought occurred to him. 'Anyway, didn't you get the sermon from John when you first got the allotment? "The Good Lord will provide." The Lord will provide . . .' And off he went, tickled pink at his little joke.

Lucy injects the sexual element into the proceedings. Chatty and flirtatious, when the weather gets warmer she turns up in her little summer dresses, and usually she has no sooner parked her bicycle by her shed (and a very good shed it is too, practically a home from home) than Michael has ambled over to tell her one of his dirty jokes, one of his absolutely filthy unrepeatable jokes. She laughs loudly, and pretends to be shocked. I am treated to the filthy jokes too, although I probably don't laugh loudly enough: I don't think he has tried them out on Eliza. He somehow senses it would be inappropriate.

As for us, I think that we are essentially regarded as the children of the allotment. Our woeful attempts to grow vegetables are watched with patient indulgence and our successes –

albeit few and far between – are greeted with something of a metaphorical pat on the head. It remains to be seen whether we will grow up to be worthy and respectable members of society, or delinquent offspring living in constant danger of being disinherited.

The thing with families, of course, is that you always think that your own is worse than everyone else's. Even so, no matter how argumentative everyone is being, no matter how cross John is about the grass paths not being cut, no matter how difficult Michael is being, at least we have never had a shotgun attack. They did on some allotments at Orsett in Essex, though, and a very nasty business it was too. A retired game beater called Ruben Bettis, aged sixty-eight, had a girlfriend, Irene, a warden in the sheltered housing where he lived, and when she dumped him for a younger man – Derek Hamersley, a stripling of sixty-seven – he got rather depressed and decided to do something about it. So he told young Derek he wanted to have a meeting at his allotment, which just so happened to be where he kept his shotgun, and instead of having it out man to man, he shot him. 'Help, help, the bastard's shot me,' shouted Derek, who really was in a bit of a bad way. He survived, however, and the police did not take long to arrest Ruben, who did the decent thing at his trial at Basildon Crown Court and pleaded guilty to attempted murder. A bit of a sorry tale, really, and I am afraid that Derek's hand will never be the same again, yet in a curious way I felt that it reflected rather well on allotment folk. All that passion amongst those old boys, who in the normal run of things would be doing nothing more constructive with their time than grumbling about modern life and watching *Countdown* – I am sure it has got something to do with the fresh air and exercise you get from running an allotment, to say nothing of the fresh vegetables you get to eat. Orsett, by the way, won the East Anglia in Bloom best-kept village award in 2005, which just goes to show that you never can tell.

We, in contrast, were never going to win any Acton in Bloom competition, no matter how hard we tried. It wasn't for lack of flowers: indeed, Eliza had been extraordinarily industrious in getting the plot planted up, and it wasn't long before all sorts of things were popping up all over the place. There were marigolds, cornflowers, nasturtiums, love-in-the-mist and salvia, and the rose which we had managed to liberate from the in-laws was coming on nicely. We even had a dahlia: it is quite easy to be snobbish about dahlias, with all their showy vulgarity, but they are the traditional flower to have on the allotment, and sometimes it is good to go along with tradition rather than just playing the iconoclast the whole time. It is simple why dahlias are so popular on allotments, other than the obvious reason that most allotment-holders are not really the sort of people to be squeamish about a bit of showy vulgarity: basically, they are troupers. With a bit of basic love and attention, they just go on producing flowers for week after week after week, and the more you cut them the more they produce. They are, in a nutshell, incredibly good value for money, and if there is anything that appeals to the average allotment-holder, it is value for money.

No, the real reason we weren't going to win Acton in Bloom was the bindweed. When we first got hold of our plot, we treated with appropriate seriousness the warning John gave us about digging up all the little bits of white-rooted weed that we could find, and indeed we thought we had done a pretty decent job of it. Every bit we had found when we were forking over the ground had gone straight into a bucket, and thence into the bin to be disposed of safely, rather as if it were the horticultural equivalent of radioactive waste.

With hindsight, it is extraordinary to think how naive we were. Remember that John Carpenter movie *Halloween*, with the young Jamie Lee Curtis doing her teenage screaming thing while an escaped mental patient goes on a psychotic murdering spree? Remember how every time you think Michael Myers has finally been killed for good up he pops again to indulge in a bit more slashing'n'stabbing? It dawned on me one day while I was doing the weeding that Mr Carpenter must have been a keen amateur gardener, and based the movie on his experiences with bindweed. Convolvulus, as it is more properly known, is essentially Michael Myers with leaves and white flowers. You dig it up, taking great care to remove every last bit of root: within a week or two, up it comes again. You dig it up again, going really deep this time to make sure you get the roots you might have missed the previous time. Then, surprise! Here's the bindweed again! You dig it up again . . . well, you get the picture. Bindweed does not die easily. In fact, bindweed may well be immortal, and never die at all. Hardliners suggest that the only way to deal with it is total war, which is another way of suggesting the Agent Orange of the vegetable patch, Roundup, but we had already decided we were not going to do that. We decided instead to adopt a more Zen-like approach to our adversary. The bindweed appears: we will dig it up. It appears again: we will dig it up again. If we can possibly do so while intoning a Buddhist chant, all the better; but the point is that we will not let it get to us. Regular weeding will keep it in check, and maybe – if we are really lucky, and keep up the war of attrition – our constant assaults will gradually weaken the bindweed. Who knows, in twenty years or so we might even get rid of it completely.

The one thing that you can say in bindweed's favour is that it is possible, at least in a theoretical kind of way, to get rid of it completely. After less than a year of looking after the allotment I came to the same tragic, unavoidable conclusion that every gardener comes to at some point in their life: that you will never, ever get rid of slugs. According to a statistic I read once, there is an average of sixty-one slugs to be found in every square metre of soil, making a UK population of nearly 15 billion, or 250 slugs for every man, woman and child – each one a relentless eating machine which consumes twice its body weight every twenty-four hours. They lie there in the dark, all slimy and secretive, and wait until it is night and your back is turned before rising up as one vast gastropod army to lay waste your carefully tended crops, destroying your seedlings, ruining your lettuces, gorging themselves on your cabbages. Almost nothing is safe from them: a row of baby lettuces can be all hale and hearty one day, and simply not there the next. At first you have no idea what has happened, and start questioning your own sanity – 'I'm sure I put the Little Gems in there . . . I'm not imagining it, am I?' Then you spot some fat, bloated slug in the corner of the plot, rubbing his belly and belching as he says, 'That was very tasty. Now, what's for main course?'

It is entirely understandable, therefore, that gardeners become completely obsessed with waging war against slugs (and snails). The gardening literature is filled with helpful articles on ways of defeating them, from copper rings to porridge oats, and hardly a month goes by without someone coming up with a new and foolproof way of keeping the mucilaginous little terrors off one's plants once and for all. So many anti-slug treatments have been proposed over the years that it is entirely possible that there are as many theories about slug control as there are slugs on my allotment, possibly more: sometimes I think about trying every one of them in turn, just for the hell of it. Then again, sometimes I think about running the London Marathon, but I find that the moment usually passes. I have, however, tried a few of them and, to save any slug-beset gardeners out there the bother, here are a few random thoughts based on my experiences waging war on slugs. (The war analogy is quite fitting. Like all wars, my attempts to defeat the slug population of East Acton involved a great deal of carnage on both sides, several false victories and a great deal of investment in the technology of death; and, in the end, no one was really sure who had actually won.)

Slug pellets

There is an admirable simplicity about the slug pellet technique. You sprinkle them on the ground, the slugs come along and eat them, having failed to notice that they are bright blue and therefore DEADLY POISONOUS, and then they die, just like it says on the tin. End of story; or at least, end of slug. What's not to like about slug pellets? Well, it turns out some people think that there are plenty of things not to like about slug pellets.

Wildlife charities say that birds and hedgehogs eat the dead and dying slugs, and are then poisoned in turn, which if true would certainly be an argument against them. There is a way round this, though, which is to put your slug pellets underneath broken bits of old pipe so that the birds cannot get to them. Garden Organic, formerly known as the Henry Doubleday Research Association, says that you shouldn't use slug pellets at all because they contain toxic chemicals. Recently I started using a more environmentally friendly type of slug pellet, which uses a different active ingredient from traditional pellets – ferric phosphate instead of metaldehyde – and is said to be less toxic to other animals.

Beer

They like a pint, slugs do. Unlike the rest of us, however, slugs have a habit of drowning in their beer, which turns out to be quite a good method of killing them. You can either make your own crude slug traps, by burying jars in the soil half full of beer (it's the yeast that attracts them, apparently), or buy specially designed slug traps. They come in all shapes and sizes: some have umbrella-like roofs to keep the rain out, others have special ramps to facilitate the slugs' journey to their beery doom, and all are remarkably expensive given that they are just a cheap piece of moulded plastic. But then there is no limit to the ingenuity of horticultural equipment manufacturers when it comes to working out new and ever more imaginative ways of parting desperate gardeners from their money. Actually, I don't begrudge them too much, because the slug pubs do work moderately well: it's just that on a decent-sized allotment you do need an awful lot of them to keep your slugs at bay, and a correspondingly large amount of beer to keep them filled with fresh ale. And the trouble with slugs is, they just never buy their own round.

Copper

Slugs really don't like copper. For some reason which my O level chemistry is not up to explaining, when they crawl across it gives them a small electrical discharge, which annoys the hell out of them. Surrounding your vegetables with copper rings is, therefore, said to be a very effective way of keeping the slugs off. I would like to try it, too, were it not for the fact that setting up a copper ring defensive perimeter is possibly the most expensive form of pest control ever designed. A pack of six small rings from the Green Gardener would cost you £16.75 (£22.50 for the large ones); I am sure that that reflects the most modest of mark-ups on the price of the sheet copper they bought from the Arthur Daley Metal Exchange, but I am afraid that with the number of plants I would want to protect at any one time I would soon be slug-free, but bankrupt. Let's see: we usually have a couple of dozen lettuces on the go, a couple of dozen brassicas, and then there are the things like young bean plants which also need protecting. That probably adds up to a minimum of sixty rings, or ten sets, which wouldn't give us much change out of £200. And if I know slugs, they would probably find a way to bypass the copper rings anyway: I would probably be better off scattering £200 in used fivers around the allotment, and hoping that the slugs ate them instead of the baby lettuces.

Barriers

Apart from copper, there are various things which slugs don't like crawling across, such as sharp gravel, wood ash and crushed eggshells. Most of these become rather useless when they are wet, however, and need to be reapplied regularly. Global warming fears aside, we still live in a country where it often rains, and I am not sure if I am prepared to eat the number of eggs required to keep every single vulnerable plant surrounded by a slug-proof cordon of crushed shells.

Nematodes

If you really, really hate slugs, nematodes are the most brilliant revenge. A tiny microscopic worm, *Phasmarhabditis hermaphrodita* is a parasite that burrows into the slug and starts to produce a bacterium on which it feeds, grows and multiplies. After a few days the slug stops feeding and burrows underground to die. The nematodes gorge themselves on the corpse for a bit, and then when they have finished that they form new juveniles which go off in search of more slugs. The other perfect thing about the nematode method is that it is as green as they come: nematodes occur in the soil anyway, and all you are doing is increasing the population for a bit. But is it the perfect method of slug control? No, of course it isn't: there's no such thing.

There are three basic problems. One is that the nematodes – which you receive in the form of a powder called Nemaslug which you mix with water – don't work when it is cold, which means that you can only apply them between March and October, which was not much use when it came to dealing with the slugs that took up residence in our Savoy cabbages one winter. The second problem is that it is quite a bore to use: you have to dissolve the powder in water, and then dilute that mixture in more water before applying it in measured doses to your soil and then watering it in. The third problem, as always, is price: to deal with our allotment we need a large-sized pack of nematodes, which costs around £20 and only lasts six weeks. It's all to do with population dynamics. In normal conditions there are a certain number of nematodes per cubic metre of soil, and they zap a certain proportion of the slugs living there. Apply your dose of nematode solution – the recommended rate works out as 3 billion per hectare, or the equivalent of thirty per square centimetre – and you create a mini population explosion among the local nematodes, which are then in a position to kill an awful lot more slugs. But as the weeks go by, they run out of slugs to infect, and their population goes down as a result. Without so many parasites in the soil, the slug population begins to recover and you are back to square one, with parasite and slug living together in some sort of happy equilibrium. Then it's off to your friendly local nematode supplier, and before you know it you are spending anything between £60 and £100 a year on slug control. And they are probably still laughing at you behind your back.

Guerrilla warfare

If you ever see someone walking round their vegetable patch in the middle of the night, torch in one hand, bucket in the other, and with an expression of grim determination on their face, you will know that they are in the late stages of advanced slug paranoia; there is probably little hope for them now. They have tried every other method of getting rid of the slugs, and found them all to be wanting, and they have now been reduced to killing them by hand, one by one. Slugs are nocturnal creatures (and who can blame them? If I was that slimy and ugly, I think I would only come out at night), and apparently if you wander around after dark with a torch they are quite easy to spot; and, given that they are not exactly quick on their feet, quite easy to kill, too. People have varying opinions as to the best method, none of which (cutting them in two with an old pair of scissors, dropping them into a strong salt solution) are for the squeamish, but then given that you have taken up skulking round at night looking for slugs to kill, squeamishness is probably no longer an issue. As a method of slug control it is almost perfect, just so long as (i) you have nothing better to do at eleven o'clock at night, (ii) your vegetable patch is outside your back door, not three-quarters of a mile down the road, and (iii) the local police are so busy chasing muggers that they do not have time to investigate reports of strange individuals wandering around late at night with a torch and a pair of rusty scissors. I think I have a little way to go before I am ready for night slug warfare, however much fun it sounds.

The truth is, there is no perfect method of controlling slugs. At the moment I favour the environmentally friendly slug pellets, but they won't solve the problem completely and no doubt there will be times when I bring the slug pubs out of retirement or, if I am feeling both flush and virtuous, embark on a programme of Nemaslug war. If we had a vegetable garden at home instead of an allotment, we might even get some ducks, which are said to be wonderfully enthusiastic consumers of slugs. As one allotment-holder put it in Chris Opperman's book *Allotment Folk*: 'You don't have an excess of slugs, you have a duck deficiency.' In the end, though, the best thing to do is to learn to live in harmony with your slugs, because you are never going to get rid of them, not ever. Protect your seedlings; grow them in pots at home until they are big enough if the slugs are a real nuisance; and if the slugs have a bit of a munch on your lettuces, then who cares? As John said to me one day – I think it was when I was feeling particularly upset about some pigeon attack or other – 'Let them have something to eat. After all, they are all God's creatures.'

7

War and Peace

Let 'Dig for victory' be the motto of everyone with a garden and of every able-bodied man and woman capable of digging an allotment in their spare time.

Sir Reginald Dorman-Smith, Minister of Agriculture
and Fisheries, 4 October 1939

Mention allotments, and the image that springs to most people's minds is of a ramshackle and usually far from charming site, most likely on the edge of town somewhere; in the shadow of the gasworks, perhaps, or next to the railway sidings. The plots are run by old boys in flat caps, pensioners with too much time on their hands who have found a harmless way of occupying the hours between breakfast and dinner: if their wives are lucky, they might even bring home a few carrots for the pot. The more obsessive ones among them grow their vegetables for show: the fattest onion, the straightest parsnip, the whitest leek. Occasionally the younger generation gets a look-in, vaguely hippyish types who like their food to be grown organically and would do anything rather than darken the doors of a supermarket. Inasmuch as the rest of the population thinks about allotments at all, it is as a quaint, rather eccentric part of the English suburban landscape, mildly amusing – what is it with these people and their cabbages? – but not really terribly important, not in the grand scheme of things. But that is not how allotments were in the beginning, back when they first started. They were a rural phenomenon, for a start, and rather than being a harmless indulgence for the horticultural equivalent of trainspotters, they played an essential role in ensuring that the rural working classes actually got enough to eat. Allotments were a serious business.

It was the enclosures that started it all. Before the great wave of enclosure acts in the late eighteenth and early nineteenth centuries, small peasant farmers and other villagers could graze their livestock on the common land, as well as using it to gather fuel. Even if he did not have much else, a chap with a pig or a flock of geese – or even better, a cow – was never going to go hungry. Then, in the interests of greater agricultural efficiency, much of the country's farming land was enclosed through a series of parliamentary acts, and those peasant farmers found themselves with no rights whatsoever, and certainly nowhere to graze their animals. People started going hungry.

It took the generosity and foresight of a couple of open-minded landowners in the Midlands to work out the way forward. In 1770, noticing that people who had land attached to their cottages tended to look after them far better than those without, the Lord of the Manor of Tewkesbury set out twenty-five acres of land for the use of the poor as an experiment. It was a resounding success: even the most idle of labourers was prepared to put in some hard work if he could reap the fruits of his labours. Over in Tetbury, which at the end of the eighteenth century was hard hit by the demise of the wool-carding industry, another landlord rented out some land to his labourers so they could cultivate it in their spare time, such as they had. Given the opportunity to grow their own crops, the peasants of Tetbury responded with enthusiasm, and before long such 'Poor Plots' started appearing all over the country. In 1806 the village of Great Somerford in Wiltshire became the first place in the country where an enclosure act stipulated that some of the land – five to eight acres of the 970 being enclosed – should be set aside as allotments for the labouring poor. It wasn't all altruism on the part of the landlords, of course: as well as the modest rent they received, the more the labouring classes were able to feed themselves, the less the parishes had to pay out in the form of poor relief. But the deal suited both sides, particularly when the recipient of the land was a man as committed as one James Croft, a miner from Swinton in Yorkshire who rented a plot of what was once unproductive moorland from his mine-owner. So keen was he on his allotment that he arranged to work the night shift down the pit so that he could tend his plot during the day. He must have been doing something right, because he ended up a prosperous tenant farmer.

In the towns another form of allotment garden began to

appear. As the towns were generally inhabited by people who had previously lived in the countryside, and had until recently enjoyed the benefits of having their own cottage garden, landlords worked out that they could earn themselves some additional rental income by providing sites for detached gardens, which became known as Guinea Gardens after the annual rent of a pound and a shilling a year. These gardens were not so much about growing vegetables to survive as providing workers with a leafy retreat; they had lawns, and summer houses, and carefully tended herbaceous borders, and for a while parts of towns like Birmingham and Nottingham became green and lovely oases in an otherwise dull and grimy cityscape. It did not last, however: industrial expansion, and the pressure on land for housing, meant that most of the gardens disappeared by the latter half of the nineteenth century.

It took a nasty outbreak of social unrest to get the allotment movement on a proper footing. In the early nineteenth century agricultural labourers worked long hours for little reward, until they finally decided they had had enough and rose up against their masters. The Agricultural Revolt of 1830–1 saw hayricks set alight, farm machinery smashed, and a general outbreak of dissent among the peasantry. While they did not succeed in getting the pay rise they were after – indeed 252 men were sentenced to death for their part in the rioting, of whom 19 were executed, and 505 transported – it gave the allotment movement the impetus it needed and plots became increasingly common. In Hastings, for instance, landowner Mrs Mary Ann Gilbert had by 1832 introduced 117 allotments of land for labourers. Farmers didn't always like it, however: they reckoned that the more labourers were given plots of land on which they could grow crops and rear animals, the less they would be inclined to work for the farmer. One cynical contemporary went so far as to say that 'The farmers are apt to think that the holding of an allotment will give the labourer a spirit of independence that will interfere with the service he owes his master.'

However, the Poor Law Commissioners certainly seemed to think the system worked. This extract, concerning some plots in Wells, Somerset, is from their report of 1834:

> The opinion expressed by the agent was that a man who works for a farmer for twelve hours, six to six, with the help of his wife and family, can manage half an acre, supposing it half potatoes, keep a pig, and support his family, and that a mechanic can do more. The continued increase in the demand for allotments is the best proof of the advantage derived from them. There is a general improvement in the character of the occupiers, who are represented as becoming more industrious and diligent, and as never frequenting those pests, the beer-houses. Frequently, they have been known to work by candle-light. Not a single instance has occurred in which any one thus holding land has been taken before a magistrate for any complaint.

Some landowners who provided allotments for the local labourers were clearly more philanthropic than others. Sir John Bennet Lawes had an allotment club for the workers on his Rothamsted estate near Harpenden, Herts, and there is a marvellous description in Steve Poole's magisterial social history of allotment gardening, *The Allotment Chronicles*, of the outing he arranged for the club members to celebrate the wedding of his daughter Caroline. It was to the Crystal Palace, by railway: many of the plot-holders had never been on a train before and most had never been so far from home.

Apart from the usual meats there was a tremendous array of sweets, including blancmanges, jellies and similar delicacies . . . Waiters at the party were quietly amused at the plot-holders' country talk. One old plot-holder asked the waiter for a second helping of a particular sweet and said, 'I don't know the name of it, but it's that shivery, shaky tackle.' Another old tenant said he would like the Squire's daughter to get married every year. John Pearce, keeper of the paths and roads, vowed that if there was ever another 'excu'sion he was blowed if he wouldn't goo' ag'in'.

Meanwhile allotments kept on growing in popularity. In 1873 there were 245,000 allotments across Great Britain: by 1890 that had gone up to 445,000. Laws were passed obliging local councils to provide allotments if there was a demand. They were becoming particularly popular with people in towns: Ealing, the borough where my allotment is situated, had 294 by the time of the 1890 census. The London County Council followed the lead set by other local authorities in buying a tract of land in Forest Hill, south London, which was once a disused brickfield, in order to provide allotments. Not that these town-dwellers needed the plots to feed their families: they might have grown potatoes, just like their country cousins, but they also cultivated roses, sweet peas and strawberries. The allotment had transformed from being the essential means of survival for impoverished rural labourers, to the chosen leisure activity of the urban artisanal classes.

All that changed with the First World War. The German submarine campaign against the Merchant Navy meant that by the later stages of the war food shortages had become a serious problem, and growing one's own food became a matter of survival once more. To give an idea of how drastic the situation was, by 1917 Londoners were regularly having to queue to buy potatoes, which were in such short supply that eating houses and hotels were only allowed to serve them on Tuesdays and Fridays. Lord Selborne, the President of the Board of Agriculture, told local councils that it was imperative to produce as much food as possible from gardens and allotments. An order was passed in 1916 allowing any land that was not in use to be turned over to the production of vegetables. Hundreds of new plots were created every week, using parks, playing fields and whatever scraps of spare land people could lay their hands on – many of them in places that had never had allotments before, such as Bolton – and even bankers and stockbrokers were to be found rushing home from the City to change into their gardening clothes and get to work on their allotments.

People went to extraordinary lengths to transform the most unpromising of sites into viable land; one, on an old rubbish tip in Battersea, was so thick with waste that most people reckoned that any attempt to grow vegetables there was sheer lunacy. But a group of volunteers set about clearing it, hauling away rubble by the barrowload, and in the end their perseverance paid off. Plot-holders did whatever they could think of to help the war effort, including organise exhibitions and shows. At the Hackney & District Plot-holders Association 6th annual show, £2 16s was raised by selling off the prize-winning exhibits, which included a 17 lb cabbage, a marrow tipping the scales at 26 lb and a pumpkin at 17 lb. The money was used to buy cigarettes for the war wounded, and surplus vegetables were given to local hospitals.

To show people how it was done, there was a model allotment in Kensington Gardens, near the Albert Memorial, and another one in Regent's Park, with an experienced gardener on hand to answer any questions from the public. Even the King, George V, was swept up in the tide of enthusiasm: he insisted on the flower beds around the Victoria Memorial being turned over to vegetables, and there is a famous photograph of the King and Queen Mary digging a vegetable patch. Allotments had never been so popular: during the war it is estimated there were about 1.5 million plots around the country, and even though many of them disappeared once peace broke out, the enthusiasm for vegetable gardening continued, and by 1920 there were still approximately 1,330,000 allotments around the British Isles. An annual show was introduced by the London Allotments and Gardens Society at the New Horticultural Hall to give allotmenteers a chance to show off their giant marrows and prize pumpkins: the prizes included a suite of furniture and a total of £100 in cash.

Cups and medals are one thing, but when it comes to people growing their own vegetables, the great motivator is hunger. In the aftermath of the war many local authorities already thought that allotments were a good thing anyway – a healthy recreation, as well as being economically useful; no doubt there was also a significant proportion of local worthies who thought they were a good way of keeping people out of the pub – but as the country slid into depression and unemployment levels rocketed, more and more people turned to allotments as a way of keeping their families fed during hard times. It wasn't always simple: in 1929 thousands of unemployed miners in South Wales and Yorkshire found themselves in danger of losing their dole money because they spent their days on their allotments instead of looking for work. It took some intensive lobbying by the National Union of Allotment Holders with the Ministry of Labour to get an assurance that they would not be docked any money as long as their gardening did not get in the way of their efforts to look for work.

In the late 1930s the popularity of allotments began to wane again. Not only were they not particularly popular, but even those allotments that were supposedly being actively cultivated all too often looked sad and neglected. As Alexander Cameron noted in the *Gardener's Chronicle*: 'Year in and year out the allotment is expected to look after itself and rapidly degenerates into a public eyesore. Many sites have badly neglected pathways, indistinct boundaries between plots, and an array of shacks, sheds and huts in every colour, shape and size are situated where they are not supposed to be, which gives the impression that the tenants can do exactly as they please.' There are, I am afraid, only too many allotments around today that fit that description: in fact, if the ghost of the fastidious Mr Cameron were to visit the allotments at Bromyard Avenue, I fear he would have rather a lot to say about the pathways and the boundaries, to say nothing of the sheds, which are indeed of every colour, shape and size. As for tenants doing exactly as they please, all I can say is that if there is anyone out there who has worked out how to get my otherwise admirable neighbour Michael to do something to which he is not inclined, they are welcome to come along and give it a go. Good luck to them.

Around this time the chairman of the Acton Gardening Association was a magnificent Scot by the name of William Strang, whose way of dealing with the problem of eyesore allotments was to write a letter to a potential benefactor asking for a small trophy to be donated which could be awarded to the neatest allotment. Noting how in recent years 'any odd piece of land, not wanted for any other purpose, was let for allotments and nobody cared very much what they looked like', he went on: 'Many of them merited the rebuke which I once received from my old Scots foreman, which I've never forgotten. Inspecting a job of mine in my apprenticeship he said, "Wullie, it may be guid, but it's not bonnie."' However, the letter has a greater significance than the question of whether the Acton Gardening Association managed to get its hands on a silver spoon for the tidiest plot: it was written in October 1939, just one month after the outbreak of the Second World War, and it was already abundantly clear that the nation was once more going to have to work hard to feed itself. As Strang wrote: 'Now we are again unfortunately in the throes of war, allotment gardening has again become fashionable.'

The Ministry of Agriculture launched its Dig For Victory campaign on 4 October 1939. There were posters, leaflets and radio broadcasts, and advice on everything from which vegetables to grow to how to build a compost heap. Two cartoon characters, Doctor Carrot and Potato Pete – who had his own song, sung by the music hall star Betty Driver, who was later rather better known as Betty Turpin in *Coronation Street* – were introduced to make helpful suggestions as to how to serve all those vegetables the new generation of kitchen gardeners was about to produce. Doctor Carrot came up with such culinary delights as curried carrot, carrot jam, and a homemade drink called Carrolade, which was made from the juices of carrots and swedes. And who could forget Woolton Pie, the vegetable pie made from potatoes, cauliflowers, swedes and carrots, and named after the high-profile Minister of Food, Lord Woolton? (Actually, people forgot it only too easily; Woolton Pie never really caught on with the great British public.) There was even a jingle to be heard on the radio:

> Dig! Dig! Dig! And your muscles will grow big.
> Keep on pushing the spade!
> Never mind the worms
> Just ignore their squirms
> And when your back aches, laugh with glee
> And keep on diggin'
> Till we give our foes a wiggin'
> Dig! Dig! Dig! To victory.

Hitler never stood a chance.

Just as during the First World War, there was a model allotment in Regent's Park Zoo, on the site of Pets' Corner, with a resident gardener to hand out advice to all those urban first-time gardeners. And who was that expert? Why, none other than our old friend William Strang. An old boy in his seventies by this time, Strang cut a distinctive figure, with his bushy beard, little round glasses and enduring capacity to produce an old Scots homily to suit every occasion. No one can have been in any doubt that he was the ideal man for the job of banging the drum on behalf of the allotment movement: in fact, reading between the lines, it would have been all that anyone could have done to keep him away. 'When I heard of the offer of the garden by the London Zoo,' he said, 'I realised it could be made into the verra finest advertisement for allotments in the country. So I found two other auld men to help me to dig it; and our combined ages, ye ken, were 210 years.' For the arithmetically indisposed, that means that their average age was 70.

Certainly the reporter sent along by the *Acton Gazette* to write about the allotment – and what an allotment it was, with its vegetables, herbs, flowers, hens, dovecote, beehive and air-raid shelter – was rather taken with Strang. This is what he/she wrote:

He looked like a story-book gardener, a lean little Scotchman with a grey beard and a bright green baize apron, surrounded with such a growing profusion of growing tomatoes and marrows and potato plants that it was hard to believe that this had been the Pets' Corner only a few months ago.

What advice did Strang have to offer the first-time vegetable-grower? the reporter asked.

I tell them to divide their gardens into three plots, one for potatoes, one for roots, and one for greens. If they forget that, they have to remember the old Scotchman and his PoRridGe. If you take the vowels out, you get P, R, G, for potatoes, roots and greens. And the potatoes need manure, greens need lime, and roots need double-digging. Therefore, if they only manure a third of their garden, lime a third and double dig a third, that is the most economical way to keep your garden clean and fertile. That is the epitome of gardening. And let the greens chase the potatoes round the garden once every year. That ensures a three-year rotation of crops.

Clearly they did not have many gardening books in those days – and indeed, who needs books when you have Wullie Strang?

Different parts of the country responded to the Dig For Victory campaign with varying degrees of enthusiasm, with parks, sports pitches and any available scraps of unused land being turned over to allotments. In Kensington Gardens the flower beds were dug and planted with cabbages. Croydon was particularly impressive, increasing the area in the borough given over to allotments from 2,500 acres at the start of the war to 8,000 by 1943. In England and Wales, the number of allotments rose from 815,000 in 1939 to 1,400,000 in 1942. At their peak, in 1942–3, allotments were responsible for producing nearly a million tons of vegetables. It wasn't just vegetables, either: people started keeping hens and even pigs, and some local authorities set up special bins in the streets for people to put their food scraps so they could be used as pig feed.

Brian Hester, who was a schoolboy in Ruislip during the war, recalled:

Vacant land was divided into allotments on which people could grow more vegetables. In some places, strips along the railway tracks were given over to gardeners. Articles and advertisements appeared in the ever-shrinking newspapers telling us how to get the most nourishment out of the food we ate. Peeling potatoes became almost a crime! They had to be scrubbed. At home, we sliced the green beans we grew and preserved them in salt for use during the winter. Boiling vegetables was discouraged in favour of steaming to preserve the food value. The water so used was saved and used for making soup.

With all this vegetable production so essential to the feeding of the nation, the courts used to take a very dim view of anyone caught stealing from allotments. When a load of carrots disappeared from some plots in Oldbury, Worcestershire, the local police viewed the matter seriously enough to take plaster casts of the footprints left at the scene of the crime; they caught the culprits, too. It was not just men who pilfered veg from allotments, either. A Mrs Cicely Graham was caught on a London allotment carrying a basket full of onions, tomatoes, carrots, parsley and other vegetables, as well as some apples and pears. She even used a little girl – presumably her daughter – to carry a bag of tomatoes. She was fined £10, the equivalent of about £300 today.

When the end of the war came, many of those wartime gardeners who had been so enthusiastic about doing their patriotic duty with spade and fork thought they had done their bit, and gave up their allotments. Half a million allotments disappeared in just two years. Hunger did not go away, however; there was still rationing, and the terrible winter of 1946–7 made the food shortages even worse. The inescapable fact, though, was that people associated growing their own vegetables with wartime austerity, and simply were not interested any more. There was pressure on land, too; a lot of councils thought it was more important to have all that open space which had been turned over to allotments available once more for recreation and walking, and there was also an increasing demand for land for town development schemes. Carrots and spuds just did not seem quite such a high priority. People were earning more, too, and food began to get cheaper and more plentiful, with the result that between 1950 and 1964 the number of allotments shrank from 1,100,000 to 729,013.

In the 1960s there were some sporadic attempts to get allotments to move with the times. A report commissioned by the Ministry of Land and Resources said they should be developed along the lines of the allotments found in Germany, Holland and Denmark, all neat and tidy and equipped with such facilities as car parks and lavatories, and renamed 'leisure gardens'. Bristol District Council embraced the idea with some enthusiasm, and created a special site with cedarwood chalets, each one with its own porch. They even had curtains in the windows. It didn't catch on, of course. Allotment-holders liked the old way, with their ramshackle sheds and general air of dilapidation and chaos. The rest of the country might have been rushing headlong to embrace all that post-war progress and what Harold Wilson would later call the white heat of technology, but the world of allotments remained stuck doggedly in the past.

8

Pick Your Own

The first gatherings of the garden in May of salads, radishes and herbs made me feel like a mother about her baby – how could anything so beautiful be mine. And this emotion of wonder filled me for each vegetable as it was gathered every year. There is nothing that is comparable to it, as satisfactory or as thrilling, as gathering the vegetables one has grown.

Alice B. Toklas, *The Alice B. Toklas Cookbook*

Summer on the allotment was a time of smells. In theory that should have meant our rose, which in its prime location next to the compost heap should have been the very epitome of fragrance. But there was just the one rose bush, and while it gave a stalwart performance there was a limit to what it could do. In theory too that should have meant our sweet peas, which were growing on the fence on the northern edge of our plot, between us and the abandoned plot next door (perhaps fence is a rather grand word for what was in reality half a dozen assorted sticks and pieces of old metal piping, all joined together by some old electrical flex). Somehow, though, we just never seemed to have much luck with our sweet peas, and by the time summer was upon us all we could muster was three rather sad-looking specimens hiding behind the raspberries. They weren't going to give the plot much fragrance, either.

Instead there were John's strawberries. His strawberry patch was just across the path from our allotment, and on a sunny day you just had to stand there doing a little light hoeing to be overwhelmed by the most gorgeous aroma of . . . well, bubblegum, actually. The first time I noticed it I could not for the life of me work out what was the source of the smell, until I looked down and saw all the fruit. John's strawberries were an object lesson in how gardening is as easy or as difficult as you want to make it. The literature will fill your head about how hard it is to grow strawberries, how you have got to protect them against the slugs, and the birds, and the frost, how they don't like it too dry, or too windy, and if you don't renew the plants every few years they will soon stop producing. I don't know if John had somehow got himself some special easy-care Caribbean strawberries, or whether his natural charm and gardening ability meant that the strawberries were just pleased to grow for him, but from what I could tell he just stuck them in the ground, waited for them to grow, picked them and ate them. Being the most generous of men, he was always offering them to anyone who looked as if they might fancy some strawberries for their tea, and very delicious they were too. One day John told me he was going away for a couple of weeks and we were to pick any strawberries we fancied. 'That's very kind of you, John,' I said, and promised myself that I would harvest a few when I had a moment.

Here is a tip for people lucky enough to find themselves in a similar position at some future date: if a friend tells you that you can pick his strawberries, and that indeed you would probably be doing them a favour if you did, because otherwise they would rot or be eaten by the pigeons, you do not make some vague remark to yourself about getting round to it some time, when you have a moment. You think to yourself: when are they going to be ripe? How do I make sure that we get the strawberries, and not anyone else? How early do I have to get there to ensure the maximum possible strawberry harvest? And can all this be achieved without resorting to physical violence? The reason I know all this is because the next time I turned up at the allotment, my head full of thoughts of how nice it would be to have a few strawberries for tea, I was greeted by the sight of John's assorted friends, relations and acquaintances all gathered round his strawberry patch – not to mention Lucy and, from what I could tell, half the congregation of his church and a number of complete strangers John had encountered in the street – all merrily picking away as though it were Open Day at west London's finest Pick-Your-Own. 'John said we could have some,' they chorused with big smiles, and I have no doubt that they were telling the truth. By the time they had moved on the strawberry patch was picked clean; there are locusts who would not have done such a thorough job.

The most lingering smell of summer, however, was Safi's lunch. Whenever the weather was nice Safi would be there in his flower garden, pottering about with his roses or shifting his latest piece of junk. Quite often he would have invited some friend or relation along to keep him company for the day, and they would sit there under the terrace he had built chatting away in Afghan. If he was alone, it would not take long for him to emerge from his little one-man shanty town and greet us with a booming 'Hello my friend! How are you?' Then he would sit himself down on our bench and proceed to engage us in conversation on some subject or other. I say this with some vagueness, because it can be hard to remember exactly what Safi was talking about; indeed, sometimes it was hard to get a precise hold on what he was saying at the time. Once I recall chatting with him about Islam and terrorism, and very interesting it was too, although I am not sure if we managed to reach any firm conclusions. One conclusion was inescapable, though: Safi liked to talk. After a while we realised that if we were ever to get any work done on the allotment, we would have to develop a technique of nodding, being pleasant and polite, but never actually pausing for a moment from the task in hand; the slightest hesitation, the mere whiff of a suggestion that we were prepared to stop hoeing – or digging, or weeding, or whatever it was – and talk to him, and we were lost. But however chatty he was, and however much a blight on our productivity, there was no denying that Safi was a good man to have around. He was kind and amusing, and exceedingly good-natured. Sometimes if the children were with us he would emerge with a couple of soft drinks and some biscuits or nuts, which Kitty and Orlando would fall on with wide-eyed grati-tude, unable to believe their luck. If it was lunchtime Safi would start cooking himself a meal, and glorious smells would waft

108

across the allotment so that you felt you were no longer in dull old East Acton but somewhere in a market in the Hindu Kush.

Occasionally he would offer us some of whatever he was cooking, and we were always too busy, or polite, to accept; it was, of course, a day when I was not there and Eliza was working on the allotment by herself that she finally ran out of excuses and decided, what the hell, maybe she would accept his generous offer after all. She found herself sitting down on his terrace, and sharing a lunch of what can best be described as some sort of chicken pilaff; as she told me later, rather annoyingly, 'It wasn't just good – it was REALLY good.' Sharing the meal with them was a young Slovak girl. It was never entirely clear what she was doing there, but I think we took it as a wholly innocent relationship; just as Safi filled the space in and around his allotment with bits of old scrap, he also liked to collect people. Perhaps none of this was really surprising, since Safi made it quite clear that he really regarded the allotment as home. As he always liked to say, the allotment was his paradise, and where he liked to spend his days, and so it was only natural that that was where he took his meals, and where he liked to invite his friends.

I call him Safi: perhaps it would be more correct to call him General Safi. He had been in the Afghan army, and had in fact risen to such august heights that he had been the Protector of the King of Afghanistan. Later he had been imprisoned and tortured before finally managing to escape the country and end up in Britain. No wonder he loved his paradise so much.

Meanwhile our own plot wasn't looking too bad either. It goes without saying it was still a constant battle, a never-ending struggle to keep the forces of chaos at bay – the weeds, the birds, the slugs – but we were also beginning to reap some of the rewards of our labours. The treats were beginning to come thick and fast;

after the delight of the early broad beans there was the harvesting of the early potatoes, one of the great fixtures of late spring/early summer. There may be things more delicious than new potatoes boiled with a sprig of mint, and served with plenty of butter; but not many. In our case they were Charlottes, one of the classic salad potatoes, and even digging them up was a pleasure. The technique seemed to be to dig a fork into the ground to one side of the plant, doing your best not to stick the fork through one of your precious spuds, and then gently lift the plant a bit. That done, you can start rummaging through the soil for the young potatoes, which are like creamy-yellow eggs against the chocolate brown of the moist soil. They look practically good enough to eat just as they are. It is a bit like digging for buried treasure, and is one of the jobs which really appeal to children. 'Look Dad, I've found one!' I may have forty-odd years on the children, but I still know how they feel. Digging up potatoes brings out the 8-year-old in all of us.

Around the time the first potatoes were coming out, the first beans were going in. While I am quite happy to eat them, runner beans are not my favourite vegetable; I find the flavour a little coarse and intrusive. It would, however, be completely out of the question to have an allotment and not grow runner beans. As well as being one of Eliza's favourite vegetables, they also occupy a totemic role in allotment culture, being the crop that you will find on almost every allotment in the country. Their pretty red flowers are an essential part of the allotment summer, and plotholders devote much of their time and energy to working out how best to grow them. Runner beans, being foreigners of a rather tender disposition – despite their traditional English image, their forebears actually came from South America – like moisture and plenty of goodness in the soil, and the way that many gardeners like to provide this is by digging a trench for their beans.

These trenches are the subject of much debate among bean-growers, who are liable to get dangerously obsessive on the subject. If you are serious about your runner bean trench, you dig it several months before you are going to plant your beans – perhaps even the beginning of the winter before. Then you start filling it with all sorts of organic matter which can gradually rot down so that by the time the following June comes and it is time to plant out your runner beans, they will be going into a lovely, rich, moisture-retentive growing medium.

So what goes into these trenches? I'm glad you asked, because from what I can gather, just about anything can. Garden waste, obviously, and kitchen waste: that goes without saying. People also put in material which is slow to decompose in the compost heap, like Brussels sprouts stems, as well as less obvious things such as newspaper, cardboard, old woolly jumpers (good for the slow release of nitrogen, according to the Woolly Jumper Supporters Club) and human hair. I did read of someone on the Allotments4All online forum who, when he did not have any jumpers he could spare, found a couple of old woollen flock mat-tresses whose contents he tipped into the bean trench; he also mentioned how the old Yorkshire show growers used to use wool shoddy, but he hadn't seen any of that for several years. Goodness me no, it's been quite a while since I've seen wool shoddy in London. Whatever wool shoddy is. Although pre-sumably back in the days when Shepherd's Bush was full of all those shepherds you probably couldn't move for the stuff.

The other subject that exercises bean growers is the question of the best structure to grow them up. Some people favour a line of pairs of sticks – bamboos are a common choice – set in the soil like a succession of capital As, without the crossbar, and with a long stick resting along the top to give it all some stability; others, perhaps rather more ambitious, have large, semi-permanent wire structures, a bit like an old-fashioned bedstead set on its side. We went for the traditional cottage garden look with three wooden tepees, each one consisting of six hazel sticks stuck in the ground and tied together at the top. The hazel sticks came from the forest next to my parents-in-law's house in Wiltshire, which as a bit of green recycling was hard to beat. We also had one tepee of borlotti, the rather beautiful beans from Italy with the distinctive red-and-white marbling which are so good in soup.

After a slightly unreliable start, our salad production was beginning to come on stream. We had had a few failures at the start, such as the Little Gems which proved to be as popular with the slugs of East Acton as they are with supermarket buyers; we also did not seem to have much luck with another lettuce which, according to the pretension level of your seed company, is called either Merveille de Quatre Saisons or Marvel of Four Seasons. Apparently it is an absolute trouper, grows practically all year round, brilliant performer in the vegetable patch, etc., etc. Not in London W3 it isn't; Débâcle de Quatre Saisons, more like. Apart from those, however, we grew some wonderful Cocarde lettuces, an oakleaf type with a gorgeous purple tint to the leaves, and some Lobjoits, which are beyond question the best Cos lettuce I have ever eaten. Crisp, and tasty, as well as being extraordinarily well behaved in that they will sit there for ages without bolting, which is more than I can say for some lettuces. However, to my slight shame and regret I have to confess that on the salad front, the star of the show during our first year was a packet of mixed salad leaves from Mr Fothergill. There we were, doing our best to buy interesting lettuces from the more credible seed suppliers (the more obscure the better, of course), only to find they were all outshone by a packet from one of the mass-market companies which had come free with an issue of my *Kitchen Garden* magazine. It was brilliant. All you had to do was sow a line of Mr Fothergill's seeds and a short while later you could, by carefully snipping a leaf or two off each little plant, pick yourself the most fantastic salad of mixed baby leaves, the sort of thing which normally comes in chlorine-pumped plastic bags in the supermarket and costs £1.99 for enough for two. Then, about five days later – and this is the glory of the so-called 'cut-and-come-again' method – you could do it all again.

It was round about this time that I began to notice some mildly disturbing changes in my behaviour. Before we started growing our own vegetables, I used to regard salad-washing as one of my least favourite kitchen chores. If there was some salad to be washed, I would often find myself with some fright-fully important task to do upstairs, or a vital phone call to make. But when it came to salad we had grown ourselves, I actually found myself enjoying cleaning it. The leaves were so perfect and tender and fresh, not to mention pretty, that it was a joy to immerse them in a sink full of cold water, swoosh them around and dry them in the salad spinner. They were my little babies, and it was only right that they should be served looking their absolute best. I did, though, acknowledge that this was not necessarily entirely normal, and resolved to monitor the situation for the development of any other manifestations of Vegetable Obsessive Behaviour Disorder.

Along with the spuds and the salad, the beetroot was begin-ning to come along too, a success about which I had decidedly mixed feelings. In fact I think that the only vegetation on the plot which I regarded with less affection was the bindweed, and even that was a pretty close thing. Still, even I had to admit that its purple-veined leaves were quite attractive, and if you picked them young enough they were a moderately pleasing addition to a salad of mixed leaves. At the back of my mind I wondered whether if I picked the young leaves aggressively enough, that might even stunt the growth of the root itself and I wouldn't have to eat any of the wretched things, but I guess that that was just wishful thinking. I was, in any case, in something of a minority when it came to the joy of beetroot. There was my wife, of course, who had a well-documented history there; unfortunately, she also managed to get to the children before I did and convince them that *Beta vulgaris* wasn't just something that should be fed to farm animals, it was actually fit for human consumption. Her trick was to bake it in a sealed pot with a bit of olive oil and plenty of salt and pepper, instead of boiling it, which obviously was a rather underhand way of brainwashing my children, who were just innocent pawns in this battle. I am afraid to say that they gobbled it all up, although whether I am prepared to accept her word for it that they also asked for more is perhaps going a little too far.

If it had just been my wife who was trying to spread the word, that would have been one thing; however, she also managed to recruit some co-conspirators. First there was her brother Piers, who – while not someone who would ever describe himself as a foodie, let along a gourmet – knows his food, and is a rather good cook. Throughout our first year on the allotment he would ring me up at regular intervals and say, 'Hello, Val, got any beetroot for us?' Fortunately for me the one gap in his expertise was the life cycle and cropping times of the beetroot, and so for the first half-dozen phone calls I was able to palm him off with 'Sorry Piers, it's not ready yet'; then, at the appropriate moment, I was able to change that to 'Sorry, Piers, it's all gone.' There was after all no way that I was knowingly going to participate in the beetroot trade; it was bad enough growing it without actually transporting it across borough boundaries.

While Piers's beetroot proclivities could perhaps be explained by some strange family trait – perhaps Eliza, while ostensibly of fairly straightforward Anglo-Irish stock, actually had some Eastern European ancestors somewhere back along the family tree – the final insult came at the school summer fair. This was in June, by which time I had finally run out of excuses and actually let myself be manoeuvred into eating some of Eliza's baked beetroot. Being an amenable sort of fellow, and seeing no reason to start divorce proceedings just because of a disagreement about vegetables, I managed to eat it all up without any unpleasant incidents; however, I resolved then to find a way of getting rid of the remains of our crop on to someone else. My chance came at our children's school summer fair, one of those occasions with a raffle and an auction and stalls selling toys and books, all aimed at raising money for the school. 'I know what,' I said brightly. 'Why don't we have a small stall selling a few of our surplus lettuces and other vegetables? Such as, for instance, oh I don't know, how about a few beetroot?' Eliza, although a bit suspicious, could not think of any serious objection, and so on the day of the fair we set up a stall with a few salad things, and two bunches of beetroot all neatly tied together.

There is, sadly, no getting around the fact that the beetroot was a success. 'Ooh, beetroot – my favourite!' gushed one mother who, until then, I had always thought to be in perfect command of her senses. 'Is there any more?' another one asked. 'I'm never allowed to have it at home – my husband cannot stand it.' She then proceeded to go into a graphic description of the effects of beetroot on the digestive system, which I have no intention of repeating here, other than to say it involves EVERY-THING turning purple. And she wonders why her husband cannot abide the stuff.

Unfortunately for me Eliza had not allowed us to sell the whole crop, and so there were a few more beetroot dinners to endure before I could declare the season over. There was baked beetroot, which once more I managed to finish, quite bravely I think; there was also a dish of beetroot baked in yoghurt which we served to friends at dinner, although how I managed to let that one slip through I really cannot imagine. They all finished their helpings, too; obviously they were being polite. Finally, to use up the last of the crop, we decided to make some soup. Instead of borscht, which sounded a bit of a palaver, we went for a recipe for a thick beetroot cream from Lindsey Bareham's *A Celebration of Soup*. Whenever one has a glut of vegetables, I usually find that soup turns out to be one of the best ways of using up the surplus, and if you make too much you can always freeze it. Lindsey Bareham, who used to write the cookery column for my very own newspaper, the London *Evening Standard*, has a soup for every occasion, and in the very rare instances when she happens not to come up with the goods there is always my other favourite soup book, *Soups* by Hannah Wright. Armed with those two volumes, no vegetable grower need ever be stuck for inspiration. Anyway, here is Ms Bareham's Beetroot Cream, which I quote not because it is in any way delicious – it's got beetroot in it, remember? – but because it is such an extraordinary shade of deep purple that I had two helpings, just to make sure that what I was eating was actually soup, and not some kind of weird reject from a Dulux paint factory. Eliza said it was particularly tasty and nutritious, but then she has to earn her retainer from the Beetroot Marketing Board somehow.

450 g/1 lb raw beetroot
1.7 litres/3 pints chicken stock
4 sprigs parsley
6 peppercorns
8 coriander seeds
½ tsp fennel seeds
1 leek, chopped
2 celery stalks, chopped
2 carrots, peeled and chopped
4 shallots, finely chopped
1 clove of garlic, peeled and chopped
salt and pepper
150 g/5 oz strained Greek yoghurt
1 tbsp snipped chives

Scrub the beetroot but do not peel or cut it. Place it in a pan with the chicken stock, and add the parsley, peppercorns, coriander and fennel seeds bundled up in a muslin bag. Bring to the boil, lower the heat, partially cover, and simmer gently for sixty minutes. Add the chopped leek, celery, carrots, shallots and garlic, and cook on for a further twenty minutes.

Remove the pan from the heat. Fish out the beetroot and leave to cool, remove and discard the muslin bag. Rub off the skin of the beetroot and trim the ends. Transfer to a processor or blender and purée with the other vegetables and the stock. Sieve into a clean pan, reheat, taste and season.

Serve the soup with a dollop of yoghurt garnished with chives. There it is. And don't say I didn't warn you.

9

Not So Fantastic Mr Fox

But Peter, who was very naughty, ran straight away to Mr. McGregors's garden and squeezed under the gate! First he ate some lettuces and some French beans; and then he ate some radishes; and then, feeling rather sick, he went to look for some parsley.

Beatrix Potter, *The Tale of Peter Rabbit*

'God,' said Michael, with a look on his face that might have been admiration or amusement, it was not entirely clear, 'would you look at those onions.' And yes, I had to admit that our onions were looking pretty good. While we had been fighting all our other battles over the year, warding off the encroachments of various pests large and small, seen and unseen, the onions had just kept on growing. I would like to be able to claim it was all down to us, that somehow we were such diligent gardeners that we just had mastered the art of onion-growing in our first season, but that would be straining credibility too far. We put them in the ground, we weeded them once or twice, they grew. We did apply a mulch of bark chippings the previous autumn, which as you may remember was regarded as a controversial technique at the time, but even at my most self-deluding I would be hard pressed to argue that that was why some of our onions were practically the size of grapefruit. 'Look at the size of them,' said Michael. 'The biggest onions on the allotment. I can't grow onions like that.' Then he walked off, chuckling to himself, although what precisely was so amusing was not immediately apparent, other than the obviously hilarious fact that two complete jackasses who had never grown a vegetable in their lives had somehow managed to produce the largest onions for miles around.

As well as onions, we were also proving passably adept at growing flowers (I say 'we', although of course if I was being honest I would say that my participation in the flower-growing division of our allotment enterprise should probably be more accurately described as that of a sleeping partner). We had lots of flowers, many of them very pretty, and some of which I could even put a name to (the salvia I could do, and the nasturtiums, and of course the marigolds, although I can only really award myself a half-credit for that one, because I still get confused as to whether they are the French ones or the English ones). It was all very pleasing, not only because it gave us a great sense of satisfaction to be able to cut our own flowers for the house, but also because it saved us a small fortune.

There was only one problem with our flower-growing efforts,

however: apart from the ones I have already mentioned, most of the flowers we were growing were black. We had black scabious; we had black cornflowers (one of my favourite flowers, which we had at our wedding – proper blue ones, that is); and we had black dahlias. It was an awful lot of black flowers. By the height of summer the allotment was beginning to look like an undertakers' convention (albeit quite a sophisticated one). I did confront my wife one day about how this state of affairs had come about: 'Eliza,' I said, 'why exactly are we growing quite so many black flowers?' I am afraid to say that she did not really have much of an explanation, other than to mutter something about some of them being quite stylish, and to admit that even for her it was causing a bit of a problem, what with the flower arranging and all that.

The passing of the weeks meant that gradually and imperceptibly the workload began to increase. The warmer it became, and the longer the days, the faster our crops grew; and the faster they grew, the faster the weeds grew, too. They weren't the only ones. Overwhelmed by the sight of all this luscious vegetation, the various pests who chose to dine on our allotment became more numerous and more voracious by the day. The result was that there was so much work to do that if we did not visit the plot for a couple of days there was a serious danger of getting badly behind with the work. It was a far cry from those idle days of winter and early spring when we could decide to go to the allotment at the weekend, or not, depending on how the mood took us, and nothing would really matter. There was always something to do, whether it was weeding or watering, thinning the lettuce or checking to see how the beans were getting on; and there was never enough time to do it all. Before we knew it, the allotment had become what is technically known as Work.

Now, I already had one job, and to be honest that was quite enough, thank you. While the world is full of people who – for reasons of ambition, martyrdom or perhaps just sheer stupidity – choose to make a virtue of working fourteen-hour days, I am not one of them. To be honest, in my view the old-fashioned nine to five is enough of an imposition as it is without trying to take on more. Yet the curious thing is that while I often rushed home from work, changed into my gardening clothes and high-tailed it over to the allotment as fast as my bicycle could carry me to put in another couple of hours, I never regarded it as a burden. If anything, it was a bit of a relief; after a stressful day at the office, there was nothing like performing a simple task such as watering or hoeing as the late afternoon sun played on your back to make your daily cares just melt away. You might even pick a little something for your supper; from plot to plate in less than an hour. How perfect is that?

As we struggled to stay on top of things, we almost forgot to stand back and have a good look at the plot – which, much to our surprise, was actually beginning to look like an allotment. What had been a cold, damp place back in January, full of weeds and stones and not a lot of promise, had by June become an Eden of lush growth and good things to eat. Here was a row of Cos lettuces, as fresh and crisp as you like, there a row of rainbow chard, thick and glossy and abundant. In one bed a patch of maincrop potatoes was doing its own special underground magic, while across the way three wigwams of hazel sticks had bean plants twining their way upwards. There were tomatoes and cucumbers, radishes and courgettes, and it would not be going too far to say (though perhaps I am a little biased) that it was all looking rather splendid. I know this because, some time around the harvesting of our much admired onions, Michael came over to have a look at our progress. 'Well, you're not doing too badly,' he said. 'For newcomers.' It may not have sounded much, but coming from Michael it was one of the greatest compliments I had received all year.

As the season progressed, one of the tricks we learned about good allotment management was the technique of successional sowing. It is a pretty simple business, really, but an easy one to overlook. The idiot gardener's approach – and believe me, this is one area where I know what I am talking about – is to sow a row of carrots, say, and then wait anxiously for them to make an appearance. When they do bother to germinate, the idiot gardener congratulates himself on his brilliant horticultural skills, and starts counting down the days until they are going to be ready. Fast-forward three or four months: up come the carrots, and then before he knows it the IG has eaten them all, and is going to have to wait until next year before he can enjoy some more. What he should have done, of course, is sow a second row of carrots a month or so after the first one, so that as soon as he finishes pulling up one row he knows there is another one that will soon be ready for harvesting in a couple of weeks.

The result of all this successional sowing was that all over the allotment there were rows and rows of freshly sown seeds, which tended to make working a slightly tricky matter: seedlings are delicate chaps, and don't take kindly to being trodden on by size 11 gardening boots. The answer was to mark each row with string – a bamboo cane at each end of the row, and a length of garden twine stretched between them.

Unfortunately, it wasn't quite as simple as that. Whenever we put up a new line, a few days later we would return to the allotment and find that it was broken in two. My first thought was that somehow it was rotting in the wet conditions, and so I went out and bought a roll of extra-thick string, the really hairy old-fashioned kind. It did not make a blind bit of difference; within a week the new line, once so taut and straight, was a sad, limp thing, lying dankly on the ground. I asked Michael what he thought the reason was and he answered without a moment's hesitation. 'That'll be the squirrels,' he said as if everybody knew who was responsible for any string-chewing antics that went on in these parts. Of course. How silly of me. Everyone knows about squirrels and their propensity to sink their teeth into any passing piece of string that catches their fancy. I am not entirely sure what exactly is in it for the squirrel, however. As far as I am aware there is not much nutritional value in string, and they did not seem to be stealing the string to line their nests, or anything useful like that. The only conclusion I could come to was that they were biting through our lines for the sole purpose of being annoying; in which aim, I need hardly add, they succeeded brilliantly.

The squirrels were not the only intruder on the allotment that summer. For the past couple of months our manure heap had been maturing away nicely. It was, though I say it myself, not a bad manure heap, with old pallets for sides, some weed-proof fabric at the bottom to stop the bindweed infesting it, a layer of plastic sheeting over the top to stop the rain getting in, and a couple of pieces of old carpet over the top of that to keep the warmth in. One day I noticed that there was a barrowload or so of my finest horse muck spread all over the path next to the heap. On closer inspection I noticed that some of the plastic sheeting had been torn to shreds, and on closer inspection still I noticed that there was a hole in the heap, just at the side near the front. It went along the side of the heap, just inside the pallet wall, and then into the centre of the heap where it opened out into a rather larger chamber, about eighteen inches in diameter. I am no zoologist, but something told me that this was no squirrel.

There was at least some kind of rationale as to why a fox should want to make its home inside my manure heap. It was cosy and warm, and contrary to what one might expect, it didn't really smell. Thanks to my admirable construction it was also as safe a home as a fox could reasonably expect, at least certainly in those parts of East Acton. In a sense, the fox was paying us a compliment by choosing to rear its family on our plot.

Cheeky sod: I served the bushy-tailed squatter with his eviction papers the very same afternoon. I filled in the hole, replaced the scattered manure, adjusted the torn plastic and laid down a barrier of bricks and old planks to make sure that any fox who wanted to take up residence in my manure heap again would have to come equipped with a JCB digger before he would be able to effect an entry. While in a sense I have nothing against foxes – apart from a lingering suspicion that they trampled my onions once – it offends my sense of territory that they should think they have a right to wander where they like. And they should be under no illusion that should my defences fail, I would have any hesitation in setting up the inaugural meeting of the Shepherd's Bush and East Acton Hunt – ban or no ban.

Human intruders are a more straightforward proposition, and like most allotment societies the Acton Gardening Association does its best to keep them out. The Bromyard site is protected by a substantial metal gate, secured with a heavy padlock and topped by some nasty-looking spikes. Anyone managing to get past that lot would have to be very resourceful and/or athletic, not to mention hungry, to the extent that if they did manage to break in I for one would be hard-pressed to begrudge them the odd carrot.

Aside from its robust attitude to breaking and entering – allotment-holders are asked to lock the gate at all times, even when they are there working their plots – the Association is a remarkably liberal and tolerant institution when it comes to rules and regulations. Some allotments have all sorts of laws about what you can and cannot do, with a thousand petty restrictions about what you are allowed to grow (no flowers), what you are allowed to keep (no livestock) and what you are allowed to build (no sheds). There are allotments where you are allowed sheds, but they must all be painted the same colour, and allotments where you are not allowed to put up any netting unless it has been approved in advance by the committee.

Still, at least there aren't any allotments these days where the members are obliged to attend church at least once on a Sunday, as was once common, or where you will be fined sixpence if you are caught collecting produce after 9 a.m. on a Sunday. The fines imposed on erring members could be quite substantial. A chap called Edwin Grey was secretary of the Rothamsted allotments in Hertfordshire at the end of the nineteenth century, and wrote in his memoirs how he found several instances in the old record books of people being fined as much as five shillings (25p), which was quite a decent sum in those days. One entry, he said, 'records the fact that the wife of a certain member shall be fined 5 shillings for cutting George Smith's cauliflowers: and yet another record wherein after serious discussion it was resolved that a man named Attwood be fined 5 shillings, for calling the Committee an ignorant set of fools'.

The attitude of my own allotment committee, which bears no resemblance whatsoever to a set of fools, ignorant or otherwise, seems in contrast to be that as long as you pay your rent, look after your plot and don't break the law, you are pretty much allowed to do what you like. Except, that is, for the bit about no cockerels. You can keep hens if you like – a couple of plot-holders do – but there is a strict rule about no cockerels. It is something to do with the noise, I expect, although the days when East Acton was some kind of rural idyll where your early morning sleep would be disturbed by the sound of roosters greeting the day are long gone; what with the traffic noise, the burglar alarms, the police sirens and the late-night altercations between drunks, it is a wonder that anyone gets any sleep at all.

Rules, however, are all very well, but they are only of any use if the potential offenders are likely to be members of the allotment association; local vandals and cauli-blaggers are unlikely to be deterred by threats of expulsion from an organisation to which they don't even belong in the first place. That explains, perhaps, the rather draconian action taken by North Avon magistrates a year or two ago when someone started stealing vegetables from the allotments in the Gloucestershire village of Iron Acton. It was the height of the summer, and the cabbages and carrots had started disappearing from the allotments at an alarming rate. That was bad enough, but then the strawberries started going too, and that was going too far: something had to be done. Plot-holders started looking for clues. They found incriminating footprints, and even managed to work out his shoe size, but a shoe size without a suspect isn't generally much use, not unless you have got CSI Gloucestershire on the case (they were probably a bit busy). Then one of the plot-holders, 74-year-old John Seymour – in a display of resourcefulness which I feel is characteristic of the can-do attitude of allotment folk – installed a camera in a neighbour's bathroom and set about catching the culprit red-handed. He would get up every morning at 5 a.m., reckoning that that was probably the sort of time that strawberry thieves went about their business, and lie in wait. He did not have to wait long. 'He would come as regular as clockwork at around 5.15 a.m. – I took four photos of him looking at people's things while my wife ran down and got his number plate,' he said. 'He must be healthy because he got a lot of cabbages. He dug someone's leeks up as well and he had a good look at the rhubarb and apples, but didn't touch them. One old chap lost his strawberries – so I don't think he spent much money on groceries.'

The villain turned out to be a 76-year-old former accountant called Phillip Powner from Yate, who when he wasn't digging up valuable brassicas was also helping himself to hanging baskets and garden ornaments without so much as a by-your-leave. When he appeared before the magistrates' court he was given a six-month interim Asbo which banned him from entering any garden or allotment in the county.

Thanks to Mr Seymour, the allotment-holders of South Gloucestershire can now sleep soundly in their beds, safe in the knowledge that their vegetables will still be there when they get up in the morning. Unless the pigeons have got to them first, of course, but they are probably on their own on that one.

10

Mind the Gap

The best thing about Grandpa's house was the wonderful garden. 'I grow all my own vegetables,' Grandpa said proudly.

'I don't eat vegetables,' Oliver told Grandpa.

Vivian French, Oliver's Vegetables

As an allotment gardener, it is easy to be seduced by the summer. It is a time of plenty, when your courgette plants are producing new fruit almost every day (and if you have made the beginner's mistake of planting too many, you are probably running out of friends to give them away to), your bean plants are laden with tender green pods and your tomatoes are ripening nicely on the vine. Everything in the garden is lovely, and it is all you can do to eat all the produce that comes off the plot. But that's the summer for you; any fool can run an allotment in the summer. The tricky bit is making sure your plot keeps on producing in the autumn and winter, to say nothing of that period in spring known as the 'hungry gap' when the autumn vegetables which the wise gardener has diligently kept in storage during the winter months have finally run out but the early spring veg haven't started doing their thing yet. That's where your winter veg come into their own, stalwarts like cabbages and leeks which will keep you fed during those cold, dark months. If you like cabbages and leeks, that is; if you don't, you'd probably better go and live somewhere else rather warmer for the winter.

The trouble with these winter veg, however, is that they do take up an awful lot of room for a very long time. My packet of Early Purple Sprouting Broccoli, for instance, says it is 'a delicious vegetable producing heavy crops of purple topped side shoots in March'; it also says that you should sow it in April. In other words, it is in the ground for something approaching a year, which is a long time by anyone's reckoning. If you compare it with the lettuce, for instance, or the beetroot, both of which can be ready in as little as twelve weeks, the old PSB does seem to take its time about things. However, as it is one of my favourite vegetables, this rather dilatory approach to the business of growing was a character flaw for which I was prepared to forgive it. Other vegetables that do not seem to be in any particular hurry to get on with things include Brussels sprouts, Savoy cabbages and leeks, so if you want to have anything to eat over the winter, you have to be prepared to plan ridiculously far in advance, and to devote a significant proportion of your plot to your winter greens.

Being of a somewhat obstinate disposition, not to say bloody-minded, I regarded these obstacles as an interesting challenge rather than an argument for not bothering, and resolved that I was going to provide winter vegetables for my family if it was the last thing I did. They were words that I would later learn to regret.

The First Great Brassica War began one afternoon in April when I made a little seed bed in an unused corner of the plot, and sowed a couple of lines each of winter cabbage and purple sprouting broccoli. It seemed a pretty uncontroversial move to me; I had, after all, sowed plenty of rows of seeds by then, and I don't think it would be going too far to say that I was beginning to get the hang of it. A week or so later the little seedlings made their first appearance: so far so good, I thought. That feeling of comfortable smugness lasted for about three more weeks, when I first noticed the tell-tale signs of flea beetle attack – tiny little holes all over the seedlings' leaves. Being a veteran of flea beetle attacks – they had by now mounted assaults on my mizuna, red giant mustard, rocket and radishes – I now knew what to do with them, and went off to the shed to fetch the derris dust. The great virtue of derris dust is that not only is it meant to deal with flea beetles, but it is also acceptable for use by organic gardeners. I have never been able to establish exactly why this should be the case, but as far as I can tell there are two possible reasons. One is that it is OK because it is a natural product, being made from the roots of a number of tropical plants. The other is that it doesn't work. The instructions say that you can harvest your plants just one day after dusting them with the stuff. That sounds all very reassuring, until you consider that if it is all right for people to eat after twenty-four hours, presumably it doesn't do the old flea beetle much harm either. For the moment, though, I decided that positive thinking was the order of the day, and so I gave the seedlings a good going-over with the derris and thought that that was that.

Wrong again. A week or two after transplanting the young plants into their final positions I noticed that holes – rather larger than the flea beetles' efforts – started appearing in the leaves. In some cases it wasn't so much a hole in the leaf as a general absence of leaf at all. It was all rather worrying, but at least I knew what was going on: the slugs were on the attack. Here were some nice juicy brassicas, as young and tender as you could hope for, and what slug worth the name could resist having the odd nibble? I saw Michael on his plot, and called him over to confirm my diagnosis. 'I think the slugs have been at my cabbages,' I said.

'Ah yes,' said Michael. 'That'll be the pigeons, then.' Until then I had had no idea that pigeons ate cabbages. Soft fruit, yes, and grass seed, and I had once lined them up as the prime suspect in the disappearance of our beetroot seedlings – but cabbages? Serious measures were called for; pigeons weren't like flea beetles, sent packing with a puff of derris dust, or even slugs for that matter, who can be more or less kept under control if you are prepared to use genocidal amounts of slug pellets. They were an altogether more resourceful and determined enemy, and defeating them would take rather more than a quick application of Pigeon-B-Gone. (Mind you, if anyone did actually manage to come up with something called Pigeon-B-Gone, and which actually worked, they could make a fortune overnight, as well as earning my undying gratitude.) Eliza and I sat down for a council of war as we considered our options. We could try making a scarecrow. It had the merits of being cheap (depending on how you dress the scarecrow, naturally), traditional, long-lasting and thoroughly organic; it was also, we feared, thoroughly useless. During the time that we had had the allotment, it had not escaped our attention that while we were working on our plot, pigeons were perfectly content to land on neighbouring plots to gorge themselves on whatever crops they could find, and so the idea that pigeons were so terrified of human beings that they would avoid a patch of ground displaying a straw-stuffed vaguely humanoid *thing* was a little implausible. I think we would have done as much good if we had put up a sign saying 'No Pigeons'.

Compact discs were a popular method of pigeon control. The idea was to string up a selection of discs over your crops so they could swing gently in the breeze, and the pigeons would be so disturbed by the sight that they would leave your plot alone and go and eat someone else's cabbages. Apart from the fundamental aesthetic objection – that having old CDs flapping around our allotment would make it look even more like a shanty town than it did already – I had a distinct feeling that in terms of efficacy it would not rank much higher than having a scarecrow.

It goes without saying that what I would most like to have done is to have lain in wait with a .22 rifle or a shotgun and sent the fat greedy monsters on their way to pigeon heaven. Sadly, that wasn't really on, and so we were left with just one last alternative – to drape netting over the cabbage plants to stop the pigeons from getting anywhere near them. Netting was purchased – at some expense, I might add, making me wonder whether this would not end up being the most expensive purple sprouting broccoli the world had ever seen – bamboo canes were procured and I narrowly managed to secure the precious brassicas before the pigeons ate them all. It was a close-run thing.

So: the cabbages were safe at last. There was simply no way the pigeons were going to get at them. But was that the end of the story? Of course it wasn't. The broccoli, you see, kept on growing taller and taller, and there soon came a point where I was going to have to raise the netting otherwise the two would get hopelessly entangled. The old, short bamboo canes were discarded and replaced with long ones, with empty plastic water bottles placed over the top so that the netting would have something to rest on. And, for a while, that did the trick, until the broccoli got so tall that even the long bamboo canes were no longer high enough. By now it was late summer and – based on a remark Michael once made about the pigeons being at their worst in the spring – I took the radical decision to remove the netting altogether. The broccoli plants were quite large now, and I thought that even if the pigeons did give them the odd peck they would probably survive. I remember thinking as I removed the last of their protection that they looked rather magnificent standing there; but also rather vulnerable. How were they going to get on? We would have to wait and see.

While the First Great Brassica War lumbered on with no clear end in sight, I learned another of the valuable lessons that allotment life has to teach you: that disasters come in all shapes and sizes. There is the brassica sort of disaster, for instance, where horrible little pests (or, in the case of the pigeons, horrible big pests) decide to make a feast out of your lovingly nurtured seedlings. There is another sort of disaster, however, in which the problem is not so much the disappearance of your crop as the fact that it seems to have ambitions to take over the whole of your plot. When we first got hold of our plot you may remember that I decided to plant some horseradish, on the grounds that I have always fancied having a bit of freshly grated horseradish sauce to go with my roast beef; you may also remember that I was given some dire warnings about how once it gets a hold on your vegetable garden you will never get rid of it. Fortunately I am careful, not to mention resourceful and enterprising, and was quickly able to come up with a solution to the horseradish problem, in the shape of the bottomless washing-up bowl (the theory being that it allows the horseradish to grow downwards but not to spread sideways). Problem solved.

Did I really say 'problem solved'? Time passed, the horseradish flourished, seemingly confined to the washing-up bowl, until one day I decided that the time had come to dig some up and have a proper Sunday roast. Armed with my best spade and brimming with misplaced confidence, I started digging; yes, there was that familiar white root, and goodness me doesn't it seem to be going down far? I dug a bit further; the root carried on going down. A large pile of earth began to appear next to where I was digging. I dug a bit further still; the root branched, and then carried on going down. And across: it had long since left the confines of the washing-up bowl far behind. My pile of earth was beginning to resemble a small hill. By this time I had dug all the way through the topsoil and was into the clay below, all thick and sticky and not really keen on being dug at all. The rate of digging began to slow down somewhat, which is just as well because I feared that if I carried on for much longer I would soon be getting through to the outskirts of Sydney, and I am not sure how I would explain that.

Eventually, partly in an attempt to preserve Anglo-Australian relations, and partly because it would soon be getting dark, and

I didn't really fancy digging by torchlight, I decided to admit defeat. I had created a monster, a monster with pungent white roots that had clearly decided it was never going to leave my allotment, no matter how much I tried to dig it out. Wearily I removed all the horseradish root that I could find, put the earth back and resigned myself to spending half a day every year fighting a hopeless battle against the condiment from hell. Although I admit that I do not come out of this escapade well, looking (i) foolish, (ii) lazy and (iii) foolish, there are two positive conclusions that can be drawn from this sorry adventure. One is that my wife never once said 'I told you so', which shows almost superhuman levels of forbearance on her part, and is yet another example of what a wonderful woman she is. No wonder I married her. The other is that the roast beef and horseradish was absolutely scrumptious, without a doubt the best I have ever tasted. So perhaps it was a sacrifice worth making after all.

During the horseradish digging exercise, Eliza had been on the plot with me, offering occasional guidance and encouragement ('Carry on, you're doing a really good job'; 'Keep on digging, don't give up'; and 'Don't you think you should dig a bit further?' – this last one when I could practically smell Australia) while she got on with her own tasks. That was a rare treat, because it is not often that the two of us manage to get down there at the same time, what with the demands of childcare and work and just life in general. Sometimes she manages to go during the day, while the children are at school and when she hasn't got any work on; sometimes I fit in a stint after work if I manage to finish early. The weekends should be easy, but aren't, mainly because I am afraid that Kitty and Orlando have got some rather old-fashioned ideas about child-rearing, namely that the parents should be around for it. Both of them. That means that slipping off to spend the day on the allotment on one's own is not really acceptable behaviour. As for the alternative – announcing brightly on Saturday morning, 'Children, have we got an exciting day for you! We're going to spend the day on the allotment, doing all sorts of wonderful things like weeding the salad beds, pinching out the tomatoes and tying in the sweet peas!' – well, it's not a stroke you can pull that often. Kitty and Orlando aren't stupid, you know.

That's not to say that they do not like the allotment; they do, they just don't necessarily want to spend the whole weekend there. Every weekend. Which is, of course, entirely reasonable, if a little misguided (I would happily spend every weekend there, except perhaps in January and February, but that's only because we haven't got a very big shed and there's nowhere to sit and read the paper). Eliza and I have worked out a strategy that as long as we take the children to the allotment only occasionally, and as long as we don't make them stay there for too long, we can have a very nice time. If we ignore either of those two rules, there is a high chance of hearing the traditional distress call of the young *Homo sapiens* fledgling: to wit, 'How much longer are we going to stay here?' Trained observers of the species in its natural habitat will also be familiar with the alternative form of the distress call: 'Dad, this is BOOOOORING!' – or, in extreme situations, 'I hate the allotment!'

In truth, they rather like it, not least because they each have their own little plot where they are allowed to grow what they like, and they also have their own tools, consisting of one fork, one spade and one pair of gardening gloves each. That's not to say that it has all been easy. Children being children, they quickly worked out that using their own tools was not nearly such fun as using Mummy and Daddy's, especially when Mummy and Daddy want to use them themselves; and anyway, the first time a child's spade encountered a particularly heavy piece of ground it bent in a rather alarming way. I don't think they will be using it for any double digging in the near future. It was also a mistake to give them their own little garden each, as opposed to one rather larger garden between the pair of them, as the existence of individual nation states led to inevitable conflicts ('His garden is bigger than mine!' 'No it's not! She's got far more than I have!'). We will, I feel, have to work on them on this one, explaining that by dismantling internal borders and removing trade restrictions, not to mention having a federated constitution and harmonious tax laws, they can soon learn to live happily together.

In the meantime, they do at least have something approaching a common agricultural policy. For a start, they like growing things. In fact I would say that all children like growing things, as long as they get a chance; there is something magical about putting a seed in the ground, and watching it change into a tiny little seedling, and then grow into a big healthy plant. It is even more magical if you feel that you can claim a little bit of the responsibility for yourself. I remember that feeling from when I was a child – sowing mustard and cress on damp blotting paper, and counting down the days before I could cut it and put it in a sandwich (does anyone eat mustard and cress sandwiches any more?). What the children like growing are things they can see, like tomatoes, or things they can dig up, like carrots, because digging things up is fun. They also like things that grow quickly, which rules out vegetables like broccoli and leeks, which are enough to test even the most patient gardener. As it is the children's enthusiasm can run away with them, so that one finds oneself explaining that no, you cannot eat the carrots today because you only planted them the week before last and they are not actually ready yet. The most important criterion, however, is the ease with which you can eat the crop there and then. In common with most other children, Kitty and Orlando's picking technique can be summarised as: 'One for me, one for the pot, one for me, one for the pot', except that sometimes they do not always bother with the 'one for the pot' bit. I can't say I blame them, either. What is better than picking a juicy, sweet tomato off the vine, all warm from the sun, and popping it straight into your mouth? If a few of the tomatoes manage to make it home without being eaten – well, that's just a bonus.

Employee theft aside, Kitty and Orlando are pretty good members of the team when it comes to harvesting. I have already mentioned the fun we have had digging up potatoes. There are even times when I would go so far as to describe the children as invaluable, such as the bean harvest. We grow our beans up wigwams, which is a moderately efficient use of space, I suppose, and without doubt an attractive feature on the allotment; the downside is that it is not always easy to reach the beans on the inside of the wigwam. That is where having small boys on the team comes into its own. Rather like the way the Victorians used to send boys up chimneys – a practice which I sometimes think they abandoned with a little too much haste – the 5-year-old Orlando was of a perfect size to be sent inside the wigwam and instructed to pick any beans he could find. It was a task he relished, even more so after we christened the little Orlando-sized chamber inside the wigwams 'Bean World'. One day Orlando was doing his bean thing when Michael happened to be passing. 'Look,' I said to him, pointing to the scarcely visible Orlando. 'A human bean!' How I laughed, although with the passage of time I cannot accurately recall whether anyone laughed with me.

Sometimes there are no beans to be picked, no potatoes to be dug; then, rather reluctantly, Eliza and I let the children play. If they put their mind to it, there are plenty of things to do on the allotment, such as digging useful holes, having fights on top of the manure heap and collecting worms. Once in a while, we have a special treat and use the camping stove to fry up some sausages for a sausage sandwich picnic. It may not be Café Safi, but it is pretty delicious all the same.

The best thing about it all, though, is that our secret plan to brainwash the children has proved remarkably successful. Kitty and Orlando now know where vegetables come from, and understand that homegrown things are somehow better than shop-bought, even if it is only because we have told them so often enough. They understand that certain vegetables appear at certain times of the year. And I cannot, without scratching my head a bit, think of anything from the allotment that they don't eat: it all gets gobbled up. Orlando, now he is a bit older, likes flicking through the gardening magazines by our bedside, and once picked up a colour supplement which we had left open at a feature about vegetable-growing. 'Mum, dad,' he said, pointing at the pictures on the page in a rather serious manner, 'I would like to grow . . . pumpkin, leeks, beetroot, sweet potato and sweetcorn.' Another time I was serving the children their tea, and brought to the table a steaming bowl of greens. 'What's that?' asked Kitty. 'Kale,' I said. 'Wicked!' she said.

11

Sex and the Allotment

CECILY: When I see a spade I call it a spade.
GWENDOLEN: I am glad to say that I have never seen a spade.

Oscar Wilde, The Importance of Being Earnest

Machete or strimmer? It's not one of the traditional allotment dilemmas – these are normally no more taxing than the question of whether to grow Moneymaker tomatoes or Gardeners' Delight (and if you ask me, I wouldn't bother with either), or whether to ditch all those pesky organic principles and bung some Growmore on your onions – but some time around July it was one that was becoming increasingly troubling.

The problem was the grass. In between the separate allotments there are grass paths (there are also grass paths in between the four beds on our plot, but that is a different matter), and it is the responsibility of the plot-holder to make sure that the paths adjacent to his or her plot do not get overgrown. Being an issue which involves both community responsibility and the potential for border disputes, it should come as no surprise to anyone that the state of the paths is the cause of some of the bitterest arguments on the allotments, and many is the time that assorted senior plot-holders on our site who, for the sake of maintaining peace and good will between all men (not that there is really much chance of that), had better remain anonymous have had occasion to complain mightily and, it has to be said, at great length, about the failure of some of their fellow plot-holders to keep their paths well trimmed. Indeed, it took a couple of gentle hints from our allotment neighbours before Eliza and I woke up to the fact that we were going to have to do something about our paths before the grass got so high that the plot disappeared from sight completely.

The question was, how? We had an old pair of garden shears at home which seemed to be the answer, so we took them over to the allotment and one afternoon I duly set about trying to cut the grass. Does anyone else remember those scissors one used to be allowed to use in primary school, the ones with round ends which were deemed safe enough for little 5-year-old hands but were in fact so blunt that they could not cut anything and struggled even to get through a single piece of paper? These shears were like them, only not quite so sharp. I did not so much cut the grass as tear it, and how we managed to get round the perimeter of the plot was a miracle of perseverance and fortitude against almost insuperable odds. By the time we finished the paths looked as if they had been suffering from a particularly nasty attack of alopecia, but at least the grass was shorter. We, on the other hand, were half dead with exhaustion, and as we crawled home that evening, scarcely able to move our arms, we decided that perhaps something would have to change.

Sharpening the shears seemed like a good start. Off they went to the sharpening man, and while I wouldn't say that when they came back they were so razor-like I could have shaved with them, they were a bit sharper. A bit. Cutting the grass wasn't much easier, however, and as I knelt there one day, hacking away like a demented barber, Michael decided it was time to take pity on me. 'Try mine,' he said, 'I think you'll find it easier.' On the allotment, there is an art to offering help. It consists of waiting until your victim is well into his chosen task, has driven himself to near-collapse/tears of frustration/the edge of madness with his cack-handed attempts to carry out the simplest job, and then stepping in with a kindly smile as you say, 'Here, why not try it this way?' Which translates, roughly, as 'I have had my fill of amusement watching you do it the stupid way, and now my natural sense of decency tells me that it is time to save you from yourself.' The key to it all is that your method should be so much better than your victim's that his gibbering gratitude is mixed with the awful realisation that for the past hour he has been making something of a plonker of himself; and in theory that is what was going on here. His shears were the long-handled type, with the blades at right angles to the handle so that you could stand up while cutting the grass, and yes he was right, it was easier. Kneeling down to cut the grass does not really count as ergonomic. But it still wasn't easy. Hacking away at grass with shears is a mug's game no matter whether you are kneeling down or standing up, and as I handed the shears back to Michael I thought to myself: there has got to be an easier way than this.

The easier way meant only one thing, of course: a strimmer. Cutting annoying bits of grass was exactly what they were invented for, and it was quite clear in my mind that with a strimmer I could shave the grass paths around our allotment – and the paths inside – to a perfect Number 1 cut in a matter of minutes. True, there was the small matter that we did not actually have a mains electricity supply on the Bromyard site – we were lucky enough to have running water – but that was just a small obstacle as far as I was concerned. A few minutes' research on the Internet established that there were several battery-powered strimmers on the market which we could recharge at home, and which seemed more than adequate for the job. The more I looked into strimmers, the more they seemed the perfect solution to our problem.

Like all perfect solutions, though, it wasn't really as perfect as it seemed. However efficient the strimmer was, however easy it was going to make the cutting of the grass, however much it was going to improve our lives, the trouble was that it just wasn't very allotment. People on allotments solve their problems with old bits of junk, with tools they have been using for decades, or – if they are absolutely forced to spend money – with equipment they have bought from the Poundstretcher store for an absolute pittance and which was probably designed with quite some other use in mind. It is not so much penny-pinching as thriftiness, not so much meanness as an approach to life that values frugality over ostentation, and resourcefulness over extravagance; how much more satisfying it is to solve your problems with a bit of artful make-and-mend than by just driving off to B&Q and waving your credit card around the place. That ruled out the strimmer, then.

It was around this time, when the grass was merrily growing away in the late summer sun, probably wondering why no one was bothering to cut it this year, that I noticed John hacking away at his paths with a machete. Chop, chop, chop, he went, and with a few deft strokes the path was transformed from an impenetrable jungle to a neatly trimmed stretch of turf. I went over to him and said something inconsequential, like 'Hello, John, you're pretty useful with that machete.' It was as if I had uttered a magic word, for he immediately launched himself into a passionate monologue on the virtues of his machete – or cut-lass, as he sometimes chose to call it – its history, its provenance and its general usefulness. Which, apparently, knows no bounds. Essentially, from what I could gather, the machete is the ultimate wondertool, something which as well as cutting and chopping can be used for weeding, hoeing, digging, planting and just about every garden job that one can think of; John even liked to eat things with it, neatly removing crops from the ground with a quick flick of the wrist and then transferring them to his mouth on the point of the blade – a manoeuvre which John made look very easy but in less experienced hands would probably have led to a visit to the local accident and emergency department. John then gave me a quick tutorial on the best way to cut grass with a machete, a technique that I may not quite have mastered on my first session, owing to a slight nervousness and a desire to return home with the same number of fingers and thumbs as when I had set out, but that John assured me would result in the solution to all my grass-cutting woes.

Now, I expect many readers will have been to one of those

outdoor markets where some stallholder is showing off a fantastic new kitchen tool, something which slices as it dices as it chops as it shreds, and which will totally transform their lives. They will also be familiar with the phenomenon of the shopper who has no intention of buying one of the said kitchen slicer-dicer thingies, and indeed would never fall for such crude and obvious marketing techniques, and yet who by the time they get to go home finds that they have unaccountably bought one of the slicer-dicers, even if they actually have no memory of the transaction. Well, something like that happened to me that afternoon with John. I didn't want to buy a machete; I never said I wanted one; in fact I would go so far as to say that I never said anything more positive than 'Gosh, that's fantastic, John' or 'Goodness me that machete is sharp, John.' But somehow – and I don't suppose I will ever get to know the answer to this one – by the end of the day John had got it firmly into his head that I was in the market for a machete, and that he was going to speak to his friend, and he was jolly well going to get me one. I considered for a moment trying to put him right, saying something like 'No, John, I was only being polite, I'm not really a machete kind of guy,' but in the end I didn't bother. John KNEW that I wanted a machete, even if I didn't, and he knew that it would transform my life, and nothing that I could possibly say would ever disabuse him of that. 'Great,' I said. 'I can't wait.'

When the machete arrived – quite where it came from was never quite clear, although I think I narrowed it down to Sheffield, Nottingham or Grenada – I could see why John used to refer to it as a cutlass. It had a long curved blade, shaped like a J, and a crudely made wooden handle, and outside of my razor was probably one of the sharpest things I had ever come across in my life. It was easy to see that it was just the thing for cutting the sugar cane back in the West Indies; easy, too, to see how buccaneers indulging in a little light piracy on the high seas might have found it a useful little persuader as they went about their business. Quite what it was doing in East Acton – where, as far as I could establish, there were neither sugar canes nor pirates – was not entirely obvious. Anyway, once I got my hands on it, and paid John the agreed sum of £9 (I think we may have given him £10 and told him to keep the change), I did what any sensible person would do on receiving a lethal weapon of somewhat dubious provenance: I stuffed it away in a corner of the shed and forgot all about it.

To be slightly more precise, I tried to forget all about it, but there was no way that John was going to let me. Every time he saw me doing a job on the allotment which could possibly be carried out by machete (which in John's eyes basically meant just about everything) he would ask how I was getting on with it ('Oh fine,' I would lie, not entirely convincingly), and then casually suggest that I would be much better off if I used the machete for whatever I was doing. If he was feeling in particularly determined mood he would come over and give me a practical demonstration. Once I was weeding the garlic bed – one of the more tedious jobs in the allotment calendar, which involves getting down on one's knees and using an onion hoe to weed between the stems without damaging the garlic plants themselves – when John came over to explain how I would really be much better off doing that with my cutlass. 'Look,' he said, 'you cut the bush like this' – as he hacked at the weeds with the end of the blade – 'and then you get up close to the garlic like this,' as he used the tip of the machete to scarify the soil around the garlic stem. Chop, chop, chop, he went, so quick I was convinced he was going to cut down one of my precious garlic plants by accident, but he didn't. It was an impressive display of advanced machete skills. 'Wow,' I said, lamely, 'that looks really, uh, good,' and then carried on hoeing. I wasn't quite ready for the machete, not yet.

I may not have been ready for the machete; Eliza, unfortunately, was. The grass on our paths was getting longer by the day – if I said that one morning we lost the children in it, and took three days to find them again, it would not be entirely accurate, but would certainly give you a good idea of how things on the allotment were getting rather out of hand, and Eliza was getting more determined that someone should do something about it. 'Someone', as in, well, you know, 'someone'. 'It's all right,' I said, 'I'll get round to it some time.' ('Some time' being the traditional riposte to 'someone'.) The weeks passed. The grass grew longer. Eliza's patience grew shorter. Finally she could bear it no longer, and one day when we arrived on the allotment she marched to the shed, got the machete out of its hiding place and started hacking at the grass. I may not be the greatest husband in the world, or the hardest-working gardener, but recognising my duty when I see it, I took a deep breath, walked over to where she was working and said: 'No, darling, let me do that.' Which is how, some months after I first found myself ordering a machete I didn't want, I found myself at last wielding it in anger as I laid into the grass like a man possessed, my left hand clad in a heavy-duty gardening glove in a rather feeble attempt to keep finger losses down to a minimum. As I hacked away I reflected that yes, women really are the superior sex; not that there had been any doubt about it. They know precisely how to psychologically manipulate us; we know they are doing it and, like a fly caught in a spider's web, there is absolutely nothing we can do about it. It is just the way things are, and no matter how hard I try to think of ways I could have outwitted her, they all seem to end with me down on my hands and knees going chop, chop, chop with that old machete.

It probably took an hour and a half of actual cutting time to trim the grass round the allotment, not including the breaks to resharpen the blade and rest my aching right arm. It wasn't a bad tool, really.

Nine months later we bought a strimmer.

My wife wasn't the only one to indulge in psychological manipulation. I was down on the allotment by myself one day when Ina – a West Indian woman who has the plot next to Safi's – wandered over from her plot and said: 'Could I ask your advice?' With the benefit of hindsight, I should perhaps have smelled a rat at this point. Ina has the neatest plot on the allotment, and grows the sort of vegetables that most of us only get to see in the catalogues; one of the other plot-holders, the charming and delightful Angelo, once told me how back in the days when they used to have an annual competition for the best plot, Ina always used to win it. She had one plot and her husband – now dead – had another, where he used to grow an impressive selection of herbs. Quite why Ina should ask me for advice wasn't so much mysterious as downright suspicious; but, being a man and easily flattered, I fell for it, of course. The advice she was after concerned the plot next to ours, the one which had lain neglected ever since we arrived at Bromyard Avenue. The first time we ever clapped eyes on it, it had been filled with a profusion of flowers, with not a vegetable in sight, and although it was already suffering a bit from neglect it was still quite a magnificent site. Whoever the plot-holder was, he had obviously put in a lot of work over the years; there was a pond, surrounded by paving stones, and a trellis supported at either end by massive wooden posts which were sitting in those special metal contraptions that you sink into the ground to provide a firm base for your uprights. 'This is my friend's plot,' said Ina. 'He's not coming back, and he said I could have the trellis. I was just wondering what you thought was the best way of getting it out?'

There were two possible responses to this request for advice. The sensible one would have been to say, 'Ooh, that looks like a big job, Ina, I think you want to get some specialist equipment to get those posts out. I'd have a chat with Michael about it if I were you.' I didn't take the sensible approach, of course; I did what Ina was clearly hoping I would do – I fetched a spade and started digging. I am not sure what I was expecting, but it was a bit like the time I tried digging up our horseradish, only without the fun (or the horseradish). No matter how far I tried digging, the posts always seemed to be buried that much deeper. Ina looked on, in an encouraging sort of way. After about half an hour I stopped to catch my breath, and to wonder how on earth I had managed to get myself into a situation where I was digging a totally pointless hole in one person's allotment for a person on another allotment, when there was a long list of jobs that needed doing on my own plot. Ina must have sensed that I was beginning to lose the will to live, for it was at that point that she decided to take pity on me and inform me that she only wanted the trellis itself, not the uprights, and so if we just separated the trellis from its supports that would be enough. Being a polite sort of person, and not prone to bursts of irrational violence, I smiled and said, 'OK, then,' separated the trellis from the posts and wondered what it was about me that made some women think that they were obliged to go round making me look like a prize chump.

It was moments like that which would be enough to make a lesser man conclude that perhaps allotments would be better off without women at all. That's how it was in the old days, when gardeners were chaps who had certainly never heard of any of your sophisticated modern vegetables like cavolo nero or Florence fennel: it was spuds, cabbages, runner beans and onions, and if they were being really fancy they might grow a bit of beetroot. Michael Wale, the secretary of our allotment association (as opposed to Irish Michael), reckons that when he first joined the association there were hardly any women there at all. Back then the vegetable plot was somewhere a fellow would go to do some digging, exchange some small talk with his neighbours, grumble about the weather and generally do anything rather than go home and talk to the wife.

As recently as 1986 the idea of a woman having an allotment, and doing rather well at it, was regarded as such an unusual phenomenon that it merited a story in *Garden News*. Mind you, this was in Lancashire, where they probably had not heard of feminism, and if they had they probably still called it women's lib. According to the paper a young woman called Mary Ellis

has been invading the traditional male stronghold of the allotment. What's more, she's also made something of an assault on showbenches around the Lancashire town of Colne – with resounding success. In 1984 she won the cup for the best exhibit in the Earby show with her three seed onions and last season came up with numerous first prizes and the top trophy in the members' section.

Well done Mary!

Nowadays women are everywhere. In our association alone there are housewives, widows, single women, gay couples, Moroccans,

Poles, West Indians, tree-huggers, middle-class dilettantes, traditional working-class plot-holders, champion veg growers . . . frankly, you can't move for women. On the Bromyard site there are fifteen plots, and women are represented on at least six of them. The idea that the allotment is a male preserve is simply no longer true; the only question is, what sort of effect has that had on the character of the average allotment? Have all these women changed things? Has the allotment been transformed from a place where a chap would come to tend his prize marrow in peace to the sort of floral haven where women grow their own cutting gardens and produce homegrown organic remedies? Not to mention rather more salad vegetables than the average man could possibly put up with?

The reality is rather more complex than one might think. Yes, it is true that on the Bromyard Avenue site there are two plots exclusively turned over to flowers – but both of them are the work of men. Yes, on our plot we do grow rather a lot of lettuce, but I am mainly responsible for that. It is true that Eliza is rather keen on salad, and so I suppose one could argue that she is ultimately to blame, but I have to carry my share of salad guilt. So what does my wife bring to the party, as it were? She has tended to grow – and this is the result of an entirely unspoken pact between the two of us, just the way things worked out – the tomatoes, courgettes, sweetcorn, cucumbers, herbs, onions, squash and, of course, the flowers. Lots of flowers, as it happens. I have tended to take responsibility for the potatoes, beans, garlic, lettuce, spinach, chard, beetroot, cabbages, broccoli and sprouts. Carrots, for some reason, have always been a joint operation. Is there a pattern in all of this? I have no idea. But if there isn't some university boffin already doing a thesis on 'Sex Differences in the Vegetable Garden', then there jolly well should be.

12

Borlotti Bean Blues

I do not like broccoli. And I haven't liked it since I was a little kid and my mother made me eat it. And I'm President of the United States and I'm not going to eat any more broccoli.

George H. W. Bush, US President, 1990

Summer, and in particular late summer, is a four-letter time of year; and that four-letter word is G.L.U.T. During the spring on the allotment you spend your time putting seeds in the ground. They grow, and then you spend the summer taking the resulting produce out of the ground, or wherever it happens to be. It's a pretty good system which works for me, and has worked for thousands of generations before I ever got here. The only drawback is that there is a pronounced tendency towards over-production at certain times of the year. Come July and August, and everything starts to come at once – the tomatoes, the beans, the cucumbers, the potatoes, the raspberries, the lettuces, the beetroot, the carrots, the onions, all ferociously producing away as if their very lives depended on it, which in a sense they do, and it is all one can do to keep up with the harvesting, let alone the eating.

Take courgettes, for instance. One of the choicest vegetables of summer, if you grow them yourself you can pick them when they are at their very best, young and tender and no more than six inches long. However, if you take your eye off the ball for more than a couple of days, or if you make the mistake of growing more than three or four plants, then you are more than likely to be overwhelmed by a glut of courgettes, a plague of courgettes, a veritable courgette mountain, and before you know it you will be scouring cookbooks as you search for new ways of cooking them, and begging your friends and relations to take them off your hands. This is not an entirely bad thing. For a start, giving away your produce is probably rather good for the soul, spreads a little happiness around the place – why should you be the only people to benefit from your homegrown veg? – and gives people a little reminder to act as an explanation for your eccentric behaviour the rest of the year. 'Ah yes,' they say, 'there are the Lows. Funny couple, completely obsessed with horse manure, but they can be counted on to give us a basket of courgettes during the summer.'

The glut thing is also a bit of a culinary incentive system, in that in normal circumstances – normal in this situation being the bad old days when you would just buy your vegetables from the supermarket, usually after deciding what you were going to cook that night – we probably never did anything more adventurous with our courgettes than braising them, frying them, serving them in a risotto or, when we were feeling particularly frisky, using them in some baked dish or other. When you are facing several hundredweight of courgettes a week, however, that simply won't do. In desperation you are forced to search out new recipes, finding ever more inventive ways of using up your courgette glut. There is even a book called *What Will I Do with All Those Courgettes?* by someone called Elaine Borish which apparently contains no fewer than 150 recipes for courgettes, including soups, salads, casseroles, breads and cakes. If you look on the Amazon website there is one review by a fellow calling himself nickforward, who calls it 'even better than Delia'. It must be good then. (Mind you, I notice that people who bought Mrs Borish's book also bought *Liquid Gold: The Logic and Lore of Using Urine to Grow Plants*, so perhaps you never can tell.) Our favourite discovery is not from Mrs Borish, but a traditional Italian recipe called *zucchini alla scapece*. Here is Antonio Carluccio's version from his book *Vegetables*, which is a bit of a favourite with us.

6 medium courgettes, topped, tailed and cut into 7–8 cm
  batons
plenty of olive oil for frying
4 tbsp extra virgin olive oil
1 bunch fresh mint leaves, chopped
2 garlic cloves, cut into quarters
1 tbsp white wine vinegar
salt

Heat a little of the plain olive oil in a pan, and fry the courgettes in batches so that they are separate rather than crowded together. Fry until brown, then drain on absorbent paper.

Put the courgette batons in a dish, and add the extra virgin olive oil, mint, garlic, vinegar and salt, and leave for the flavours to combine before eating.

If it's not courgettes, it's beans. There was a bit of a debate within the Low household as to which beans we should grow, French or runner. Eliza, being something of a traditionalist, is a keen advocate of the runner bean, a vegetable which for me brings back somewhat unwelcome memories of school dinners, but which I am prepared to tolerate (I am afraid there is no index in this book, but if there were I would refer you to the entry marked 'author, tolerance displayed by, esp. towards beetroot and other horrors of the kitchen garden'). I, on the other hand, would sing the virtues of the French bean, a vegetable which I will for ever associate with summer sunshine and holidays in Provence. Not that I can remember the last time I had a holiday in Provence – perhaps it is just a collective consciousness thing, a folk memory of the English middle classes for holidays we never had. It probably comes from reading too many Sunday newspaper travel supplements. What we are agreed on, however, is that whatever variety one prefers, beans are a class act and an essential part of any self-respecting allotment. So, rather than argue about it, Eliza and I decided we would simply grow both types of bean, which would have been the end of it if one of us hadn't mentioned borlotti beans. Well, we simply had to have some borlotti. Not only are they very Italian, an essential ingredient in such dishes as the traditional pasta and bean soup, *pasta e fagioli*, but they are also very pretty with their red and white marbling, making them among the most aesthetically pleasing of beans. You can see how we couldn't resist them.

There is just one problem with all these beans, however, and that is that they are sometimes just too jolly productive, and if you are not careful it can be quite hard to keep up with the harvest; once they get going, they really get going, and if you are not out there two or three times a week you can find your precious beans getting old and stringy before you have had a chance to pick them. That makes going away for the weekend somewhat tricky; it makes a full-blown summer holiday the subject of much heart-searching and familial angst. That summer we had many an agonised debate about whether we were actually up to leaving the allotment for two whole weeks. It wasn't so much the question of how we would get the plot watered and the weeds kept under control – those issues were important, but did not prey on our minds in the same way as the question of who was going to eat it all. We certainly did not mind that we would be missing out on some of the harvest: that was fine. What was upsetting, though, was the idea of crops going to waste, the notion of having spent all that time growing these beans and courgettes and tomatoes only for them to reach maturity and then just sit there, unloved and unwanted and slowly becoming more and more inedible by the day. That, not to put too fine a point on it, would be a crime against vegetables.

Fortunately my old friend Jeff was out of work at the time. Well, perhaps not so fortunate for him (although he has since got himself a job), but it did mean that he had a lot of time on his hands and, being a helpful and accommodating sort, was prepared to come over from West Hampstead three times a week to water the allotment and pick anything that needed eating. After a thorough and extensive briefing that may, or may not, have stopped short of an identification chart to help Jeff tell the difference between all the different vegetables (in my anxious state I may have informed Jeff that the tomatoes were the red ones and the cucumbers the long green ones), Eliza and I finally summoned up the courage to go off on holiday with the children. I think we had a very nice time, too, even though it did take me about six days to overcome the desire to text Jeff every few hours to check that everything was OK with the lettuces.

When we got back everything was OK with the lettuces, and the tomatoes, and all the rest of it; despite our nervousness, it turned out not to be that difficult looking after a vegetable plot for a couple of weeks. Jeff had even done a pretty good job of keeping up with the courgette consumption, one of the biggest challenges of his fortnight as a babysitter. As for the beans – well, you can't do everything, and Jeff had performed such sterling service with the rest of the plot that it was entirely understandable that he had been a little distracted when it came to the French beans, which had clearly decided to go into hyperdrive while we were away. A couple of days later, when Eliza had taken the children to stay with her parents in Wiltshire, I decided to attack the beans properly, and picked six pounds off one wigwam. I ate some myself, gave a couple of pounds away to colleagues at work, and froze the rest. Not exactly agribusiness, perhaps, but a crop I felt inordinately proud of for several weeks to come.

With the French and runner beans, preserving is something you do as a means of dealing with the surplus; with borlotti beans preserving them is pretty much the whole point. You can eat borlotti fresh, and people do – you can even eat them in the pod, if you pick them young enough – but the vast majority of the borlotti crop is consumed as dried beans, soaked in water overnight before cooking the next day. The secret, I was told, of successful borlotti drying is to make sure they are thoroughly dry before putting them into a jar in the larder, or however it is you are going to store them, otherwise you are likely to find them attacked by mould, and I was going to make sure that my borlotti were going to be the driest beans this side of the Apennines before they got tucked up for the winter. This involved first letting them dry on the plant in the late summer and early autumn sunshine, so that by the time we picked them the pods were brown and crackly and as dry as paper. Inside the beans were smooth and dry to the touch and every bit as beautiful as I had imagined, and landed in a bowl with a satisfying click that suggested that they were already well on the way to dehydration. I wasn't taking any chances, though, and after spreading the beans out on a baking tray I put them into the airing cupboard and left them there for a week. That's how to dry beans, I thought to myself smugly as I weighed them up and put them into ziplock plastic bags. Admittedly there weren't quite as many as I would have liked – slightly less than two pounds after drying, which would probably be good for about four meals – but they looked, and felt, gorgeous, and I could practically taste the *pasta e fagioli* and *minestrone* and *insalata di borlotti e radicchio*. From the outside, I was still the same journalist, putting up with the traffic and noise and general urban tawdriness of west London; inside, I was an Italian peasant getting ready for the winter.

These days people don't really go in for preserving. In the past, when rather more people grew their own vegetables, preserving was a part of the season, something you did when the harvest was over and you were laying down stores for the long dark months ahead. My mother-in-law remembers helping her mother during the war as she salted the runner beans – a forgotten technique if ever there was one; we all have freezers now, which may be rather more convenient but is, I feel, probably rather less energy-efficient. The first time I saw John Roberts's sweetcorn crop I remember being astonished at how much he had grown. Even for someone brought up in the West Indies it seemed a lot, row after row of plump yellow cobs ripening in the sun, and I really couldn't see how one elderly man and his wife could possibly get through all that lot. Well, he explained, as well as the ones they ate, there was the corn they gave to their children, and to their grandchildren, and then there were the barbecue parties they had where everyone ate corn. 'And,' he said, after a moment's pause, 'we have two freezers.'

We only have the one freezer, and not a particularly big one at that, but that was not going to prevent us from preserving what we could. Beans (French and runner) were easy – they just went into the freezer, as did some of the raspberries we failed to eat (it is, I know, hard to imagine the concept of failing to eat raspberries there and then, but it is a tribute to the productivity of our autumn-fruiting raspberry canes that there came a point when we felt we just had to put some aside for later). Eventually, though, we realised we just had to get involved in some serious preserving and jam-making if we were going to make any inroads into our various gluts – particularly our tomato glut – and when that moment arrived there was no real choice about what we had to do. Who you gonna call? Why, Marguerite Patten of course.

Every cook in the country knows about the influence and importance of Elizabeth David, and for sheer popularity and all-round good-eggery it is hard to beat Delia Smith, but whenever these titans of the kitchen come up for discussion people often overlook the great-granny of them all, Marguerite Patten. A

160

celebrity chef long before anyone invented the term, she first surfaced during the Second World War when she was working for the Ministry of Food and started dispensing cookery advice for all those housewives struggling to feed their families under rationing. Immediately after the war she presented her first cookery programme on BBC television – this was 1947, which is probably before Jamie Oliver's dad was even born – and simply never stopped. She has written more than 165 books – including one dedicated entirely to Spam recipes – and carried on broadcasting long after everyone else would have given up. At the time of writing this book she was still going strong, even making the occasional appearance on BBC Radio at the age of 91.

What she does not know about preserving is not worth knowing, and there is in our bookshelves a copy of her *Jams, Preserves and Chutneys* which gets dusted down every summer and does not go back onto the shelf until the last jar of green tomato chutney has been sealed and labelled and put into the cupboard under the stairs. Raspberry jam, gooseberry and rhubarb jam, just about any chutney you care to mention – if it wasn't for Mrs Patten, our winter stores would look distinctly on the sparse side. It is entirely fitting, of course, that a writer who first came to prominence during the Second World War should be our guide and mentor during the preserving season. Not only was the war a time when allotment ownership was at its peak, but that sense of thrift and careful household management that was the rule during the years of rationing and food shortages still prevails on the allotment; it may be the twenty-first century on the outside, but down on the allotment it's still 1942. Marguerite Patten is essentially our way of connecting with a past that so many allotment owners feel a part of.

Not that we are stuck in our ways, however: I do not think,

for instance, that they were particularly organic back in the 1940s. Growmore, the fertiliser which is regarded as a bringer of miracles by so many gardeners, and viewed with such deep suspicion by the organic brigade, first came to prominence during the war, when it was known as National Growmore and was seen as an essential tool in helping the new generation of gardeners get the most out of their soil, which was often not of the best quality. So, just to remind ourselves that the war is actually over, occasionally we branch out. For tomato ketchup, for example, we turned to Fergus Henderson's *Nose to Tail Eating*, which proved to be a massive success in that not only did we make more than enough to keep us going all year, but the children actually liked it. It is coarser-textured than the commercial gloop, sweet-sour rather than just sweet, and a browny-red rather than the highly artificial colour of Mr Heinz's finest, but much, much more delicious. All right, I'm prejudiced. But if a man cannot be prejudiced in favour of his wife's homemade tomato ketchup, what's the point of it all? The clincher is the children's verdict, of course: if they didn't like it they would say so, and keep on saying so until we finally gave in and bought them what they wanted. The truth is, however, that I cannot remember when we last bought a bottle of shop ketchup, which is great by us although it does cause the occasional difficulty when the children have some of their little friends around for tea and they have to explain why there isn't any Heinz to go with their sausages. 'It's homemade!' I once heard Kitty saying to one of their guests, in what she hoped was an encouraging and supportive way. 'I don't like homemade food,' he said, grumpily.

We do, though, and Mrs Patten is the writer who has – how can I put this? – helped us out of many a pickle. When one of our allotment neighbours gave us some tayberries, we could not find a decent tayberry jam recipe anywhere until we consulted Mrs Patten. Marrow and ginger jam? Pumpkin butter? Apple struper? (No, I've no idea either.) Whatever your preserving needs, Mrs P is unlikely ever to let you down. Occasionally, when the jam production is getting particularly frenetic, or the smell of vinegar in the kitchen is becoming rather overpowering after the chutney pot has been simmering away on the stove for a little too long, I look at Mrs Low and wonder whether she isn't in fact turning into Marguerite Patten. So far, though, there haven't been any signs of that familiar snowy-white hair, or those pearl necklaces, or those well-enunciated BBC vowels, and I haven't been asked to try out any new Spam recipes, so I think we are in the clear. But perhaps it wouldn't be an entirely bad thing.

I have, meanwhile, been undergoing my own transformation. Like rather too many over-educated husbands, I have long had a complete abhorrence of DIY, and the story of my marriage is a long and sorry tale of walls unpainted, broken fences unmended and dripping taps left unrepaired. I would as soon consider putting up a shelf as I would design and build my own proton accelerator. I am not quite sure whether my hatred of DIY is caused by my incompetence at anything related to manual work, or whether my reluctance to wield hammer or drill or paintbrush is the cause of my ineptitude, but the fact is I don't like it, and I'm no good at it, and that's that. (There is in fact a third possible explanation for my DIY phobia, which is that I have a fundamental and principled objection to it, based on my hitherto untrumpeted admiration for Keynesian economics, and the notion that if I spent the entire weekend doing the spare room, I would put a man out of work for about two and a half hours. Of course, it probably wouldn't matter anyway because I would no doubt have to call him on Monday morning to get him to come up and sort out the appalling mess I had made of the job; but you get the idea.)

On the allotment, though, the avoidance of DIY is altogether harder. Not only is one not going to find a handyman who would be prepared to come down and do your little jobs for you (although that is not strictly true, as I was to find out later), but there is also a spirit of enthusiastic amateurism which means that DIY is part of the fabric of allotment society. Over the years, the thriftiness that was born of necessity has become part of the very culture of the allotment, so that even if I could afford to buy a fancy new shed, for instance, or a specialist contraption from some gardening catalogue for keeping the birds off my brassicas, I would never dream of doing so.

This enforced DIY regime should have been anathema to me – but it wasn't, and for two reasons. One is that on the allotment, lessons are free. All around you are examples of how other plot-holders solved their various problems, and if you see a solution that appeals, you can simply copy it. If you are lucky the originator will come and show you how to do it, or tell you where he got his netting, say; and if you are really lucky, when you are in the middle of making a complete dog's dinner of the whole operation, he will come to your rescue and show you how to do it properly. The other reason is the one that swung it for me, however, and it is this: on the allotment, the bodger is king. It does not matter if your compost heap is held together with packing crates and old string. No one cares if your brassica cage looks like an explosion in a netting factory, or if your shed makes the average shanty town look like Chelsea Harbour; as long as it does the job, or at least does the job for a bit before falling down in an embarrassing heap, that's OK. There are no building regulations on the allotment, no snobbery, no keeping up with the Joneses. DIYwise, it's my kinda town.

When we first took over the allotment, there was a compost heap of sorts down one end, a three-sided construction made up of a piece of unidentified panelling, some rusty corrugated iron and an old door. It looked not much more than an accidental falling together of random objects, which somehow served as the structure for a compost heap, although a particularly wonky one even by the extremely lax standards of the genre, lacking entirely in straight lines, right angles, stability, strength or even charm. Nevertheless, for the first six months or so it served its purpose as somewhere for us to dump our cuttings and kitchen waste.

When we first started composting, it was a casual kind of thing. We needed somewhere to put all the green rubbish you generate on an allotment – the weeds, the old cabbage leaves, the lettuces that had bolted – and it is only sensible to put them on a compost heap so that when they rot down you can use them to improve the soil. It is a rather wonderful arrangement, in fact, this idea that you are constantly recycling the things that grow on your allotment, and that no sooner are you taking the goodness out of the soil than you are putting it back in again. But you cannot just stop at composting your garden waste – there's all the kitchen waste to consider, too: onion skins, potato peelings, carrot tops, less than perfect lettuce leaves that didn't make it into the salad. There are other kitchen candidates, too, such as tea bags and coffee grounds, and even eggshells, as long as you scrunch them up a bit. All sorts of things can go into a compost heap, and every time you put something in the compost bucket that would once have gone straight into the bin, on its way to some landfill site or other, you feel a little tingle of satisfaction that not only are you doing your bit to save the planet, but you are also fattening up the cabbages for the year after next.

My favourite compost ingredient, though, is human hair. For reasons that are too complicated to explain, but are to do with the fact that the same bloke has been cutting Eliza's hair since about for ever, we all have our hair cut at home as a family, one after the other. At the end of the session we end up with a decent-sized pile of hair in the corner of the kitchen – part honey blonde, part little boy blond, part little girl curly, and part, well, a sort of distinguished salt-and-pepper, albeit a little heavy on the salt. We consulted the books, and apparently hair is perfectly all right for compost, and so when Barry the scissors packs away his gear we get out the dustpan and brush, sweep up the hair and put it into the compost bin. It reminds me of a remark Michael made one day, when someone saw him pushing a wheelbarrow full of manure. 'What are you doing with that?' they asked. 'Turning it into human flesh,' he replied. Which, when you think about it for a second, is a pretty succinct summary of the process. If anyone asks, we're turning human hair into, well, human hair.

The one thing you cannot get away from is the smell. We happen to have two bins in our kitchen, because the bin that was built into the fitted kitchen we inherited when we bought the house was ludicrously small, so patently not up to the job that we bought another free-standing bin. That meant that when we started composting it involved no great sacrifice – and indeed no great leap of the imagination – to decide that the old fitted bin could be for compostable waste, and the new bin for everything else. We then bought an old-fashioned metal dustbin, which Eliza proceeded to paint in a rather tasteful shade of green. When the little bin is full, which sometimes takes a week, sometimes less, it gets emptied into the big bin, where it sits decomposing in thoroughly satisfactory manner, although once it has been sitting around for a few weeks, it starts to get distinctly ripe. Dark, slimy things start happening at the bottom of the bin, and if we are really lucky tiny little flies have taken up residence inside the bin, which usually means it is time to heave the bin into the car – a two-man job, this, as even a small bin of kitchen waste is incredibly heavy – and take it over to the allotment to be emptied on to the compost heap proper. Even in the depths of winter the five-minute car journey is conducted with all windows wide open, and once the whole nasty mess has been dumped on top of the heap we do our best not to stand downwind of it for the whole of the rest of the day. The only consolation is that the smellier it is, the better it is for the compost heap, or so I like to tell myself.

The more serious we got about our composting – and believe me, it is a subject on which people get very serious indeed – the more we realised that having one compost heap (which was in danger of collapsing under the weight of its own uselessness at any moment) was no longer good enough. We needed a second compost heap.

It was blindingly obvious, of course. How anyone could possibly hope to survive with just the one compost heap is such an affront to the natural order of things that it seems astonishing now that it did not occur to us earlier, but I suppose we were young and naive then, and only just embarking on our journey of discovery through the world of gardening knowledge. Or something like that: perhaps we were just stupid. Once you think about how composting works, it all seems rather obvious. You make a compost heap. You add stuff to it. It rots. After a while, it turns into compost, and you can start using it on the garden.

But what do you do with all the stuff you want to keep adding to your compost heap? You don't want to add it to your nicely rotted old compost, do you? No. You need a second compost heap, that's what you need.

In fact, I could without any effort whatsoever construct a perfectly decent argument for having three compost heaps – one for adding to, one for rotting down and one for using. Even I would be prepared to concede that that is where madness lies, however. But that's the trouble with composting; once you start, madness is only ever a step away.

While I regard my compost heap as an essential part of the allotment and a thing of great inner beauty, I try to keep my feelings in check. Some people, I am afraid to say, let themselves get rather carried away when it comes to compost. Entire books have been written on the subject, most notably the one by the great Dick Kitto, a gardener so knowledgeable and wise that a base amateur like myself can only bow his head in humble veneration. People talk about adding different material in layers, no more than a couple of inches deep – a scattering of grass clippings, say, followed by a bit of kitchen rubbish, then a layer of shredded newspaper – as though one was making a cake, not a compost heap. Garden centres will try and sell you compost activators, just in case nature isn't speedy enough for your composting needs. Some people become obsessed with the idea that their compost heap does not contain enough nitrogen – you are, I presume, already making sure your compost heap has the requisite ratio of twenty-five parts green material to one part brown, to guarantee the correct balance of nitrogen to carbon – and try to correct this by adding a solution of $(NH_2)_2CO$, also known as urea, also known as . . . Well, put it this way, if you ever heard of gardeners going off to visit their compost last thing at night, that's the reason. It's to add nitrogen. Michael Wale, the secretary of our association, saves up all his in a bottle and takes it to the allotment to be added to the compost bin. I have not yet got to that stage, and with any luck I never will – I fear Mrs Low would not be quite so tolerant as Michael's wife seems to be – although if I get caught short on the allotment, and if I think no one is looking, I am not above indulging in a little nitrogen enhancement of the compost heap on an ad hoc basis. Well, you don't want to waste it.

Becoming a compost aficionado has its hidden dangers, how-ever. Bob Sherman of Garden Organic once told of a Liverpudlian allotment-holder who constructed an incredibly complex com-posting system out of the salvaged remains of several houses. It was raised up so that a large plastic sheet could be arranged underneath to channel the liquid that came off into bottles, which were then stored in the shed for the summer. His teenage son once mistook a bottle of this pungent brew for cola, unable to detect any difference other than that it was 'a bit flat'. Dead nutritious, though.

Although I was doing my best not to become a compost obsessive, I knew that I had to build myself a second compost heap, and that once I had done that it was inevitable that I was going to have to rebuild the first one, on the grounds that you cannot have your smart new heap living next door to a slum. I started scouring the skips of west London for suitable material, and over a period of a few days found enough bits of wood to be the uprights of my new heap, and also an old table that, if sawn appropriately, could serve as one of the sides. I appropri-ated a pallet, too, on the principle that even if I could not find a role for it immediately it would be sure to come in useful later. I still didn't have a front, and was despairing that I would ever find one when Eliza pointed out an abandoned door in the street next to ours. 'That'll do,' I said, and by the next morning I had taken the door round to our front garden, sawn it in half and taken it over to the allotment, where Phase II of the Bromyard Compost Heap Development Scheme was about to begin.

The next couple of hours were a blur of sawing, banging, swearing (where the banging didn't go entirely right) and crashing as I dismantled the old compost heap and built two new ones. The entirely new one had half of someone's old front door as its front, with a brilliantly clever (that's how it felt at the time, anyway) arrangement that meant that I could slide it in and out of place; the new old one had for its front a pallet which I had disconstructed, reduced in size and then rebuilt so that the slats were nearer together. The two constructions were sturdy, square and looked like they would last a thousand years – or, at any rate, at least until the Christmas after next – but best of all, they were mine. I felt like Christopher Wren, Richard Rogers and the chap who designed the Great Pyramid at Giza, all rolled into one.

It was round about this time that I went to go and see how the purple sprouting broccoli had been getting on since I took the drastic step of removing the netting because it was starting to interfere with the plants' growth. The answer was certainly clear, if nothing else. The whole of the tops of the plants had been completely stripped bare by the pigeons, in what I can only describe as a frenzied attack. Not a leaf remained, and where the broccoli had been beginning to sprout – well, let us just say that the pigeons were commendably thorough. What was that that John Roberts once said to me? 'They are all God's creatures.' All I can say is that God was having a pretty off day when he came up with the pigeon. They are ugly, greedy and fat. I can see little

170

excuse for their existence other than as a test for gardeners' patience and resourcefulness. I wasn't going to be defeated, though; next year I was going to have another go at growing PSB, and God's creatures were going to have to go elsewhere for their dinner.

That was not the only surprise I had that year. One day in early autumn Eliza and I decided to make some pasta and bean soup and, full of anticipation for the rustic Italian feast we were about to enjoy, I went to the cupboard to get out the jar of borlotti beans we had dried during the summer. With their red and white marbling they looked just as pretty as I remembered. What was new, though, was the fact that they seemed to be moving, wriggling away as if they were alive. On closer inspection it wasn't the beans that were moving, but the tiny wormlike creatures that were all around them, hundreds of the little sods. From what I could tell they had been having quite a laugh at my expense, gnawing little holes in the beans and leaving the bottom of the jar filled with a fine dust which was, presumably, the stuff that they couldn't be bothered to eat. They were – I found out later – bean weevils, crafty little devils that lay their eggs in the bean while it is still on the plant, and then wait a while before hatching and causing borlotti heartbreak for the poor sap who has spent all that time growing them. My dreams of hearty soups and delicious stews lay in tatters. Outside, I was grim-faced and as set in my determination to outwit the bean weevil next year as I was resolved to keep the pigeons off my broccoli; inside, my inner Luigi wept.

13

Rainbow Chard Nation

No occupation is so delightful to me as the culture of the earth, no culture comparable to that of the garden ... . But though an old man, I am but a young gardener.

Thomas Jefferson, *Garden Book*

It was Michael who got me going. I was out on the allotment one day, hoeing the weeds, when Michael walked over to see what I was up to. 'Oh, you've got a lovely action with that hoe,' he said, in that way he has which might have been a compliment, or might have been Michael's way of taking the mickey out of the newcomers. One was never quite sure. Anyway, it had been a rather dry couple of weeks, and the surface of the soil had formed a bit of a crust, which it tends to whenever there is rain followed by a dry spell. The ground was dusty, and hard, and didn't really give the impression that it was all that keen on supporting any kind of plant life. 'No,' said Michael, 'it's not terribly good soil around here. This used to be a brickworks, you know. We do our best to improve it, and it's slowly getting better.' Then, without any further explanation, he turned his back and went off to go and examine his parsnips, which had been causing him a bit of trouble.

A brickworks? I had never even considered what our allotments might have been before they were allotments; to me they were just the allotments, and the nearest I had come to expressing any curiosity about the past was to enquire about who had had our plot before us (Paddy, who grew potatoes and came from Kerry, and was now in a home in Hounslow). The notion that there might have been a brickworks on or near the allotments was at the very least consistent with my observation that a couple of feet below the surface was some premium-grade London clay, which from what I could tell was responsible for the fact that whenever there was heavy rain it would sit on the surface for hours if not days on end, stubbornly refusing to drain away. The brickworks story would seem to suggest that I wasn't the first person to notice the clay.

It turned out that bricks used to be big in Acton. In Victorian times there were at least three brickworks around the place, and at the height of the Victorian brick boom, in the last quarter of the nineteenth century, when they were building houses as fast as they could – including the one where I live now, and where I wrote this book – some nine to twelve million bricks were made every year in Acton. The clay came from brickfields in the immediate vicinity, and so it would not be too far-fetched to imagine that my house was built with bricks that came from my allotment. The Mr Big of the Acton brick scene was a chap called George Wright, who owned a lot of the land in the neighbourhood and was quite an influential figure. He was not, though, entirely popular – but then again making bricks was not an entirely popular activity. It was a smelly old business, which involved mixing clay with burnt fuel extracted from refuse, which would end up in huge great stinking heaps, and annoy the neighbours. Tenants would sometimes complain about the stench, especially in summer, and if it was particularly bad they would get a reduction in their rent by way of compensation. Reading between the lines, however, it seemed that George Wright found additional ways of his own of upsetting the local populace, over and above those involved in his chosen trade, and there really wasn't a lot of love for him locally. For a while he used to sit on the local council, but then he failed to gain re-election; according to the *Acton Gazette*, 'The news was received with the greatest delight in East Acton.'

If the man who used to turn the local clay into bricks was not a popular figure, then the fellow who was actually responsible – in a roundabout sort of way – for the allotments existing in the first place was a different matter entirely. He was called John Perryn, a seventeenth-century goldsmith and local landowner, and also an alderman of the City of London. When he died in 1656 he bequeathed his estate to the Goldsmiths' Company, to be used for the benefit of the people of Acton (although being a decent enough chap, he stipulated that his widow Alice should be allowed to enjoy it in her lifetime). It was quite a considerable chunk of land, and there are reminders of his generosity in the names of local streets: there is a Perryn Road, for instance, and Bromyard Avenue is named after the village in Herefordshire where Perryn was born.

Back in Perryn's day Acton was quite a smart sort of place, being close enough to London to be a convenient summer retreat for the capital's courtiers and lawyers. It is hard to imagine, looking at the Uxbridge Road now, with its bendy buses and kebab shops, that it was ever deepest countryside, let alone that it was ever fashionable among high society: even in Victorian times it was hardly a rural idyll, what with all those brickworks and factories. Before all that industrial expansion, though, it was a quintessential part of the English countryside, and did its part to keep the city fed. *A History of the County of Middlesex* notes: 'In 1706 Acton was said to be sown every year with all sorts of grain, for which its soil was very suitable; crops were good, especially peas, and intermixed arable and meadow produced a chequered landscape.' Which is all very interesting, but does not shed any light on when the allotments came into being.

Fortunately our old landlords, the Goldsmiths' Company, are the sort of people who don't like to throw anything away, and their archives are full of material – letters, maps, contracts – which shed a fair amount of light on the history of allotments in Acton. A map of the Perryn Charity Estate from 1887 shows that the land where the allotments are now was then open fields, although whether they were arable land, meadows or even brickfields is not clear. It also shows what looks to be a cutting for the Latimer Road and East Acton Railway, a line that I had never heard of until I started researching the subject. As for Bromyard Avenue, the road simply did not exist yet; it was just a footpath, called Crown Lane. The next map, from 1902, shows a large area given over to allotments, right where the Bromyard Avenue site is now – only much larger. Of the railway cutting there is no trace. It seems to be the case, then, that our allotments came into being somewhere around the 1890s, significantly before the great allotment boom of the First World War. By the beginning of the Second World War the Acton Gardening Association had 150 plots, spread over various sites dotted around Acton: my own site had by then shrunk to something like its current size, hemmed in to the south by the new houses which had been built along what had by then become Bromyard Avenue. Opposite was a rather large, impersonal lump of a building occupied by the Ministry of Pensions, which is still there to this day, only now it is a block of recently converted flats, the sort of place which the developers try to market with pictures of couples drinking wine in fancy brasseries.

Everything was taken frightfully seriously. One legal document from 1942 shows the contract drawn up between 'George Ravensworth Hughes, Clerk of Goldsmiths Hall London EC2, and acting on behalf of The Wardens and Commonality of the Mystery of Goldsmiths of the City of London (hereinafter called the landlords) of the one part, and William Strang, Henry William Pettit and Michael Ryan, of behalf of the Acton Gardening Association'; the land occupied by the Acton Gardening Association extended to 13 acres, 0 roods and 27 poles.

William Strang was, as we have already seen, a bit of a poster boy for the allotment movement. Not only did he supervise the model allotment established in Regent's Park Zoo as part of the Ministry of Food's Dig For Victory campaign, but he was also to be seen on the front of a leaflet distributed by the Quakers. Next to the picture of this bearded Scot in his pinstriped waistcoat, white shirt and hat appeared the words: 'A Typical

Allotment Holder appealing on behalf of the Unemployed Gardeners who are helping in a practical form of National Service ... Help the unemployed and you help the country!' One shilling and sixpence (7½p) would set someone up with vegetable seeds (twelve varieties), while a shilling (5p) would be enough to buy a stone of seed potatoes.

In common with what was going on around the country, the Acton Gardening Association expanded apace. In just two years from the beginning of the war the association had grown nearly sevenfold to 1,039 plots. Some 700 of these were on local playing fields, and a 9½ acre site was set up on land which had once been the home of the East Acton Brick and Tile Works, which had long since moved west. By the end of the war, the Association had no less than 37½ acres under management. For some reason – perhaps inspired by William Strang's pioneering work on behalf of the nation's allotment-holders – the Ministry of Information decided in July 1940 to send a photographer along to Acton to make a visual record of what the plot-holders were getting up to, to encourage other would-be gardeners to follow their example. The resulting black-and-white photographs are a wonderful treasure trove of images from the days when gardening was a pastime indulged in by chaps in ties (judging by these pictures it was almost unthinkable to garden without a tie) and even in bicycle clips. Then, as now, the old gits' brigade was well represented among the ranks of the plot-holders. 'Jimmie Lowe, 75 years of age, and once a soldier of Queen Victoria,' read the caption to one of the pictures. 'Now he plants cabbages, but he has seen service with the Hussars.' A chap with a pipe was pictured looking out over his leeks: he was J. H. Tendal, sixty-eight, a former sergeant-major with the Northumberland Fusiliers who had seen service in Egypt and

Sudan. Best of all, though, was a picture of Mrs May Segrott, a widow of fifty-nine, who was photographed wearing a chunky sweater and a rather jaunty-looking beret as she trained her runner beans up some sticks. According to the caption she had worked on allotments for sixteen years, during which time she had won more than fifty prizes, four cups and one medal – a statistic that seemed to suggest that while there might not have been many women who had allotments in those days, those that did were more than capable of holding their own against the men.

After the war the land held by the association began to be whittled away, piece by piece, as parks and playing fields were taken back by the council. There was pressure, too, to use land for much-needed housing and within eighteen months those thirty-seven acres were down to twenty-two. For plot-holders, meanwhile, there were often rather more immediate problems to be considered. A letter from the association secretary to the Clerk of the Goldsmiths' Company in 1960 drew attention to a line of tall trees between one of the allotment sites and a local sports ground, 'in which a large number of wood pigeons make their nests'. The letter went on: 'These pigeons cause quite considerable damage to the crops growing on the allotments. One of the members of the Management Committee of this Association, Mr Baudrey, is in possession of a licence to use a sporting gun. I have been instructed to request permission from the Goldsmiths' Company for Mr Baudrey to be allowed to use his gun on the sports ground side of the trees in order that the number of pigeons may be reduced.'

Quite a few plot-holders with shotgun licences made similar requests, which suggests the pigeon problem in the early sixties must have been bad. The Goldsmiths turned down the requests, which was a shame because a brief but efficient pigeon blood-bath would have saved everyone a great deal of bother. They might even have got a nice pigeon pie out of it all.

What was also striking about the Goldsmiths' files was the number of letters from members of the public complaining that they had torn their coats on stray bits of wire poking out of the fence as they walked along the pavement next to the allotments. A Mrs Peggy Stancombe wrote to say that she had been walking along the footpath with her friend Mrs Nolan 'when a piece of wire protruding from the fence caught in the sleeve of my coat, causing a three-cornered tear in the main material and also the lining, about 6in in length. My rough estimate of the cost of repair is between 30 shillings to £2.' They must have been a wild and dangerous place in those days, the East Acton allotments.

In October 1968 the allotments made the local paper, when vandals broke in and 'all but destroyed' every building and greenhouse on the site. It was big news for the *Acton Gazette*, which reported the attack in colourful terms: 'Sheds smashed, glasses kicked in, prize-winning blooms crushed, the main pavilion wrecked and set on fire. Not one building was left untouched, not one greenhouse left unmarked. But one man's property suffered more than the rest.' That man was the association secretary George Spriggs, and there was a picture of Mr Spriggs in the paper, wearing dungarees and holding two broken flowerpots. Mr Spriggs told the paper: 'I could cry, I really could. Who could do a thing like this? What manner of person could walk on to an allotment and just tear it apart?'

Looking back through those archives, one is struck by various differences between allotment gardening as it was practised in the first half of the twentieth century and how it is now. There are superficial differences, such as the fact that the men dressed far more formally – I think that if I wore a tie to the allotment, somebody would have me sectioned – and that, Mrs Segrott notwithstanding, there weren't that many women about. Those were the days before plastic, too, so seed trays were made of wood and flowerpots of clay, and no one was able to enjoy the benefits of plastic polytunnels, a boon to horticulture if not to the landscape. The most striking difference of all, however, is that everybody was white. There would have been a few Scots and Welsh in among the English, of course, and I would not be going too far out on a limb if I suggested that the Irish were possibly quite well represented; but allotments now are very different places from how they were back in the days of William Strang. Michael Wale counted up the number of different nationalities represented in the Acton Gardening Association, and came up with a total of sixteen, and I am not sure if the number has not increased since he carried out his straw poll.

London has changed, of course, and it would be easy to assume that the changes in allotment ownership merely reflect the transformations that have occurred in the city as a whole; London has become much more ethnically diverse, and so has its gardening population. However, I believe that there is more to it than that. Looking around the Bromyard Avenue site one day, I did a quick headcount of my own, and realised that Eliza and I were the only permanent plot-holders who were born in the UK. Who were the others? The West Indians were the biggest single group – John Roberts, from Grenada, Monty the callaloo-fancier in the corner, Gladstone with the plot between us and the gate, and Ina in the other corner. Then there were the Irish (Michael and Tim) and the Moroccans, Mr T and the Mysterious Bean Woman, who, once I had established her nationality, should perhaps be allowed the dignity of being renamed the Moroccan

Bean Woman. On the other side of the gate from Gladstone there was Safi from Afghanistan, with Lucy from Poland down the bottom next to Michael. Finally there was Angelo, a faintly shambolic but utterly charming figure who works in the maintenance department of one of the large local hotels. He was brought up in Tanzania although his family originally came from Goa, and is one of the longer-established plot-holders on the Bromyard site. Over on the main site there are also Iraqis, Portuguese, Italians, Libyans and Spanish.

I have a theory, which perhaps does not amount to a hill of beans but is at least worth discussing, that there is a reason for all of this. Ethnic minorities are disproportionately represented among modern allotment folk because growing your own vegetables is a way of keeping in touch with your roots (for which pun, which was almost entirely unintended, I apologise wholeheartedly). Sometimes this can be true in a pretty literal kind of way. Take John, for instance. I once asked him the name of the beans that he grows on his allotment (a habit I have long since grown out of, having learnt from bitter experience that almost without exception the old hands don't have any truck with fancy stuff like varieties. If you ask one of them what kind of potatoes they are growing this year, they will say either: 1. They don't know; 2. The same ones they grew last year; 3. Red ones (or white, depending); or 4. The ones they got from their friend next door. None of your rubbish about Belle de Fontenay or Pink Fir Apple or Linzer Delikatess), and he told me they were called Cry-Baby beans, and he had brought them over from the West Indies many years ago. Why Cry-Baby beans? Well, it turns out that there was this chap, who really loved his beans, and liked one particular variety more than any other, which he used to grow to the exclusion of anything else. One day when he was out, his cousin came to visit, and his wife thought she had better give him something to eat, and so she cooked up a big pot of beans. The cousin was so hungry, and the beans so delicious, that he scoffed the lot. When the husband returned home he saw what had happened, and was so upset that he wailed 'Why did you have to give him those beans?' and burst into floods of tears, completely inconsolable. So there you have it. Cry-Baby beans: they're really good.

John is also a bit of an expert on sweetcorn, as we have seen, which does not sound so remarkable these days; however, a generation or so ago virtually no one grew it here. Wullie Strang would have as soon grown Indian hemp as he would have grown sweetcorn; its popularity on allotments today is as much due to people like John Roberts as anything else (although I don't suppose that all those sweetcorn-growers out there follow the advice that John passed on to me once, which is that back home everyone knew that you had to have your sweetcorn sown by Fisherman's Day, a national day of celebration in which there are church services to bless the boats and the nets, followed by fishing displays and boat races and parties which go on late into the evening, and altogether what John described as 'a good jump-up'; I will do my best to get my corn in by then next year, just as soon as I find out when Fisherman's Day falls in these parts). Other allotments also reflect the ethnic backgrounds of the people who tend them; both the Moroccans have given over a large part of their plots to broad beans, underlining the importance of beans in North African cuisine (although I notice that they don't share our obsession with picking them as young as possible, instead letting them grow to full maturity – perhaps if you are going to cook them for two or three hours, as in the ubiquitous *ful medames*, you don't need to worry so much about them being tender).

Mr T also grows a lot of mint, to which he generously allows us to help ourselves whenever we want. And while I am on the subject of cultural heritage and ancient traditions being passed down from generation to generation, it would be churlish to forget the Irish and their potatoes. I don't think I will ever be allowed to forget how our predecessor Paddy grew virtually nothing but potatoes while Michael himself is never short of instant wisdom on the planting, cultivation and harvesting of potatoes. Red potatoes suffer less from slug damage is one that I particularly remember; perhaps the slugs mistake them for beetroot, and are understandably put off.

One has to be careful, however, not to take too literally the idea that immigrants are consciously preserving the traditions of their ancestors when they take on an allotment; sometimes they are just growing vegetables. But there is a deeper, more fundamental truth involved, in that while the likes of Mr T and Angelo may have left their homelands when they were too young to grow anything, they do at least carry with them a memory of a society where people grew their own crops, where people were still in touch with the land and beans weren't something that came plastic-wrapped on polystyrene trays that had been flown halfway round the world. For them, growing their own vegetables is an entirely natural thing to do, and even if they cannot remember exactly what it is that their grandmother did to get such tasty tomatoes, they do at least feel some sort of connection with those generations who simply grew their own food because the only alternative was starvation. For too many twenty-first-century Britons, we are so detached from our past, and from the land which supported our forebears, that even to grow something as simple as a spud we have to go scurrying to our *Gardening Which? Guide* to look it up. And yes, I suppose I was one of those people. Before we got our allotment, I had no idea what a seed potato was, or how people grew onions, or what cucumber plants looked like. In a sense I still know nothing, but at least these days I am well informed about my ignorance.

Allotments would be nothing if it were not for people like Michael and John; not because they are colourful characters, or are part of what we think an allotment should be like, but because with their generosity they encourage a spirit of cooperation and mutual support that means that the allotment is more than just a collection of vegetable patches gathered together in one place, it is a community, a collective enterprise where people who would otherwise have nothing in common gather together and help each other out without a second thought. It was halfway through that first summer when we had our first taste of that, one day when Eliza had been working on the allotment during the day. She fell into conversation with Michael, who had by this time decided that we were not complete time-wasters, and were even beginning to show the first signs of promise. Michael had shown Eliza how to string onions, and she had left the finished strings hanging on the allotment to dry in the sun for a few days, with the result that whenever Michael passed them he would say, 'God, I will say this for your other half, she knows how to grow her onions, she does,' or 'Look at her, showing off with her onions again.'

Impressed enough to decide we needed a bit of help and encouragement, Michael told Mrs Low that a lovely pile of manure had just been delivered at the main allotment site further up Bromyard Avenue, and that if I came down to the allotment he would show me how to build a manure heap. This, thought Eliza, was an obviously splendid idea, and considerably better than the alternative of him showing *her* how to build a manure heap, so she immediately rang me at the office on her mobile phone. 'Hello,' she said, 'what are you doing after work?' Whatever I replied, it obviously did not count as more important than a free course in manure management, and so no sooner had I finished work than I rushed home to change and get over to the allotment as fast as I could to meet Michael. He was already there waiting for me, with his specially adapted manure barrow (like a wheelbarrow, only with an extension on top to give it more depth, and a modified wheel arrangement which seemed as far as I could see to have been made out of the moving parts of an old pram and which meant that you did not have to lift it up in order to push it). We walked the two hundred yards up the road to the main allotment site as Michael gave me a short lecture about the shortcomings of the fork I had produced, which might have been perfectly sufficient for general gardening work, but was not really up to snuff when it came to transferring manure, for which task I should clearly have a proper manure fork like they have in Ireland, with a good long handle and long, curved prongs. I wasn't quite sure which was worse – the fact that I did not have a manure fork, or the fact that I had never heard of such a thing, but as I had long ago realised that there was really no end to my ignorance about allotment matters, and probably never would be, I tried not to let it distract me too much from the task in hand.

Upon arrival at the main site, I found that there was indeed a pile of new manure. This, it turned out, was no ordinary manure: it was royal muck. The allotment used to have its manure delivered from a riding school for the disabled run by a nun on Wormwood Scrubs, but that arrangement came to an end when their trailer succumbed to old age. When Michael Wale tried to find a new supplier he discovered that London

186

allotments had the right to apply for deliveries of royal manure free of charge, and so rang up Buckingham Palace and had us put on the list. I am not sure if royal shit is any better than the common kind, but Michael seemed to think it was quite good quality – lots of straw, which is apparently what you want, as opposed to wood shavings, which is what you don't – and anyway, I felt it couldn't be any worse. I made a mental note to tell my cabbages that they would be getting some pretty classy muck to help them along, and that to be honest there wasn't really any excuse for not growing nice and big. I hoped they weren't republicans.

Michael turned out to be quite a good teacher, patiently walking up and down the road with me as I filled the barrow first with manure, then general compost, then manure again, occasionally putting in a modest layer of grass cuttings, which Michael assured me was an important part of the mixture. Each time we emptied the barrow on to our manure heap Michael would get me to water it with the hose ('It won't rot if it's too dry,' he said) and then stamp it down, and if I looked slightly ridiculous dancing around on top of a big pile of manure in my wellington boots while Michael leant on the fence and gave a running commentary on my performance ('You're not doing too bad,' he said, only slightly grudgingly), anyway, at least I had my manure heap.

If Michael and John were generous with their time and advice, they were also generous with their produce. 'Could you use some onions?' Michael would say, or parsnips, or tomatoes, or whatever it was he had a surplus of, and felt that you were lacking. We would say yes – we didn't dare say no, not for fear of offending him, but out of concern that if we ever refused him, the offers might dry up, and that would never do – and he would walk over to his shed with his slightly rolling gait and come back with a bunch of whatever was on offer that week. Occasionally he would not even bother with the offer stage of the process, and would simply leave a pile of vegetables for us on our bench, like some South Sea Islander leaving an offering for the gods. After a while Michael's generosity began to prey on our conscience, and we decided it was necessary to give him something in return. We tried offering him some of our raspberries; no thanks, said Michael, he didn't really eat raspberries. Some time later we tried offering him some tomatoes. We were on safe ground there, we thought; after all, he grows his own tomatoes. 'No thanks,' said Michael, 'I don't really like tomatoes.' Cucumbers? No thanks, don't eat them. Sweetcorn? Never touch the stuff. In the end we decided to give him some chutney we had made (Green Tomato Chutney, made from the tomatoes which fail to ripen by the end of the season, and very good it is too). It was, of course, a racing certainty that Michael did not like chutney either, but we managed to outwit him by thrusting it into his hands and saying 'HelloMichaelhere'ssomechutneywemadefromourtomatoeswethoughtyoumightlikesome,'only really really quickly, and then running away as fast as we could before he had a chance to give it back.

Michael's generosity would also take other forms. As well as showing us how to do things, like make manure heaps or string onions, he would also be notably generous with his praise, although there were times when I wondered whether this wasn't actually Michael's way of conducting – for reasons which were entirely beyond us – a rather subtle and sophisticated form of psychological warfare. When he said, 'Oh, she's showing off again with her onions,' what did he mean? What was he after? Would we only find out when it was all too late? Once I was

188

sowing some seeds, and was feeling rather pleased with myself because I had just mastered the technique of raking back the soil over the drill and then gently firming it down with the back of the rake. Michael must have smelt the air of self-satisfaction coming off me, because as he passed along the path he said, 'Oh, you've got a lovely gentle action there.' The idea crossed my mind that he meant it: perhaps Michael was just a man with a proper appreciation of advanced rake-handling techniques. I dismissed the thought from my mind, though, on the grounds that thinking about these things too much would probably send me mad in the end.

Sometimes his generosity could be rather more straight-forward, such as the time soon after we arrived when he gave us a garden bench to go with the other bench we had made (two pieces of four-by-two sitting on top of some old plastic bread crates), which was very kind of him, except for the fact that the bench is so wonky that you cannot really sit on it with any confidence. It looks nice, though. Perhaps his greatest act of generosity was to set up the system of water tanks on the Bromyard site which saved our lives during the hosepipe ban. Unlike some sites around the country, our allotment does have a tap, so that we are never short of water, and there is even a hosepipe rigged up so that anyone can water their vegetables whenever they want. So far, so standard; any fool can have a hosepipe on their allotment. Michael went one further, however, and set up a series of water tanks around the allotment, connected to the mains supply by hidden pipes and rigged up with ballcocks and valves cannibalised from old lavatory cisterns which meant that they automatically filled up with water every time you took water out. When the hosepipe ban was in force they proved an absolute god-send, because while it was perfectly legal to water your plants by filling a watering can at the tap, it was incredibly time-consuming. Filling your watering can by plunging it into a tank was about a hundred times quicker, and probably the one thing that kept us this side of howling insanity during the long hot summer when we weren't allowed to use the hose.

Other people could be equally generous. Angelo had a rhubarb patch which was much too prolific for him to get through, and said we should take as much as we like. Which we did, regularly: that's what we are like. The generosity of allotment folk is partly down to enlightened self-interest: they have a glut of something, and are desperate to get rid of it, and who better than some fellow plot-holder who has already shown an appreciation and taste for fresh, homegrown produce? But there is more to it than that. Allotment-holders love their vegetables, and get great pleasure from them, and like nothing better than when other people share that pleasure too. So if I grow some particularly gorgeous courgettes, for instance, and can give some of the surplus to someone else – well, that makes me very happy. If they are polite enough – or smart enough – to comment afterwards on how delicious they were, then they will have earned themselves a place on the official Allotment Donation Register, and be guaranteed a sporadic supply of free veg for life.

There are limits, however. There is a very nice woman called Corinne whose daughter has swimming lessons with Orlando. She has an allotment down by the river, and while she and Eliza are waiting outside the pool they occasionally get to talking about allotment matters. One day Corinne talked about her Jerusalem artichokes, and whatever Eliza said must have sounded encouraging because the next week Corinne turned up with a plastic bag full of artichoke tubers – not to eat, but for us to plant. Very easy to grow they are, she said – just stick them in the ground

190

and watch them come up. They also make a great windbreak, she added. Now, while Corinne was being typically generous and kind, and while she only had the purest intentions, I felt that her description of Jerusalem artichokes and their growing habits could benefit somewhat from translation. 'Easy to grow' and 'makes a good windbreak': what that really means is that they are enormous, grow like crazy and once they are in the ground, you will never get rid of them. I had already been there with the horseradish, and was not inclined to make the same mistake again.

That would possibly be acceptable, even so, were it not for the fact that I would quite happily pass the rest of my life without ever eating a Jerusalem artichoke again. It's not as if I don't like them. Some people say that Jerusalem artichoke soup is the most delicious thing in the world, and while I think they are guilty of mild exaggeration – haven't they had broad beans with feta and mint? – I can see where they are coming from. No, the problem is not that Jerusalem artichokes are in any sense horrid: it's the inulin. For reasons best known to themselves, they store their carbohydrate not as starch, as most sensible plants do, but as inulin (not to be confused with insulin). Because our bodies are used to digesting starch, the inulin passes through most of the gut intact until it reaches the colon, where the bacteria get to work on it, releasing what have been described as 'significant' (I would prefer the term 'industrial') quantities of carbon dioxide and methane. For people who are particularly sensitive, or just unused to it, the experience of eating Jerusalem artichokes can be a little gassy. Or indeed very gassy. As for my own experience, I can do no better than refer you to Gerard's *Herball* from 1633, which quotes the English planter John Goodyer on the subject: 'Which way soever they be dressed and eaten, they stir and cause

a filthy loathsome stinking wind within the body, thereby causing the belly to be pained and tormented, and are a meat more
fit for swine than men.' After an extended debate with Eliza, it
was agreed that we were probably not going to grow something
that would (i) take over the allotment, (ii) prove impossible to
remove, and (iii) cause a filthy loathsome stinking wind, and the
bag of artichokes ended up sitting in a corner of the shed, while
we rather conspicuously failed to confess our ingratitude to
Corinne.

Some weeks later we happened to have a spare squash seedling
in a pot, which we agreed to give to Corinne. A short time after
handing it over, we bumped into her again and she told us how
she had planted the seedling, which was growing away nicely. I
probably do not need to spell out how guilty that made us feel.

14

Mimi and Charlotte

Only two things in this world are too serious to be jested on – potatoes and matrimony.

Irish aphorism

If running an allotment is like driving a racing car – which is, I admit, not necessarily the first image which springs to mind, but bear with me – then the start of autumn is like the end of the big fast straight, the one with the grandstand and the pits and all. At the end of the straight you are slowing down, putting your brakes on for the slow corner which is winter, but if you want to be in a good position for the next fast bit (spring, of course: do try to keep up) you have to start thinking about it quite early, making sure you take the correct racing line into the corner so you can come out the other side with the maximum acceleration. The autumn may appear to the untrained eye like a time when you can sit back and enjoy the last of your crops – the carrots, the squash, the last of the autumn raspberries – and prepare yourself for a period of enforced idleness over the winter months, but in reality it is quite a different story. Next season is around the corner, and you won't get off to a flying start unless you are well prepared.

There are onion sets to plant, and shallots, not to mention our old friends the broad beans; that's the obvious stuff. Then there are the more specialist crops, like lamb's lettuce, which while not being the fastest-growing salad crop or indeed the most prolific, does have the virtue of being pretty much winter-proof. Snow, sleet, frost – it takes them all in its stride, so you can plant it in the autumn and be guaranteed some kind of green leaf in your salad literally all year round. There are winter lettuces, too, which won't necessarily crop during the winter but will be the first things to be ready on the allotment come the following spring. Other questions raise themselves, too, such as: do you manure now (so it can be worked into the soil by the worms) or later (so that the goodness does not get leached out by the winter rains)? And that's without even mentioning the old-fashioned winter crops, like leeks and cabbages and sprouts. Autumn: it's busy, busy, busy.

This autumn, however, I had my sights set on grander things than just a bit of lamb's lettuce to get us through the winter months: I was going to stage my own garlic festival. It is the sort of thing they have been doing in towns in south-west France for years, showing off their finest produce, gorging themselves on garlic soup and seeing who can make the best garlic tart. But why should such celebrations be confined to France? They are not the only people who can grow garlic. So, on the patriotic – if possibly misguided – grounds that anything France can do Shepherd's Bush can do better, I decided it was time for *La Grande Fête d'Ail de W12*. This seeming madness was prompted by the fact that, just when there was a bit of a glut of seed garlic waiting to go into the ground on the Low family allotment, they were experiencing a shortage on the other side of the Channel, making it the perfect opportunity to show the French that there really isn't anything where they would not benefit from being exposed to our superior skill and expertise.

Our own glut had started when I began developing an obsession with the challenge of ensuring a year-round supply of garlic for my family. (The story of my allotment life is essentially a list of various obsessions, as I become completely absorbed in the idea of producing the finest garlic crop, or the perfect lettuce, or the best squash, or whatever it is that has caught my interest that year.) To make sure you have your own garlic for twelve months of the year you have to plant a number of varieties, which led that autumn to our purchasing some Early Purple garlic (which is early, and purple), some Solent Wight, which stores well through the winter, and one called Albigensian, which is the garlic of the Cathars, those heretics who flourished in the Languedoc region of France in the twelfth and thirteenth centuries; I think it is important to have at least one crop every year named after a religious sect. Anyway, we thought that that would probably be enough to see us through, until we visited the Garlic Farm on the Isle of Wight and came across yet another variety from the village of Lautrec in the Tarn, which has cloves of the deepest purple and is, according to those in the know, the champagne of garlic. Well, we just had to have some, didn't we? The question of which is better – *l'ail rose de Lautrec* or *l'ail violet de Cadours*, which comes from a village the other side of Toulouse and which was the variety that the French had run out of that autumn – is one of those thorny issues that divide garlic connoisseurs the world over, and I am not entirely sure whether I would ever be able to settle the question with any degree of certainty. But I think we had a pretty good garlic selection, given the circumstances, and if things went our way there was no reason to think that we would not have the finest garlic crop in all of Shepherd's Bush and East Acton. That posed its own challenges, however, because there is no point having terrific garlic unless you are in a position to show it off to its best advantage. Thanks to Michael's tutorials, our onion-stringing skills were by then second to none, but our garlic-plaiting still left something to be desired. It wasn't entirely awful, in that it hung together, and looked almost respectable, but it certainly was not up to the standards of those beautiful plaits you see in French markets. The record at the *Fête d'Ail* in Lautrec for a garlic tress is 21.66 metres. I was not sure what the Shepherd's Bush record was, but I felt it was ours for the taking.

As well as preparing for my conquest of the garlic world, the autumn was also the time of one of the most significant events in the gardening calendar: the Acton Gardening Association Annual General Meeting. It is held at the Acton Working Men's Club, a rather sensible choice of venue I thought to myself when I turned up, because it meant that I was able to buy a drink at the bar and take it into the meeting, and so would be in a position to drink myself into a stupor if the meeting turned out to be boring. Which, to be honest, is what I feared it would be.

Minutes of the last meeting. Presentation of accounts. Election of officers. It did not exactly have enthralling written all over it.

That, however, turned out to be somewhat misleading, because the only interesting item of the evening's proceedings had not, for some reason, been included in the meeting's agenda – to wit, the airing of grievances. And boy, were there some grievances that needed airing. Gates that had been left unlocked. Complete strangers turning up on the allotment, almost certainly as a result of the aforesaid gates being left unlocked. (As a veteran non-locker of gates, at least when I am on the allotment, on the grounds that I can see everyone who comes and goes from our vantage position slap bang in the middle of the site, I felt a little shifty at this point, and stared fixedly at the head on my pint of Guinness.) Worst of all, it seemed that some people were turning up on their plots with THEIR ENTIRE FAMILIES, and letting their children run riot all over the allotments. Crops were trampled. Entire plots were laid waste, or at least something like that: I wasn't entirely sure, because I had stopped listening by this point. I buried my face in my Guinness, and hoped that no one would mention that day of infamy on the Bromyard site when Kitty and Orlando had decided to relive England's Rugby World Cup victory on our allotment, or indeed the time they discovered that the manure heap made a very serviceable castle to be defended against the scurvy knaves with whatever weapons came to hand, chiefly being the fork, the trowel, the dahlia stakes and any of the numerous bamboo canes that litter our plot.

The council officer in charge of allotments at the London Borough of Ealing, a very nice chap called Stephen Cole, once told me that there were two sorts of allotment-holder: those who thought that there were far too many rules and regulations, and those who thought that there were nowhere near enough. It struck me as a very perceptive remark, never more so than at that meeting, when the militant wing of the Rules Are Good tendency proceeded to mount a determined assault. Among them were two women, who from what I could tell shared a plot, and who were very much part of the new breed of allotment-holder: youngish, probably *Guardian* readers, and absolutely chock-full of opinions. (Of course I am youngish, although perhaps more 'ish' than young, read the *Guardian* and even grow rocket on my allotment, but for all that I feel that fundamentally I am on the side of the Old Gits, or at least the Old Gits who cannot be doing with all these rules and regulations.) The two women, and their allies, presented an unanswerable case. 1. People running riot was clearly a bad thing. 2. Something had to be done. 3. I know what – how about a new rule? The suggestion was that the gate on the main allotment site should be kept locked at all times, even when people were there, so that there was no chance of anyone running riot on the allotments, ever. At this point I decided to mount a last stand against this heinous assault on liberty, free speech and the allotment way. The proposed new rule was all very well in principle, I said, but it posed a problem to people like me, who have plots on other sites but often want access to the main site for things like manure and wood chippings. We don't have keys to the main plot, I said, and could well find ourselves locked out. Don't worry, someone from the association committee said, there is always someone there on the main site who will let you in.

The new rule was, of course, voted through: I will leave it to the reader's imagination to work out whether the next time I wanted to get on to the main site to get a barrowload of manure, there was anyone there to let me in. Or the time I wanted to get some wood chippings. Or the time I went to pick up a pallet from the pile that is always there to make a front for my manure heap. Still, at least no one was running riot.

Not all allotment AGMs are the same. At Fulham Palace Meadows, two or three miles from where I live, there are some rather delightful allotments, which were a gift from the Bishop of London in 1916. They are more interesting than the average allotments, because they are on the largest unexplored Anglo-Saxon site in the country, which means that they are protected under the Ancient Monuments Act 1979. It also means that plot-holders are not allowed to dig any deeper than eighteen inches, to stop them from disturbing anything interesting down below. In fact the Rules Are Good tendency seems to have been rather dominant over the years at Fulham Palace, to judge by their association's old AGM minutes. For instance, an amendment to the rules from 1955 states that 'No persons other than a married man or widower shall be granted tenancy of a plot on this Meadow.' The first female tenant was not admitted until 1970. On the other hand, the bishops seem to have had a rather more robust attitude to the question of pigeons than the Goldsmiths' Company: in October 1962 a Mr Parker (Plot 103) was thanked for his efforts shooting wood pigeons, and the committee voted to buy more cartridges for his shotgun, so that he could continue. They seem to have drawn the line on culling the pigeons on the Sabbath, though: in 1965 there was a complaint by the bishop about shooting early on Sunday mornings. As recently as 1973 the rules about what people were allowed to grow were particularly stringent: no soft fruit, no permanent crops, and all vegetables to be planted in double rows. Quite what rule was being breached when this note was written is, though, beyond me: 'Plot 82 suspected of growing King Edwards.'

At a recent AGM, however, they had rather more important matters to discuss than whether some rotter was trying to sneak King Edwards on to their allotment: they were there to discuss The Fulham Palace Poisoning Mystery. A couple of old boys had been enjoying a cup of tea in the allotment shed when they were taken seriously ill and had to be rushed to Charing Cross Hospital, where for a while it was all a bit touch and go. They survived, and the source of the poison turned out to be the sugar bowl in the shed, where police found a white powder which was not sugar at all but a chemical which had been banned from garden use many years earlier. Accident or deliberate? The sort of thing that happens when you have dangerous herbicides hanging around in unlabelled containers, or a villainous attempt to settle an old allotment score? I do not know, and indeed the police do not know, for no charges were ever brought, but when the matter was raised at the AGM and was being treated with perhaps a little less gravity than some might have wished, one of the elderly victims got to his feet and, his voice quaking with indignation (I think it is good to imagine here Private Frazer of *Dad's Army*), said something to the effect of 'You laugh if you will, but it is no laughing matter. There is . . . a MURDERER IN OUR MIDST!'

The period when autumn gives way to winter is when most allotment-holders' minds turn to the subject of potatoes, and in particular what they are going to grow and where they are going to get them from. It is a very exciting time of year. No, really, it is. There are all sorts of decisions to be made when planning your potato crop, and none of them are easy. Do you want first earlies? Late maincrop? Red ones? White ones? Floury ones? Waxy ones? Is your chief concern making sure you have potatoes with good flavour? Or are you more worried about good disease resistance? How do you feel about growing funny knobbly potatoes, like Pink Fir Apple? Or groovy coloured ones, such as Vitelotte, which according to those in the know makes wonderful purple mash? Decisions, decisions, decisions.

There are about 150 different varieties available to amateur growers in the UK – which sounds quite a lot until you consider that in Peru they have got about 3,000, with names like 'Best Black Woman' and 'Makes the Daughter-in-Law Cry' – and for just about every one of them there is an enthusiast somewhere who will tell you that it is the best spud in the world. A gardening friend of my parents-in-law once wrote a speech entirely using the names of different rose varieties, and I have often been tempted to do something similar for potatoes, which would lend themselves very well to a work of romantic fiction. There are plenty of suitable names for heroines, for instance: Catriona, the wilful Scottish lass from the Highlands, Belle de Fontenay, the mysterious French beauty, and her friends Charlotte and Desirée. How many hearts have been broken by the lovely Mimi? Or matches arranged by the scheming Lady Balfour? As for heroes, Buchan sounds like a fine, square-jawed kind of fellow, and there have been no warriors braver than the Dunbar Rover, slain under the Arran Banner at the battle of Ballydoon as he defended his master, the Ulster Chieftain, against the armies of that most dastardly of villains, the evil Sarpo Mira. After his body was borne back to Carlingford, a haunting lament was played by the Maris Piper . . . and, well, you get the idea. I haven't yet sorted out a role for the Pink Fir Apple, but I'm working on it.

Choosing your varieties is closely tied up with the equally vexing question of where to get them from. You can buy them from the mail order companies – several of the seed catalogues, such as Tuckers, sell seed potatoes – but you generally have to buy them in 3 kg bags, which is quite economical but does mean that you end up with a rather large quantity of just one or two varieties. Our allotment shop also sells potatoes, but only a relatively small number of varieties. Thank heavens, then, for the greatest thing to happen to *Solanum tuberosum* since Sir Walter Raleigh: the potato fair. Every year, around the end of January or beginning of February, a number of organisations around the country hold special events where they sell seed potatoes by the individual tuber, so you can buy as many different varieties as you think you can manage. As the London Potato Fair is held in a school in Peckham on a Sunday morning, that meant we were going to have to take the children, and while Kitty and Orlando are quite happy to help out with the allotment from time to time, buying seed potatoes in a school hall in south London may not have been their chosen way to spend their weekend. On the other hand it happened to coincide with my birthday, which offered me something of a lifeline. 'This morning,' I told them a touch disingenuously, 'as it's my birthday, we're going to a fair.'

'What kind of fair?' they chorused.

'Er, a potato fair.'

They took this cruel parental deception quite well. Singularly devoid of merry-go-rounds, dodgems and candyfloss, the fair turned out to be quite fun, if you regard a large room laid out with tables bearing endless containers of seed potatoes as fun, which I do. There was just about every variety you could hope for, from Accent to Yukon Gold, although no sign of Makes the Daughter-in-Law Cry: perhaps I will be able to persuade them to get it in for next year. A small catalogue – think cheap photocopy here, not glossy colour brochure – gave tasting and

202

growing notes on each variety, which in a way was very useful but really just served to make it all much more difficult. I am not too good at being decisive at the best of times, but faced with all that potato choice I became almost catatonic with indecision. Belle de Fontenay or Pink Fir Apple? Edzell Blue or Golden Wonder? Or perhaps we should just play safe and get some Desirée, which everyone says is good and reliable but which Eliza was firmly opposed to on the grounds that you can get it in the shops, and we weren't there to grow stuff you could get from any old supermarket. I was particularly taken with a variety called Kestrel, which according to the blurb not only has excellent flavour and beautiful blue eyes but 'matures gracefully to be a general purpose chipper and baker'. I like a touch of graceful maturity in my potatoes.

I was not the only person who regarded the potato fair as one of the highlights of the allotment year. The school was packed with spud fanciers of every shape and size who had come from all over London to stock up for the coming season, from stout matrons in sensible shoes to sweet old couples in matching anoraks, a definite smattering of *Guardian* readers and even one or two vaguely hippyish-looking types who looked as if they probably planted their potatoes according to the cycles of the moon. People consulted lists and poked around in the boxes of potatoes as they looked for their favourite varieties, chatting enthusiastically to total strangers as they discussed the growing qualities of Red King Edwards, and whether Charlottes or Rattes make the best potato salad. There was one group that was missing, however: the Old Gits. I don't think that Old Gits would have regarded 15p a tuber as a bargain in any sense of the word, and neither are they as interested as I am in growing as many different varieties as can possibly fit into one modestly sized bed. Old Gits tend to find one variety, or possibly two, and then grow as much of it as they can possibly manage. I spent about £7 on buying enough seed potatoes to fill a quarter of our allotment: any Old Git worth his salt could have filled his entire plot for about half that.

They wouldn't have had as much fun, though. Kitty and Orlando proved to be remarkably enthusiastic members of the team, and were signed up to go round the hall looking for the different varieties on my list, treating the whole exercise as almost as exciting as an Easter egg hunt, only without the chocolate bit. 'Dad, Dad, shall I go and find the next one?' Orlando would shout out every few minutes, tugging at my elbow to get my attention, and it was all I could to do to ensure that he did not start loading up with varieties that we had no intention of buying but had somehow acquired because Orlando liked the look of them. Eventually, and not without a certain amount of cross-checking, double-checking and any other checking we could think of, not to mention a fair bit of 'No, darling, shall we put the Golden Wonder back?' (I managed to draw the line at forcing Orlando to turn his pockets out: sometimes you just have to trust people), we came away with a bag full of Charlotte, Kestrel, Picasso, Merlin, Kerr's Pink and Pink Fir Apple, which I felt would not only make a good potato selection for the following year but also the outline for a rather gripping novel (the scenes involving the magician and the painter had particular promise).

The potato fair was not just about potatoes. There were seeds, too; and not just seeds for sale, but seeds to swap. Having already been fully imbued with the allotment culture of getting as much as you can for free, I found the idea of a seed swap – where you take along your spare seeds, and in exchange help yourself to the seeds other people have donated – particularly appealing. Thanks to my slight Puritan streak – I blame my great-grandparents on my father's mother's side, who were Quakers – I get somewhat upset by the waste involved whenever you buy seeds. With some types of seed, of course, there is little or no waste. Take carrots, for instance: with successional sowing it is very easy to use up the whole packet in one season, and indeed if you are not careful you can even run out. Lettuce, too: over a couple of seasons you will run out before the seeds get too old and lose their vitality. With some other seeds, like courgettes or squash, you get so few in the packet that you treat every seed as if it were some precious treasure; no waste there. But peas and beans? Oh dear. The estimable Tuckers, for instance, gives you around 500 seeds in a packet of peas, which for £1.50 is a veritable bargain, but I would have to turn our plot over to industrial-scale pea production if I was going to get through that number of peas in one year. As for runner beans, you get 100 seeds in a packet, which does not sound too bad until you consider that in an average year we sow no more than about fifteen seeds. As the seeds don't last for ever, with the best will in the world I am only going to get through about half the packet before I have to replace it. So it was hooray for the seed swap – or Seedy Sunday as the organisers chose to call it, which may have been their idea of a joke – and a happy hour or so the previous evening spent going through our box of seeds working out which ones we could spare, putting them into envelopes and labelling them.

I am not sure exactly what we were expecting to find at the seed swap, but it certainly wasn't the sight which greeted us in that Peckham school hall. There, on a table just down from the potato section, were all the seeds laid out in boxes; and there, three deep all around them, were all these gardeners practically coming to blows as they struggled to get near to the display. It was like a cross between the first day of the Harvey Nichols sale and a scene from one of those David Attenborough documentaries where the lions gather for a slap-up feed courtesy of some wildebeest who was a little slow off the mark. By the time I had managed to work my way to the front of the mob – having jabbed only a few sweet old dears in the ribs with my elbow, and trodden on only the barest minimum of toes – I discovered exactly what the problem was (apart from the fact that here was something going for free, in a room 90 per cent filled with allotment gardeners, and well what did they expect?). The seeds had come from a variety of sources – some homegrown, some unwanted commercial seeds – with somewhat varying labelling techniques, which meant that it had been impossible to sort them into any coherent order. The result was that anyone interested in picking up some seeds was going to have to rifle through the lot, packet by packet – and, being allotment folk on their big day out, they weren't going to be in a big hurry about it. So, with a couple of precautionary elbow jabs to clear a space around me – whoops, sorry madam, was that you? – I set myself up to go through what must have been a few hundred packets of seeds to see what I could find. It wasn't a bad haul in the end: we got some lamb's lettuce, orange poppies, marigolds and a packet of mixed salad leaves described on the back as 'an innovative blend to add something different to your high-class salad creations'.

What pleased me most of all, though, was the borage. I had been looking for some ever since some seed supplier or other let us down, and so it was rather satisfactory to find a small hand-labelled envelope stuffed full of borage seeds. What was even more satisfactory was to find the man who had grown the borage, a fellow called Lindsay Wright who had launched the London Potato Fair five years earlier and was obviously a bit of a good egg. How come he grew all those seeds, I asked? Well, he said, he had an allotment almost wholly given over to seed production, just in order to put them into seed swaps. He was able to do this because he actually has three allotments. *Three.* Me, if I had three allotments I know exactly what I would do. It would be Belle de Fontenay *and* Pink Fir Apple, Edzell Blue *and* Golden Wonder, not to mention all the lady spuds – Mimi, Charlotte, Desirée, Agnes, Annabelle, Catriona, Colleen, Nicola, Simone, Vanessa and, if it is not being too presumptuous, Lady Balfour. I hope my wife will understand.

As well as the potato fair, winter is also the time for that most enjoyable of gardening activities, the perusal of the seed catalogues. To open a seed catalogue in the middle of winter, when the allotment is a cold and forbidding place where the soil is heavy and wet and impossible to work, and nothing much grows aside from a handful of leeks and some rather battered-looking Brussels sprouts, is to enter a glorious, colourful world of opportunity and hope where every tomato is red and juicy and full of flavour, every carrot a perfect specimen of crunchy carrotness. How I love my catalogues. At home we have a drawer full of them, each with its own particular brand of seductive allure, from the wholefood worthiness of the Organic Catalogue to the beguiling visions of Mediterranean sunshine proffered by Seeds of Italy (which distinguishes itself from all other catalogues by using as its front cover illustration not some bounteous shot of garden produce, but an eighteenth-century view of Venice).

On those long winter evenings there is nothing I like better than to get out our catalogues and begin the long and indulgent process of deciding what to grow that year. Courgettes, of course – they are what summer is all about. But which ones? Green? Yellow? Striped? The American hybrid called Eight Ball, which is perfectly round? Or, if we are feeling particularly brave, *Rugosa Friulana*, the only courgette found in the Venice region, which Seeds of Italy describes as 'ugly, but very, very tasty'? Then there are the lettuces. There are so many varieties out there that it makes my head spin, which makes me think that the rational thing to do would be to stick to the ones we grew last year, which were pretty successful. But that would be boring. Shouldn't we be trying the Italian heirloom variety called *Ubriacona Frastagliata* (which, according to Edwin Tucker & Sons of Devon – 'Tuckers Trustworthy Seeds' – translates as 'drunken women')? Or how about Rubens Red? Tom Thumb? Tintin? (Which is, according to the catalogue, resistant to downy mildew, root aphids and leaf aphids. Nothing about going round with a little white dog called Snowy, though.) There are too many varieties and not enough time, and what the gardener needs is help and guidance as he tries to make his way through the jungle that is the modern seed catalogue; what he gets, unfortunately, is smoke blown in his eyes.

Every time you open a catalogue you are pitting yourself against the seed companies' copywriters, a desperate breed who will stop at nothing to get you to buy their wares. Do you ever come across a catalogue which says 'this lettuce grows well but is rather dull and frankly best fed to your pet rabbit', or 'one of the finest peas on the market, assuming you are looking for ammunition for your peashooter. Could be used for soup, if you have run out of old socks'? No you do not. What you get is a load of old flannel, fancy words which sound impressive but mean nothing, and are designed to convince you that every single vegetable in the catalogue is delicious, nutritious, easy to grow and resistant to all known pests and diseases. It's not easy, of course, especially when you have a couple of dozen different lettuces to describe (thirty-four in the Thompson and Morgan catalogue, not including all the packets of mixed salad leaves), and in a way one has to admire the copywriters' skill in finding ever new and imaginative ways of saying 'this stuff is really nice, and even a five-year-old could grow it'. From the reader's point of view, however, one needs to be able to distinguish between all the different grades of flannel, a knack which requires experience, level-headedness and finely honed deductive powers. I am not sure I am quite there yet. One day, perhaps, I will learn to distinguish between 'excellent quality', 'refreshing taste', 'remarkably sweet flavour' and 'one of the best garden lettuces', but for the moment seed ordering – however enjoyable – remains a bit like floundering in the dark.

There are ways round the problem, though. This is the point in the book where I put in a good word for Sarah Raven. Now, readers may have got the impression that I regard Ms Raven's business with a suspicion bordering on mistrust, which isn't the case, because fundamentally she is a good egg: it's just that when it comes to the important questions in life one has to define where one stands, and where seeds are concerned I feel deep down that I am a Tuckers man rather than a Sarah Raven man. But she has done some good things, and one of them is to have a seed catalogue which does not overwhelm the reader with forty-six varieties of lettuce and twenty-seven different tomatoes; instead she just puts in the varieties that she tried and tested herself, and that she reckons are the best of their type. So, just eight lettuces, three cabbages, three carrots, one Brussels sprout; which makes choosing a more streamlined process.

A rather more interesting alternative is the Real Seed

Catalogue, a not-for-profit company run by a couple in Wales called Ben and Kate. The website describes the catalogue as 'a private collection of rare, heirloom, and unusual vegetables selected particularly for the home grower', with all the varieties chosen from Ben and Kate's personal experience. I am not sure why I have never ordered anything from them, because there are just too many ways in which I find them totally lovable. If you are not happy with what you have bought – even if you just don't like the flavour – they will replace the seed or refund your money. If they reckon something is too difficult or fiddly to grow, they won't stock it. They even give seed-saving instructions with some of the unusual plants so that you can produce your own, a philanthropic gesture which I cannot see being emulated by Messrs Thompson and Morgan. Most charming of all, they publish a list of the people who supply them with seed, experienced growers who choose one or two varieties they are enthusiastic about, and grow them just for seed. Even if we don't know who grows the cabbages and who grows the squash, it is good to know that Barbara Morrison and Fred Coleman and David and Val Taylor are all out there, growing away; and if I ever manage to find out what Sister Anselma Scollard of the Abbey of St Cecilia is responsible for – well, I'll be first in the queue.

Not all of my fellow allotment-holders are as obsessed with the question of varieties as I am. While I was writing this chapter I had to pop over to the allotment to pick something up, and spotted Angelo. I wandered over for a brief chat – not always the easiest thing to do on the allotment, because different plot-holders' ideas of what constitutes a brief chat tend to vary somewhat. As it was a hot day, and he was doing some fairly heavy digging, Angelo seemed quite happy to stop and chat. We talked about this and that – the state of the potato crop, the height of his sunflowers, the fact that he had bumped into the man who used to have the plot next to ours, the one with all the flowers and the pond – and then I asked him about the potatoes he was digging up. 'What variety are they?' I said. He paused for a moment, stroked his chin and said: 'They're the red ones.'

A part of me admires that approach. If I go to a shop, or a market, I don't go round obsessing about what sort of courgette is on offer, or whether those tomatoes are Ferline or Gardeners' Delight. Growing vegetables is quite easy, despite the fuss that people like me make about it, and if you grow it yourself it usually tastes pretty good. On the other hand, I do find it almost impossible to resist the temptation to say to myself (and anyone else who might be listening): 'Those French beans we grew last year were all very well, but shouldn't we be trying Cherokee Trail of Tears?' According to legend they are the beans the Cherokee Indians took with them when they were driven out of their homelands on their 'Trail of Tears', and in the view of the people at Real Seeds are simply the best bean there is. Hard to resist, isn't it?

Thank heavens, then, for the Internet. When I am on the allotment I come across no more than about half a dozen fellow plot-holders on anything like a regular basis, and they certainly cannot be relied upon to have informative views about the relative virtues of different vegetable varieties. On the Internet, however, I can talk to hundreds of gardeners, many of them with more opinions than they know what to do with. From time to time I like to have a look at the discussion forum on a website called Allotments4All, where people can sound off about anything they like, from their battles with the local slug population to the detrimental effect of the Jerusalem artichoke on the gastrointestinal system. Sometimes they moan (they are gardeners, after all); sometimes they just like to show off, and post photographs of their produce, which in theory should be annoying but is in fact rather heart-warming. Look, they say, I grew this: isn't it great? And you have to agree.

What I like most about the forum, though, is the fact that it is real people sharing real information. They talk about pests, and how to make a runner bean trench, and whether there is going to be a frost tonight, and they are only too happy to share the benefit of their experience. That's how I learned what had been attacking my borlotti beans after I had dried them and, better, how I learned how to deal with the offending bean weevil (dry the beans in the normal way, then put them in the freezer for a few days, which should kill off any lodgers lurking within; after that you can take the beans out of the freezer again, dry them a bit more just to be on the safe side, and then store them in the larder safe in the knowledge that if anything is going to eat them now, it will only be the Arctic Bean Weevil and, as far as I can tell, you don't often see them in these parts).

Sometimes people start off a thread with something as banal as 'What are your favourite potato varieties?', and before you know two dozen people have chipped in, saying what they grow and why – and often including the sort of insights that you never see in the books. Plenty of people like Pink Fir Apples, but whoever knew they made great chips? Similarly, if several people mention that a particular sort is one of their favourite potatoes, it is a fair bet that it must be doing something right. Then, when people have run out of things to say about vegetables, they write about themselves, which isn't a bad thing either: it's good to know that this virtual friend appearing on my computer screen is a real human being after all. I saw this post once, from a

Londoner who has been living in Norfolk for fourteen years, and never forgot it: for sheer life-affirming wonderfulness it is hard to beat.

I am 80 and have just turned half of my 20 pole plot into raised beds, to make life easier. There are 20 of them, 4ft × 15ft, made of scaffold boards. It took me all winter to make them. I am going to grow all tall veg e.g. sprouts, sweet corn etc. in the other half, and the short veg like carrots, parsnips & lettuce etc. in the raised beds. Am I doing it right? What a wonderful life it is having an allotment. All the Norfolk old boys are very friendly to me, even though I am one of those b- - - - - Londoners.

All the best,
cockneycarrot.

15

Renewal

The nailes, that is, the white and thicke parts which are in
the bottome of the outward scales or flakes of the fruit of
the Artichoke, and also the middle pulpe whereon the
downy seed stands, are eaten both raw with pepper and
salt, and commonly boyled with the broth of fat flesh, with
pepper added, and are accounted a dainty dish, being
pleasant to the taste, and good to procure bodily lust.

John Gerard, *Herball or Generall Historie of Plantes*, 1633

The winter trudges on, dull and bleak and cold and wet, and the allotment becomes a foreign land. We rarely make it up there, and when we do it is to carry out some perfunctory task and then return home as soon as possible. It is not that I have any great objection to working outside in bad weather – on the contrary, I adhere firmly to the dictum I first heard from the head of my children's nursery school, that there is no such thing as bad weather, only inappropriate clothing – but rather that it has become a rather depressing place, occupied by the sorry remnants of the purple sprouting broccoli and a few brave leeks. Under the ground there are some broad beans preparing to do battle, and a few rows of onions and garlic, but they aren't much to look at and certainly are not enough to entice me up to the allotment. There is not much work to be done, either. When there is some task that needs doing, some bed to be dug over, or a few sprouts to be snapped off their stem, it makes for a lonely hour on the allotment: in the soggy depths of winter we hardly ever seen any of our fellow plot-holders.

Soon, but perhaps not quite soon enough, spring comes. The exact moment of its arrival is hard to pinpoint; somehow it just slips in, unnoticed. One day it is winter, then things start changing in a rather elusive, ill-defined way, and you know that spring is about to make an entrance. It is not a question merely of the calendar, or of the temperature; you just know that suddenly there are things to be done – beds to be prepared, seeds to be sown – and that imperceptibly your mood has begun to change. Gloom is replaced by hope, torpor by action. Things look up. Although this was, technically speaking, our second spring on the allotment, it felt like the first because it was the first one we had known which had followed the proper cycle of autumn and winter, of plants settling for a bit of downtime before launching themselves back into action when the weather warms up. Perhaps because of this it found me in philosophical mood, my thoughts meandering through such notions as the universal nature of the cycle of life, and how when it comes to the seasons plants and people have really got quite a lot in common. During the winter you clear the plot of all the dead plants, and when spring comes you start putting in new ones, and it didn't take much of a leap of the imagination for me to start wondering if all of my fellow plot-holders had made it through the winter. They are pretty old, after all, and while they looked hale and hearty the last time I saw them, that was several months ago.

Sometime during the winter Safi died. Rationally speaking I knew it had been nothing to do with the weather – I knew he had a dodgy heart, and the last time I had spoken to him he told me that he had to go into hospital for an operation – but all the same his passing felt somehow connected with the passing of the seasons, part of nature's eternal pattern of death and renewal. Even though we did not have much of consequence to say to each other, I would miss his stout cheerfulness, his booming voice greeting my arrival with a jolly 'Hello my friend! How are you?' Perhaps most of all I would miss the simple, boundless pleasure he got from his allotment, his 'paradise'. I don't know where old Afghans go when they die, but I hope they have lots of flowers there.

Fortunately the other old boys on the Bromyard site managed to make it through the winter months, not just surviving but returning with a renewed vigour that made me suspect that in fact they had not been spending their winter the way the rest of us do – trudging to work, grumbling about the weather, wondering whether to turn the central heating up a notch – but had in fact been hibernating. I don't think I would have been at all surprised if I had learned that Michael had crawled under his duvet on the first of December, his flat cap securely on his head to preserve valuable body heat, a pile of carrots and parsnips next to him in case he ever woke up feeling peckish, and had not emerged again until the beginning of March.

The first of the senior Bromyard-dwellers I came across that spring was John, who positively bounded over to me with a big smile on his face and declared 'Touch the flesh!' – not, I must admit, a greeting I was familiar with, but I still had a lot to learn – as he stuck out his hand for me to shake. His smile, the warmth of his greeting: if anything said that spring had well and truly arrived, that was it. As we stood there in the thin March sunshine, we chatted about his upbringing in Grenada, and the time he used to work for a tailor in Savile Row; he also told me a long and complicated story which revolved around his various visits home to the West Indies, and a hat which had remained lost for seven years. I am not sure now what the point of the story was, or indeed if there ever was a point, but the way John told it it was a cracking good story, and I think I managed to laugh at the right point. I didn't get an awful lot of work done that morning.

An hour or so later John came back over to my plot once more and asked, casually like, if I followed Formula One racing. I confessed that no, I didn't, and kept to myself the thought that it was a rather strange thing for John to be asking. Well, he said, he has a brother, and his brother has a grandson, and this boy was driving for one of the teams, and was beginning to do quite well. Apparently the young man in question had wanted to race cars ever since he was a boy, and had badgered the boss of the race team until he got taken on. John seemed rather proud of him. I wasn't quite sure what to do with this information, but presumed his great-nephew had some kind of trainee position, and maybe had even completed a race or two. Even if he was fairly obscure, I reckoned there might have been some kind of mention of him in the sports pages, and made a mental note to look him up in our electronic cuttings library when I next had a spare moment at work.

Shortly after our conversation Lewis Hamilton began to do quite well.

Later the same day Michael arrived, full of bonhomie and jokes (Irish, or filthy, or if he is on particularly good form, both). I was planting my seed potatoes at the time, and there is nothing like the sight of someone like me (English and ignorant, an unbeatable combination in Michael's eyes) planting spuds to get his interest going. Over he came, and cast a long cool look at the trenches where I was mixing in some lovely well-rotted manure – all dark chocolate brown and crumbly – before putting in the potatoes. 'Oh,' he said, 'you treat yours a lot more nicely than I do mine. I just bung 'em in.' It was another stellar Michael performance. The new gardening year was just a few hours old – or so it felt – and already the Irish sage had got me into an advanced state of paranoia as I tried to work out what he meant. Was he congratulating me for the painstaking care I took with my potatoes, or taking the mickey at the way I was wasting my time? As ever, it was impossible to tell. He followed with a few nuggets of homespun Michael wisdom about the cultivation of potatoes in East Acton, a subject on which I am usually prepared to bow to his authority. First there were the Kerr's Pinks. I cannot remember why we bought them, and I would like to think it was because they were a good all-round potato with an excellent flavour which fitted well into our growing plan, although a small part of me is concerned that the purchase decision might have been affected by the fact that Eliza thought they were a nice colour. 'Oh, they'll never grow here,' announced Michael. Why not? I asked. Well, he explained, people had tried to grow them before, and had never got a decent crop out of them, and it must be to do with the soil, or something like that. It all sounded a bit nebulous, and when Michael said 'people' I suspect he meant Michael. I was in any case committed to my Kerr's Pinks, and made a secret resolution to investigate every way I could possibly think of of getting the greatest possible bumper crop of Kerr's Pinks that East Acton had ever seen.

Michael's other offering of potato lore concerned the subject of organic potatoes. He had once bought some organic seed potatoes – Cara, I think they were – only to find that when he came to harvest them they were totally riddled with eelworm. Or was it wireworm? One is more properly known as the potato cyst nematode, and makes tiny little holes in your potatoes, while the other is the larva of the click beetle, and makes slightly larger holes in your potatoes. I must admit I do get them confused sometimes, although it is safe to say that both are very annoying. Whoever the culprit was, the point is that Michael lost virtually his whole crop, and was very upset about it. That much is understandable, of course: what is a little harder to take on board is the lesson he drew from it. 'I've never grown organic potatoes again,' he said. I may not know much about potatoes, or indeed about the preferred breeding conditions of the potato cyst nematode/click beetle larva, but I do feel that the organic movement may have been judged slightly harshly here.

It being the time of year to start thinking about sowing root vegetables, Michael got to reminiscing about his time as a young man back home in Co. Monaghan when he would work in the fields – sowing carrots, harvesting swedes, that sort of thing.

From Michael's description it was a pretty cold and miserable way of earning a day's pay; as we all know, they had proper winters back then, with proper cold, not the silly damp things we have to put up with now. They also ate swedes, which these days is something of a minority activity. Michael tried to explain the brilliant contraption they had for sowing the carrot seeds, but not being particularly mechanically minded I failed to grasp some of the finer details, although suffice it to say I got the general drift, which is that it placed the seeds at the correct depth and the correct spacing, and meant that all one had to do was sow the seeds, forget about them, and then come back a few months later and harvest the carrots.

If growing carrots is so simple, the reason why Eliza and I have so much trouble getting them to germinate is, therefore, a bit of a mystery; perhaps a short working holiday in Monaghan would put us right. Weed control was also easier in those days, it seems. Michael recalled how there was something they would spray over the carrots which would kill all the weeds but somehow leave the carrots unscathed. What was the name of this miracle preparation? He scratched his head for a moment, and said: 'TVO.' TVO? He could not recall for the moment what it stood for, but it was fantastic stuff, and if I could get hold of some perhaps I should try it. He pondered again for a moment, shook his head and started to walk off. After a couple of paces, though, he stopped; it had come to him. 'Tractor Vaporising Oil,' he said, triumphantly. 'That's the stuff. Killed all the weeds.' Possibly not organic, though. (Technical note: Tractor Vaporising Oil is a mixture of petrol and heating oil which used to be a common tractor fuel. It was withdrawn in the 1970s.)

While an application of TVO might solve our weed problem – and perhaps give us the world's first vegetables which you

221

cook by simply holding them next to a naked flame – it was never going to address the more fundamental issue, which is that Eliza and I are simply rubbish at growing carrots. In our first year on the allotment we must have tried at least three sowings, if not four or five, managing only to get out of it the grand sum of about eight carrots. In terms of effort expended per carrot harvested – and indeed money spent on packets of seed – we would have been better off sending a limo to go and pick up a bag of carrots from Fortnum & Mason. It's not as if we didn't persevere. We tried planting early; we tried planting late. We sowed them in neat, regimented lines; we sowed them freestyle, in bands. Nothing seemed to work. Carrots just weren't interested in us. In comparison with parsnips, though, our track record with carrots made us look like world-class experts. First year on the allotment, number of parsnips successfully grown: 0. Second year on the allotment, number of parsnips successfully grown: 0. Occasionally Michael would offer us a few of his, brilliantly getting over the message – without actually saying so – that parsnips were so easy to grow that he had an absolute glut of them, so many he had to give them away. Thank you, Michael, they were delicious. Once we were with a friend of Eliza's, a rather talkative feminist and class warrior of the old school who has an allotment in south London, and I happened to mention our problems in getting parsnips to germinate. 'Really?' she said, with a look of wide-eyed innocence. 'I've always found parsnips easy – practically grow themselves.' If ever she falls victim to a mysterious parsnip-related injury, I shall plead justifiable homicide.

Whenever I am feeling plagued with self-doubt about my vegetable-growing abilities I usually find a quick trawl of the Internet makes me feel better. Among their many other uses, the allotment forums and blogs are always full of tales of woe from people who are similarly afflicted, and no matter what your problem – can't grow parsnips, don't know how to get rid of your bindweed, don't know what that nasty growth on the leaves of your courgette plant is – there is always someone else out there who is suffering in just the same way.

Sometimes you just have to plough on regardless, doing your best to ignore the slings and arrows of gardening failure. One of the first things we sowed was a globe artichoke from Italy called *Violetta di Chioggia*. The seed germinated well; we even managed to transplant the resulting plants into the allotment without any great disasters. But after that, nothing. The plants sat there doing not an awful lot other than looking sickly. One of them died. The second year, which is when they should start producing fruit, they looked even more poorly. Then, just when we were about to give up and throw them out, they started producing artichokes. Quite small ones, but very pretty and quite delicious, as long as you were prepared to overlook the occasional blackfly. (Memo to self: next time try soaking in salted water before cooking them. Apparently it's what old hands do.) We felt quite pleased with ourselves, all in all – or at least we did until we visited our friends Barbara and Eugen at their home in Italy, just outside Orvieto, and saw their artichoke bed, which seemed to stretch halfway to the Amalfi coast and was positively groaning with artichokes. They were enormous, too, several times the size of ours, and I would like to be able to say that their flavour was somehow inferior to that of the *Violetta di Chioggia*, which is known as a very sophisticated artichoke, except that it wouldn't be true.

The other announcement Michael made that spring day, as well as the ones about the finer points of Monaghan agricultural techniques and the frailties of organic potatoes, was about his growing plans for the year. 'I'm growing melons this year,' he said, looking rather excited at the prospect. 'Just you wait! I'll be tucking into them with a big spoon!' Rather taken aback by this – Michael's interests seemed at face value to extend no further than cabbages and carrots, spuds and onions and other suchlike allotment stalwarts – I quizzed him further. It seemed he hadn't grown melons before, and when I expressed some mild surprise at this he said that he always liked to grow something new every year. Now that he mentioned it, I remembered how the previous year – when we had only had our allotment for about six months – he had come up to me with a handful of courgette seeds and asked what the instructions on the seed packet meant when they said that the seed should be sown on its side. Fortunately I was able to explain: courgette seeds are flat, and allegedly if you sow them on their flat side water can collect on them, making the seed rot before it has a chance to germinate, and so the thing to do is to sow them on their edge.

I must admit that the whole theory all sounds a bit far-fetched to me, but I of course religiously sow all my courgette seeds – and squash, and cucumber – on their side, just in case I am wrong and everyone else with their centuries of accumulated wisdom is right. Michael wasn't just growing any old courgette, as it happens; they were round ones, which you virtually never see in the shops but are said to be great for stuffing. When they were ready later that summer Michael left a few on our bench for us, which Eliza took home, stuffed and then ate with the children while I was at work. They were very good, she said.

I found the whole idea of Michael and his melons incredibly heartening. There was something very uplifting about this ancient Irishman who has been growing vegetables all his life still finding the whole thing exciting, and it proved that just because you have a flat cap and fifty years of spud-growing under your belt does not mean to say that you have to become set in your ways. I, in contrast, am about a quarter of a century younger than Michael (let's not get too specific about this), do not own a flat cap and have no intention of doing so, and have about twelve months of potato-growing under my belt, and so there is absolutely no danger of my becoming stuck in my ways. Well, no excuse, anyway. Just to make sure, though, I resolved to grow something I had never grown before: a giant pumpkin. It was, I concede, a bit of an odd choice, because as everyone knows giant pumpkins are no good to eat and in fact are really only good for carving scary faces on at Hallowe'en and putting a candle inside. That, and showing off. The real *raison d'être* of the giant pumpkin is to get all competitive and see how big you can get it to grow, and while I have never seen the point of growing vegetables for show – all those massive onions and absurdly long carrots, which probably have the taste and consistency of the average length of four-by-two – there is something about pumpkin-growing which appealed to the competitive streak in me. I was going to grow a giant pumpkin, and it was going to be the biggest one ever. Or perhaps the biggest one in East Acton; let's not get carried away here, particularly since the largest pumpkin ever grown weighed 1,502 lb (or 666 kg, which happens to be exactly 1 kg more than one of those G-Wiz electric cars, including batteries; not a lot of people know that). That pumpkin – a variety known as Atlantic Giant – was grown by Ron Wallace of Greene, Rhode Island in 2006 and had to be forklifted on to a meticulously calibrated digital scale at the Rhode Island Weigh-Off. Later it went on display at Grand Central Station in New York.

As I do not own a forklift and do not really have the time to take my record-breaking pumpkin over to New York, I decided to stick to the traditional variety used for giant pumpkins in the UK, known as Hundredweight, which sounded quite big enough for my purposes. I knew that it could not be that difficult, because Angelo once told me that when he first got his allotment he grew a pumpkin plant, and without actually doing anything special to it he produced an absolutely massive pumpkin. I also had a target to beat, thanks to Terry Walton, the chap who makes occasional appearances on Jeremy Vine's Radio 2 programme talking about his allotment in South Wales. He grew a giant pumpkin, feeding it with the slops from his local pub – three pints a day, but then that's Welsh pumpkins for you – and it grew so big that by the time it came to be removed from the allotment it took three policemen and three firemen to shift it. Or at least that's what the story on the BBC website claimed, but as the pumpkin weighed a relatively modest 32 lb I have my doubts. Either that, or those Welsh coppers need to get down the gym a bit more often.

Still, it did not seem too ambitious a target to aim for. Could I beat the 32 lb achieved by the BBC's champion, Mr Walton? Could I manage it without the help of Welsh beer? And would Michael be impressed? It was going to be an interesting summer.

16

Allotments Under Threat

I used to visit and revisit it a dozen times a day, and stand
in deep contemplation over my vegetable progeny with a
love that nobody could share or conceive of who had never
taken part in the process of creation. It was one of the most
bewitching sights in the world to observe a hill of beans
thrusting aside the soil, or a row of early peas just peeping
forth sufficiently to trace a line of delicate green.

Nathaniel Hawthorne, *Mosses from an Old Manse*

Some allotment sites are so big that you can get lost in them. Not
literally lost, but so surrounded by plants and greenery that it is
possible to forget all about the outside world for a while; all you
can see is bean poles and potato beds and people tending their
plots, and the grey gritty reality of city life – shops and buses and

crowded streets – is somehow far, far away, the other side of the fence that keeps such little havens safe and green. To be on the allotment is to forget all the petty unpleasantnesses of urban existence; locked inside the site – and perhaps there is more than one reason why most allotment associations insist that gates are kept locked, even when people are there – you feel protected, shut away, happy that nothing can disturb the peace you have found.

There is none of that on the Bromyard site. Certainly you can get so absorbed in your work that you forget about the rest of the world, but the site itself is so small and compact that reminders of real life – or perhaps I should just call it non-allotment life, for what is more real than growing the food you eat? – are only ever a few yards away. Sounds constantly filter through – traffic from Bromyard Avenue, tennis and five-a-side from the Virgin Active health club and the regular comedy of people using the intercom when the club's entrance barrier doesn't work. ('Are you a member?' squawks a bored female voice over the barrier's tinny speaker. 'Swipe your card through the slot . . . no, the other way round . . .') A malign conspiracy of sights and sounds ensures you never forget that you are digging your potatoes in East Acton, not some romantic fantasy of the English countryside; and, in a funny way, that is just the way I like it. It may sound perverse, but the geographical situation of the Bromyard site – hemmed in, an allotment under siege – and the ever-present signs of city grot are a salutary reminder of the precarious position in which allotments find themselves in early twenty-first-century Britain.

In 2006 the London Assembly produced a report into the decline of allotments in the capital. Entitled 'A Lot to Lose: London's Disappearing Allotments', it made for sorry reading.

Although demand for plots was higher than ever, with the interest in organic food leading to a renaissance in allotment gardening, and waiting lists in some boroughs as long as ten years, the number of allotments in the city was steadily declining. The reasons were not hard to identify. Peter Hulme Cross, the author of the report, wrote: 'The relentless pressure on land in the capital, the need to build at high densities, and, in some cases, neglect and disuse, mean that allotments are slowly but surely being eroded.' The last major survey of allotments had been carried out nearly a decade earlier, in 1997, when the National Society of Allotment and Leisure Gardeners revealed that plots across England were disappearing at a rate of 9,400 a year. The NSALG also found that the number of people waiting for an allotment site had more than doubled since 1970. Within London, the survey identified over 36,000 allotment plots, of which almost 31,000 were in outer London, and a waiting list of 1,330.

Since then, the Assembly report discovered, the situation had only got worse. The number of allotment sites in the capital had fallen from 769 to 737 over the last ten years, a decrease of 4.2 per cent. The number of plots had gone down by even more – to 20,786 plots across the twenty councils for which full figures were available, compared to 22,319 in 1996. The reason why the number of plots had fallen faster than the number of sites was because allotment sites were often chipped away a few plots at a time – five shaved off the periphery to make way for a new road, say – a practice which the report described as 'the real threat to allotment provision in London'.

But I didn't need an official report to tell me all this: for it is only thanks to the tenacious resistance mounted by my fellow Acton allotmenteers that I am able to have an allotment at all.

As I mentioned earlier, until the 1990s the land on which our allotment stands was part of the Perryn Estate, owned by the Goldsmiths' Company. Since the 1967 Leasehold Reform Act the estate had been gradually whittled away as tenants bought their freeholds, until it reached a point where the Goldsmiths decided that the estate was no longer economically viable. A deal was struck in 2000 to let half of their land in East Acton – the bit containing the allotments – to something called the Park Club, an upmarket health and leisure club which was about to be built on the outskirts of Acton Park. It was owned by one Colin White, who also owned a similar place in Chiswick called the Hogarth Club. The next that the allotment-holders knew about it was when they were given notice to quit by the Hogarth Club. There were nearly 200 of them, and they had been given just three months to get out. Allotments that had been tended by the people of Acton and Shepherd's Bush for 100 years – providing food, and fresh air and exercise, not to mention peace of mind and the sort of well-being that money cannot buy – were about to be bulldozed so that the haute bourgeoisie of west London could pedal away on exercise cycles listening to their iPods, or play tennis with their fellow lawyers and bankers and television producers; or perhaps more to the point, so that Colin White could become an even richer man than he was already.

The allotment-holders did not really have a leg to stand on, mainly because they were on private land – as opposed to statutory allotments, which are provided by local authorities and protected by the law – but they resolved to fight anyway. They found a friendly (i.e. allotment-owning) lawyer, and started the battle to save their plots. It was a battle which was to last three years. The Goldsmiths – motivated perhaps out of a slight feeling of guilt about the way the plot-holders had been treated – agreed to pay their legal costs, and Michael Wale and others set about trying to negotiate a new lease and to get the notice to quit lifted. They launched a press offensive, and recruited the local councillors and the constituency MP to their cause. Even while all the negotiations were going on, Colin White kept up the pressure with what the allotment side felt was a series of totally unrealistic demands. In turn Michael Wale and the allotment-holding solicitor developed their own strategy, which in Michael's words involved going along to negotiations, sitting there and listening and, by never saying anything of any consequence whatsoever, boring everybody to death. The tactic – along with a sneaky secret meeting Michael managed to arrange with Colin White's younger son Patrick, the most reasonable member of the enemy camp – seemed to do the trick, because in the end the Acton Gardening Association managed to win a reprieve for the majority of allotments under threat. Not all of them, mind; they had to give up an allotment site next to the Park Club, but in return they were able to keep the rest of the allotments for a peppercorn rent. The notice period was changed from three months to twelve, and a guarantee instituted that all the remaining allotment land under cultivation would be protected and used only for allotments for the next ninety years. A peace of sorts broke out, although one can never be sure whether hostilities might be resumed at some future date.

When the allotment-holders at Manor Gardens in the East End faced the threat of losing their plots, they were pitted against an opponent even more formidable and intransigent than Colin White and the Hogarth Club: they were up against the London Development Agency, a body armed with statutory powers and rather more highly paid lawyers than Colin White could ever dream of. Their aims were also rather more significant than just building a health club: as the Mayor of London's agency for economic growth, they were charged with the task of acquiring the land for the 2012 Olympics – and the allotments were in their way. Trying to get the Manor Gardens Allotment Society to resist the will of the mighty LDA is like putting a small kitten into the ring with Muhammad Ali in his prime; not so much an unfair fight as not really a fight in any normally accepted meaning of the word. But, being typical allotment-holders – obstinate, resolute, and not really impressed with things like money and power, or even expensive lawyers and their big expensive lawyer talk – they decided to have a go anyway.

Until they were cast in their unhappy role as the martyrs of London's Olympic dream, the Manor Gardens allotments were one of London's best-kept secrets. Tucked away in the wastelands of east London, where dual carriageways criss-cross a landscape of factories and warehouses and backstreet breakers' yards, the allotments are so well hidden that no one would ever stumble across them by chance; even equipped with directions, it is no easy task to find them. In fact the surprise was not so much that the LDA wanted to use the land for the Olympics, but that anyone in authority actually knew that the allotments were there. They looked like an oversight, ignored for years by the outside world and quite happy to remain so – the allotments that time forgot.

To find them, you first had to find the First Capital bus garage on Hackney's Waterden Road, a bleak industrial no man's land, and then Wani's Cash and Carry warehouse to its right, at which point you might spot that there is a small gateway in the metal fencing which separates the two of them. From there a meandering path takes you to a narrow bridge over the River Lea, up a brief slope and then suddenly you are – well, where? It's a funny little spit of land between the Lea and the Grand Union Canal, and you certainly didn't notice it from the road. You didn't notice the fig trees, either, or the runner beans or pumpkins, or any of the other wonderful things that people grow up there. You didn't notice Tom Norris's shed, with its long row of awards for the prize-winning vegetables he has grown over the years, or Reg cooking up lunch, or John Matheson's pine tree grown from a seed his son brought back from a holiday in Tunisia some fifteen years ago. No one ever notices the Manor Gardens allotments, but in their rough and ready way they are one of the most charming idylls one could imagine, a rural haven in the midst of some quite staggeringly unprepossessing urban dereliction.

They owe their existence to a philanthropist called Major Arthur Villiers, one of the founders of the Eton Manor Boys' Club in Hackney Wick, an attempt to bring a bit of public school enlightenment – and football and boxing – to the impoverished youth of the East End. Villiers was a friend of Winston Churchill, and in the allotment hut, hanging above the cushioned bench, there is a group photograph from the early 1900s of them together in military uniform. Some of the older plotholders remember Villiers visiting the site on his bicycle. 'He used to come up here on his rusty old bike,' recalled one old plotholder, Reg. 'We would give him a few carrots, or a cabbage. We would say, "Help yourself." If you saw him you would not believe he was an entrepreneur. To put it bluntly, he looked like a bit of a tramp.' He was very protective of the allotments, though. There is a story that the nearby Oxo factory once wrote to him suggesting they buy a piece of the allotment land so that they could extend the factory; Villiers wrote back suggesting that they sell him the factory so that he could extend the allotments. When he died he bequeathed the site as allotments 'in perpetuity', telling plot-holders 'You'll never be thrown off here . . . you'll be here for ever'; but perpetuity, it seems, ain't what it used to be.

The allotments have changed significantly since Villiers's day.

Back then they were solely the province of working-class East Enders, men who saw the chance to spend a few hours at the weekend tending their vegetables as a welcome break from the hard grind on the factory floor; now there are middle-class interlopers, and women, and of course all manner of ethnic minorities – West Indians, Greeks, Turkish Cypriots, Italians. Sam Clark – one half of Sam and Sam Clark, of Moro restaurant – got a plot there a few years ago after hearing about the site from a friend who was a waitress at the River Café. 'Having this allotment made me fall in love again with London,' he told me. 'It let us into this multicultural world which was every bit as good as the romance we have sought abroad. It was this fantastic community, very varied; old-fashioned cockneys, and then this wonderful wave of Kurds and Turkish Cypriots. Apart from that there is the growing of some of the best vegetables I have ever grown in my life. Sweetcorn, courgettes, cucumbers, sunflowers, incredible strawberries, twenty different varieties of tomato, each one with their own personality.' When I asked him what would happen if they lost their battle against the LDA and they were offered an alternative site elsewhere, he sounded so upset it seemed out of the question. 'The idea of moving somewhere else is too distressing. I don't think I could move, and a lot of the people are too old to move.'

He wasn't the only one. John Day, seventy-seven, a retired Post Office worker, has been going to the allotments for thirty-three years. He had one plot, his wife had another, but she died about five years ago, so he just comes up by himself now. He is big on fruit, is John: there are gooseberries, red and blackcurrants, an apple tree, and cherry plums at the back. 'I've got a freezer full of fruit at home,' said John. 'I would be really gutted if this went. This is my summer. It is like the holidays over here. I've got a deckchair at home. I bring it over in my car. I sit here and watch it all growing.' When I met John they were under notice to leave, but still fighting a last-ditch battle to be allowed to stay; inevitably, though, many people had started to let their plots go. John pointed to his neglected strawberry beds. 'I will miss that this year. All the pounds of strawberries I used to have off there. Sometimes there were so many you almost thought, oh no, not another strawberry.'

Perhaps because it is so remote, when people go up to Manor Gardens to visit their plots they tend to make more of a day of it than other allotment-holders elsewhere; and when they do, they have lunch. Reg and Hassan are famous for their lunches now, cooked on the allotments over a Calor gas stove with whatever ingredients are in season. Reg Hawkins was seventy-five when I met him, a former compositor and graphic designer who has had a plot for fifty-four years; his father had one before him, and Reg remembers coming up to help him when he was eight years old. 'That was what started my passion for gardening,' he said. 'There is no other place like this. We call it our Shangri-La.' For the last fifteen years he reckons to have spent just about every day on the allotment. His friend Hassan Ali, a Turkish Cypriot, is about ten years younger, a former mechanic, and whenever they are both on the allotment they cook lunch together. Reg has got quite a reputation for his salad nowadays; the recipe has appeared in the *Guardian*, and also in Sam and Sam Clark's book *Moro East*. Reg and Hassan's culinary fame took off after Rick Stein heard about the food they produced at some allotment barbecue or other – they are a sociable lot at Manor Gardens – and decided to come up to the allotments to make a television programme about their al fresco creations, part of his series *Food Heroes*. Reg said, 'Rick Stein said to me, "Where did you learn to make salad like that?" I said, "Hackney Marshes."'

Here is Reg's special salad, Hackney Marsh-style. For best results, assemble and consume on an allotment.

4–5 cloves of garlic, finely chopped
1 Cos lettuce, outer leaves removed, cut into 1 cm slices
2 small new season's onions or spring onions, sliced into
    thin rings (with a little bit of green stem, too)
2 small red onions, finely chopped
2 beetroots, raw, grated or cut into matchsticks
2 carrots, grated
2 handfuls purslane, chopped roughly
6 cherry tomatoes in quarters or 3 large tomatoes
    chopped
1 large cucumber, peeled, chopped roughly
1 kohlrabi, grated
2 sweet peppers, green or red, chopped
1–2 fresh chillies (optional)
1 bulb of fennel and leaves, chopped
1 handful sorrel, shredded
3 tbsp chopped flat-leaf parsley
1 tbsp chopped fresh mint

dressing
6 tbsp olive oil
juice of 1 lemon or 1 tbsp red wine vinegar
sea salt and black pepper

Put all the vegetables in a large salad bowl. Pour over the dressing, season with salt and pepper. The salad will have a purple/red hue from the beetroot.

It is good to have things like that recipe to serve as reminders of Manor Gardens, because the allotments aren't there any more. The bulldozers came along in 2007 and flattened the place, the first stage of the process of turning it into a walkway for the Olympics. The last time I saw it they were having a summer open day, part of the tireless propaganda campaign they waged against the LDA but also a way of trying to keep their spirits up as they fought a war they were always going to lose. Hassan and Reg cooked up a storm, and Sam and Sam Clark grilled *pinchons* – delicious little pieces of spicy marinaded pork – and chorizo. Children ran along the paths between allotments playing hide and seek, while a three-legged lurcher trotted about the place, sniffing things in a busy, doggish way.

Perhaps the most heart-breaking thing was to watch people working away on their allotments, painstakingly cultivating ground they knew they were going to lose for ever in a few weeks' time. I met a teacher called Cynthia, who spent most of the day with her husband Mark working their plot, making it as immaculate as they could get it. 'Nobody is going to tell me I cannot plant,' she said with a slightly stroppy smile. 'My plot is probably tidier now that it has been for years. I've got onions in, and potatoes chitting, and I've just gone and bought some more seeds. I want it to be looking as good as it can when it finally goes, so that when the builders come and bulldoze it all they feel really guilty.' As they worked, a friend of theirs called Tracey leaned over the fence to chat to them. She told me proudly about her shed, which had been built by one of her predecessors on the allotment way back in the 1950s and was still going strong. It probably took the bulldozer about eight seconds to reduce it to matchwood.

After they were evicted from Manor Gardens, the allotment-holders were given another site where they could grow their veg; the LDA was at least good for that. It was about a mile away, a place called Marsh Lane Fields in Leyton. It was what was known as Lammas Land, given to commoners in the reign of King Alfred to graze their livestock from 1 August (Lammas Day) until the following spring. Getting the land was a bit of a struggle, though, as the local residents understandably rather resented losing such a sizeable piece of common land. They walked their dogs there, played football and other games and did not see why they should have to hand it over just so a few cab-bage-fanciers could carry on growing their own veg instead of buying it at Tesco like normal people. Waltham Forest Council refused planning permission for the proposed allotment site, and for a while it looked as if the plot-holders would not have a home to go to at all. The LDA reapplied for planning permission, did a rather better job of buttering up the council and was eventu-ally granted permission. The plot-holders – organised by a rather doughty campaigner called Julie Sumner – also managed to wring one more concession out of the LDA, being allowed to stay on at Manor Gardens until the growing season was over and the Marsh Lane site was ready.

So, in theory, everyone should have been happy: the LDA got

238

their land for the Olympics, and the allotment people got somewhere to grow their vegetables. But Manor Gardens – the trees,
the landscape, the wildlife, everything that made it special – they
are all gone. The sheds too; the plot-holders will just have to start
again, but then allotment folk are good at that. When I was
writing this I presumed – prompted, I suppose, by that remark
by Sam Clark – that many of the older boys would not be taking
up the offer of a new plot. They would be getting on in years,
and probably would not feel like starting all over again from
scratch, and anyway the new place wouldn't really feel the same.
Just to be sure I rang up the chairman of the association, John
Matheson, to check. Was Reg going to move to Marsh Lane, I
asked? Oh yes, he said, and so would John Day, and Tom Norris,
who had had a plot for sixty years and was, at eighty-four, the
oldest member of the association; he was looking forward to
making a new start, apparently.

The saga of the Manor Gardens allotments attracted a lot of
attention because the Olympics made it a high-profile story (the
presence of the Sam Clarks, not to mention Reg and Hassan's
minor culinary fame, probably helped too). But all over the
country allotments are slowly disappearing, unnoticed save for
the occasional story in the local paper. If they are on privately
owned land, there is little that anyone can do about it; if they are
statutory allotments, on council land, they are supposed to be
protected by the law, and any allotments that get handed over to
developers are supposed to be replaced by new plots somewhere
else. It does not always work like that, though. The councils only
have to respond to demand, and if they bulldoze 100 allotments
but show that there is only demand for seventy – well, that is
thirty allotments that have disappeared for ever.

When one considers the future of allotments in this country, there is a simple fact of life which is hard to ignore. Land given over to growing vegetables is worth virtually nothing – I pay £25 a year rent for the use of my five-rod plot – while land made available for housing is worth an awful lot of money. Given that there is a huge demand for new housing, and therefore land, the pressure on councils and private landlords to sell allotment sites to developers is immense. The situation became even worse thanks to a High Court ruling in summer 2007 when a group of allotment-holders in Hampshire finally lost the battle to save their plots in Eastleigh.

The fight was spearheaded by Marian Hatt, who has tended an allotment on the South Street site for the past twenty-five years. Eastleigh Council wanted the land for new housing – 140 affordable homes – and offered the allotment-holders alternative plots on various different sites around the town. But Mrs Hatt reckoned that that was not good enough; she had a rather large allotment – 75 rods – because she was a vegetarian, and considered that the offer of a 10-rod plot was completely inadequate. There was another offer of a 40-rod plot, but Mrs Hatt said she could not get there by bus so that wasn't good enough either. The situation was even more critical because the council was going to close another site in the town, meaning that more people would be chasing after a diminishing number of plots, putting ever more pressure on the waiting lists. The case ended up at the High Court after Ruth Kelly, the Environment Secretary, gave the green light to the council's housebuilding scheme and the campaigners tried to get permission to challenge it. Mr Justice Calvert Smith thought about it, and then ruled that although there was a 'looming crisis' with regard to the allotments waiting list, Ruth Kelly's decision could not be condemned as unlawful. The Secretary of State was not obliged to take into account the situation regarding every single allotment-holder, he said; all she had to do was satisfy herself that the majority were given suitable alternatives, and that was a good enough basis to give the scheme the go-ahead. The allotment-holders were pretty furious about the decision, and Tim Holzer, chairman of the Eastleigh and Bishopstoke Allotments Co-operative Association, claimed it would undermine the protection currently offered to allotments nationwide. He said:

It is our firm belief that the decision was flawed. It is a huge disappointment for the plot holders and supporters who have fought tirelessly for more than four and a half years in a campaign, not only to save the threatened sites in Eastleigh, but also to prevent the basis of protection for all statutory allotments from being undermined. The decision increases the uncertainty surrounding the protection that can be expected for statutory allotments across the country. Should it result in, or even encourage, the erosion of the country's allotment resource, it will have helped to achieve precisely the opposite of the government's stated intention in 2002 to provide better protection for allotments and ensure that future demand for allotments can be met.

So, another defeat for the good guys. The enemy have got the money, the lawyers and now precedent on their side; we have got some not particularly effective legislation, which in essence says that if the council wants to uproot you from the allotments you and your fellow vegetable gardeners have been tending for the past century or so and dump you in some godforsaken site the other side of the old gasworks, then that's fine. And yet it is perhaps important to remember that these councils are often in an impossible position, desperately needing to build more homes but without the land to do it on. As Kevin Warren, Eastleigh Council's chief valuer, said after the High Court decision, 'the new housing . . . is urgently required to help reduce the enormous current demand for housing in the borough. Around 140 affordable homes will be built on the site, which will be of considerable assistance in reducing the more than 5,000 family groups registered in the borough as people in need of social housing.'

Of course I do not really mean to be quite so reasonable. Are we going to carry on building houses all over England until the last sod has been paved over? There are, after all, other things in life just as important as the provision of bricks and mortar – health, well-being, social cohesion, self-sufficiency, taking responsibility for what you eat, even maintaining some kind of link with the land. These are all important considerations, and if we lose the ability to grow what we eat, we lose a vital part of what it is to be human and become little better than battery animals, passively consuming whatever slop our masters choose to feed us. So, no, I don't feel particularly reasonable about it, and should anyone ever have the temerity to try to build over my allotment, I will chain myself to the bulldozer and not move until they drag my lifeless body away.

Around the time I wrote this, Redbridge Council on the London/Essex borders announced proposals to sell off some allotments in order to fund its capital spending programme.

Naturally they were going to give the displaced allotment-holders new plots; naturally the councillor in charge of selling the idea to a suspicious populace sounded the very epitome of reasonableness. Ronnie Barden said he totally understood why the plot-holders were so upset: 'If it was my allotment I would probably be saying the same thing.' It all came down to money in the end; doesn't it always? The council wanted to build a new school and a leisure centre, and they reckoned that the only way they could raise the money to do that was by selling off some of their land. 'A plotholder is going to say, "I don't want to move, I've been here for 10 years,"' said Barden. 'I don't have an argument about that. They are right. What I am trying to do is balance everyone's interests. I appreciate very much what allotments provide. I want them to continue. They are good for the environment. But we have to balance the needs of the whole borough.'

Yes, yes, be reasonable, balance the needs, see both sides of the story – and guess who's on the losing side yet again? Yes, that's right, it's people like Roger Backhouse, who has been running a plot in the area for thirty years and doesn't see why he should give it up now; and also people like Ambiah Khatun, a Bangladeshi woman in her thirties who moved with her family into a house in the neighbourhood just so that she could get an allotment. 'It's not the best-looking plot in the world,' she said, 'but it is lovely. From having no garden to having such a big space is wonderful. There's sweetcorn, and runner beans, and tomatoes and potatoes. The children love digging the potatoes. They get so excited when they find a big one. It has changed all our lives. Our family life has improved because of the allotment. My husband is a lot happier, the whole family is a lot happier.'

Because I am perpetually fascinated by what people have on their allotments, I asked Ambiah if she grew any traditional Bangladeshi vegetables. Yes, she said, she had some beans which as far as I could tell were called *uri*, and also something which I think she called *pani khodu*, which she said translated as water

pumpkin and was very traditional in Bangladesh. Being somewhat partial to a bit of pumpkin, I tried looking it up on the
Internet to see if I could find out more about it. I didn't manage
to dig up anything useful, like a growing guide, or any recipes,
but I did find this – the definitive cultural guide to the role of
khodu in Bangladeshi life. It came in the form of a forum where
some disaffected Bangladeshi youth were sounding off about
their parents' *khodu*-growing habits; this is an edited and
(slightly) cleaned-up version, although I have left most of the
teen spellings . . .

Do ne of you guys or ur parents grow the famous bangladeshi KHODU?
   My parents do! It's so funny, there like so obsessed!
When some1 comes round like some relatives, they have to
show em. we got 5 really big ones in r back garden – it's
mad! They've even taken some pics! my parents took 1
down the other day and we been eating it since coz its soo
big. its not just my parents tho – their bengi mates and relatives too. Its like theyre all competin and they share it out
within the fam. I dont know how im gonna stand it for
another 5 more khodus including the one that theyve taken
down and we cant finish yet. I dont even like the stuff!
from anisa22

In the light of all that, I only have two questions to ask: (i) can
anyone possibly think that a new swimming pool in Ilford is more
important than Ambiah Khatun's *khodu*? (ii) Does anyone know
where I can get hold of some *khodu* seeds?

17

Eggs and Tayberries

The cure for this ill is not to sit still,
Or frowst with a book by the fire;
But to take a large hoe and a shovel also,
And dig till you gently perspire.

Rudyard Kipling, 'How the Camel Got His Hump', *Just
So Stories*

Occasionally in my darker moments I wonder whether life on the
Bromyard Avenue allotments isn't perhaps just a little bit dull.
I'm not saying that I find it boring; on the contrary, the unpre-
dictable mix of triumph and disaster makes running an allotment

a perennially fascinating activity, and anyway I do not think I will ever tire of the joy of digging up the first of the new potatoes, or picking a basket of perfect young French beans. All the same, I cannot help noting that as far as I am aware, no one on our allotments has ever: (i) had sex on the allotments; (ii) died on the allotments; (iii) grown drugs on the allotments; or (iv) gone to prison as a result of allotment-related fraud. All of these things and more have happened on the allotments in *EastEnders*, culminating in the sad death of that eternal loser Arthur Fowler, who succumbed to a brain haemorrhage on his plot after he was struck on the head during a prison riot.

The Walford allotments were always good for a bit of dramatic plot development whenever the storylines looked like drying up, whether it was sex (a bit of how's-your-father in the shed), drugs (the short-lived allotment cannabis patch), drink (the local youth binge-drinking vodka on the allotment) or just good old-fashioned mindless vandalism. In between all that sex'n'boozing, some people actually managed to grow a few vegetables. Arthur, who was basically never happier than when he was tending his plot, was particularly proud of his leeks and marrows, although being the hapless character he was, it was Tom Clements who won the first prize for the best leeks at the Walford & District Allotment Society Show; the rotter had stolen them from Arthur when the leeks he had been hoping to enter were damaged by Roly the poodle the night before the competition. That sort of thing would, of course, never happen with the Acton Gardening Association; no poodles.

Arthur may have loved his allotment, but it did for him in the end. When funds went missing from the allotment fundraising kitty the theft got blamed on Arthur, who ended up being jailed for it: cue mental breakdown in prison, riot, that nasty blow to the head and, finally, Arthur's sad demise on the allotment. On the whole, I think I prefer life in Bromyard Avenue, thanks all the same.

The point, though, about *EastEnders* and the late lamented Arthur is that the programme portrays a very traditional view of allotment life. The allotment is where sad old men go to escape the wife, where there is skulduggery over the prize leeks and where people get up to all sorts of unmentionable things in the privacy of their sheds (or, indeed, someone else's shed). It took a more recent film to portray the vegetable-growing tendency in a way that was at all realistic, or to reflect the fact that not everyone who tends a plot these days is a member of the white Anglo-Saxon working classes. That film was *Grow Your Own*, a 2007 comedy about the effect of a group of asylum seekers on a city allotment, and if I say that it did not have quite the same impact on the box office that year as the likes of *Harry Potter and the Order of the Phoenix* and *Rush Hour 3*, you may not be overly surprised. I suspect the cinema audience was not really ready for a movie where most of the dialogue occurred inside, next to and around the back of a series of all-but-identical garden sheds. Or indeed a movie where one of those same garden sheds played a key role in the film, standing as a metaphor for conformity, repression, rebellion and the liberating qualities of a fresh coat of paint.

The movie originally started life as a documentary, based on the work of Margrit Ruegg, a psychotherapist and director of the Family Refugee Support Unit in Liverpool, which works with people who have had terrible experiences in their home countries. Asylum seekers often have difficulty sleeping and are liable to depression, and Ruegg's idea was to help them cope not by giving them drugs but by giving them allotments. As the co-writer Frank Cottrell Boyce put it, 'Gardening provides structure, social contact and a drug-free path to total exhaustion.' The trouble was, making a documentary about asylum seekers is harder than it sounds. Often they don't want to be filmed. Sometimes they do and then change their minds, depending on how their cases are progressing. Sometimes, Cottrell Boyce said, they even suspected that the film-makers were working for Immigration. In the end it was easier just to turn the documentary into a normal feature film, centred on the tensions that arise when a group of asylum seekers are given plots on an established inner-city allotment to help them overcome their trauma (with an avaricious mobile-phone company to add some spice to proceedings).

Grow Your Own wasn't really a film about gardening, then. But then gardening isn't really about gardening, either; it's about life. When people go down to their allotment at the weekends, more often than not they are doing more than just providing fresh fruit and vegetables for the table, they are escaping the drabness of everyday life, finding a way to forget the pressure – or tedium – of their job, or even attempting to connect in some atavistic way with the seasons and the earth in a way that we, as city dwellers, have fundamentally forgotten.

Such concerns are not normally the province of your average film-maker. Movie directors, as we all know, hang around places like Soho House drinking skinny lattes and swapping industry gossip: they do not spend their weekends getting dirt under their fingernails and worrying about whether they have got blight on their spuds. They know as much about growing cucumbers as I do about shutter speeds.

It was, therefore, with a certain sense of trepidation that I went to see *Grow Your Own*: the risible clichés about allotment life which it was likely to perpetuate were too awful to contemplate. Fortunately it managed to avoid them. The first sight we had of the Blacktree Road allotments was an intriguing one. This was no picture-book allotment, with rough-hewn beanpoles festooned with sweet peas in among the runner beans; instead it was a rather grim, urban place, with row after row of plots set in the shadow of a huge gasometer. The docks – huge, impersonal – were just around the corner. I have seen some more unprepossessing allotments in my time; but not many.

As for the people, they were as grumpy, maladjusted, obstreperous and downright peculiar a bunch as ever planted a row of lettuces. Typical allotment folk, really. There was the cranky Scot who would go to extraordinary lengths to assert his individuality, and who spent his leisure hours watching gardening programmes and shouting at Alan Titchmarsh; the old boy who planted his tomato seeds on Boxing Day and put them on the television to keep warm; and, at the head of it all, the overbearing committee chairman, Big John, who ran the allotment as his own personal fiefdom. The committee members on my own allotment are, I am pleased to say, models of tolerance and understanding, but I have also come across places where a bullying autocrat like Big John would be welcomed as a kindred spirit.

Overall, *Grow Your Own* was amusing, original, and shed light on an aspect of allotment life – the way that growing vegetables can help the psychologically traumatised – that would never occur to most of us. Inevitably it bombed at the box office. But while the story – albeit fictionalised – of Margrit Ruegg's project might not have had mass popular appeal, it is not the only example of the way that growing vegetables can be used to help people. In the mid-1990s a group in the US city of Detroit called Gardening Angels were trying to heal their city of the ravages of declining industry, depopulation and drugs by planting gardens on derelict sites. One unforeseen side effect the Angels – mainly pensioners – discovered was that it was an effective way of driving out the local crack cocaine dealers who had set up shop in an abandoned house next to one of their gardens. 'The boys that sold the drugs had taken the place over,' Jim Stone, one of the Gardening Angels, told a journalist.

There had been fires there and fights, and every weekend there were dice games upstairs. What we found, though, was that when we put compost on the garden we started getting complaints from these kids about the smell. So we contacted our friends at the Detroit Equestrian Police Unit and arranged for them to start dumping their hay and manure on our garden. Soon the drug boys found their customers didn't like coming there because it smelled so bad – and so they ended up moving out.

After watching these unarmed pensioners drive out the drug dealers by sheer manure power, a group of young kids – aged around nine to twelve, young enough not to have fallen into the thrall of the drugs world – came forward and offered to help. 'We called them the Cucumber Kids, because they loved to eat the cucumbers,' said Stone.

We gave them their own patch and told them, 'This is your section, you maintain it.' Next, we set them up on a stall at the crossroads, selling peanuts we'd bought in bulk at the East Market, as well as the tomatoes and cucumbers they'd grown themselves. The first day they did it, they made $40 in three hours. I think for the first time ever they saw another possible direction for their lives.

Detroit street kids aren't the only ones who can sell their produce, of course, and around this time – mid-spring – my thoughts were concentrated firmly on how many vegetables we could get ready in time for Kitty and Orlando's school summer fair. The previous year, you may recall, we managed to sell a few things at the fair and it seemed only sensible to try to do a repeat performance. Being of a mildly competitive nature, however, this year I was determined to do it even better, partly because all the money raised would be going to a good cause in the shape of the school's PTA fund and partly because if you are going to have a vegetable stall, you might as well have it looking as good as you possibly can. Right from the outset, then, I was working out how to maximise crop production in time for June, carefully timing my sowings so that the early summer vegetables would be reaching their peak of perfection on the very Saturday morning of the fair. There was salad to sow, and carrots, and of course beetroot, which as I had already discovered revels in an inexplicable popularity. Meanwhile, just as I was trying to juggle all these complicated sowing schedules, I also had to bear in mind another bit of advanced planning: the sowing of the giant pumpkin. Very particular they are, giant pumpkins. You cannot sow them too early, otherwise the late frosts will get them, and you cannot sow them too late, otherwise they just won't have enough time to reach their maximum potential and become the sort of record-breaking, Welsh-beating monsters that will have the neighbours staring in astonishment and television crews beating a path to the allotment to put me and my pumpkin on the local news. According to a pumpkin enthusiasts' website I found, Pumpkin Nook, you should sow your pumpkin seeds indoors any time between 25 April and 15 May, which sounded fairly convincing to me, except for the fact that when I looked into it the website turned out to be run by a bloke in upstate New York. As I had no idea of how the late frost times for Rochester, NY, compare to those for East Acton, it would be hard for me to work out whether in fact I should be sowing my pumpkins on 16 May or even 24 April; but hell, early May sounded about right. I would go for it.

Meanwhile out on the allotment, there was exciting news: we had new neighbours. The plot next to ours, the one that had been abandoned for ages, and where Ina had got me to remove the trellis (mission abandoned due to operator incompetence), had finally got a new tenant. What's more, apparently we knew them. 'I see your friends are moving in,' said Michael, with the air of someone who wants you to know that nothing gets past him. Unfortunately I had absolutely no idea what he was talking about. 'Our friends?' I said dumbly. Who on earth were these friends of mine who had got themselves the allotment next to ours? And why hadn't they told us about it? Then, gradually, the penny began to drop. We had been having dinner with our neighbours a few months earlier; there had been another couple there, Julia and David, who had said something about trying to get an allotment, and could they mention our name? It seemed they did mention our name, although I would be flattering myself if I thought that that was the clincher that somehow got them to the top of the waiting list. 'Oh, you know the Lows, do you? Plot number eight over on Bromyard? The one where they let the pigeons eat all their brassicas? Oh well, if you know them you must have a plot immediately!'

The truth is that it has become increasingly hard to get an allotment. We were lucky, in that we only had to wait around six months or so, but since then the situation has got a lot worse and most people have to wait significantly longer. I have heard of people receiving letters from their local council ten years after they applied for an allotment, informing them that a plot had now become available. When I spoke to Lindsay Wright at the potato fair he told me he had had his allotments in south London for about nine years, and that when he first turned up there were so many vacant plots that he was able to take on as many as he could manage. Nine years after he got his three plots there were so many people wanting to have an allotment that his association had closed the waiting list.

When Julia and David first turned up at their plot with their two young children in tow, I must admit I felt a twinge of sympathy for them. Getting hold of a plot might have been hard work, but it was nothing compared to what awaited them. Their plot had been neglected for about two years, and it showed. It was thick with weeds, big tough ones with thick stalks and deep roots that weren't going to give up without a fight, and of course there were the foundations of that trellis still to remove. As if that was not bad enough, hidden behind all those weeds was a concrete pond which the previous tenant had somehow been allowed to install. Michael looked at it knowledgeably and said, 'They are going to need a Kanga to get that out.' I nodded and said, 'I think you're right, Michael.' I did not have the faintest idea what a Kanga was, but it sounded like just the ticket.

Whether or not they got themselves a Kanga I have no idea; what they did get themselves was a couple of Poles. There I was, sowing some carrots, or battling with the bindweed, or something, when I noticed two strapping young lads stripped to the waist who were clearing weeds from our neighbours' plot. I know they were Polish, because at one point Lucy went over to talk to them. There are a lot of Poles in our part of west London, always have been, and there were even more after they joined the EU. I wonder what those boys working on our neighbours' plot told their families just before they left home. 'Goodbye *Mama*, goodbye *Tata*, I am off to England to make my fortune. I hear there is much money to be made working on the collective farms of East Acton.' I tried not to look too disapproving, and wondered secretly if they were free later in the year for a little light winter digging.

As I mused on the ways of young allotment-holders these days, I realised with a bit of a soggy feeling inside that I was in distinct danger of exhibiting classic Old Git symptoms; which was a bit premature, seeing as how it felt like we had only had the plot for about ten minutes and still didn't even know how to do a simple thing like grow parsnips. It was, though, long enough to have been accepted as part of the allotment scene; and long enough to have been roped into doing a stint in the allotment shop.

'Shop' is perhaps a grand term for an old lorry container – *sans* lorry – which sits on the main allotment site, next to the manure heap, and which is open every Sunday morning during the growing season for the sale of things like onion sets, seed potatoes, fertiliser and slug pellets. Normally it is manned by Doreen, one of those selfless people who are the backbone of every voluntary organisation, but recently she had come to the belated but entirely correct conclusion that she really ought to spread the load a bit and see if she could persuade some other members to take their turn at being shopkeepers for the morning.

That, then, is how Kitty and I arrived at the shop all bright-eyed and bushy-tailed one sunny Sunday morning at three minutes to ten o'clock, anxious not to be late in case there were any enthusiastic allotment folk queuing up outside the shop who needed to get a bag of compost before they could get on with their work. We needn't have bothered. No one was hanging round outside the shop, and indeed the only people on the allotment – I think I counted three – seemed to have no interest whatsoever in buying anything. Come to that, there wasn't even any shop as such, as John

Roberts – who had the key – had not turned up yet to open it up. He finally made an appearance after about a quarter of an hour, smiling that benign smile of his and acting for all the world as if there really wasn't any reason to hurry. Considering the lack of anyone who might be described as a customer, he was probably right. I installed myself behind the counter, doing my best to familiarise myself with everything, while Kitty settled down outside to read her book. By the time I had worked out where the Blood Fish & Bone was, and the slug pellets, and the bags of composted horse manure, there still weren't any customers. I studied the pictures on the wall – there was a *Guardian* poster of different tomato varieties, which I suppose might have been useful, and a black-and-white picture of a 1930s couple in their party finery, which perhaps wasn't quite so useful; it turned out John had put it up once because he thought it looked nice. Still no customers. One of the stalwarts of the Association, Joe, a magnificent Irishman who despite being essentially blind still makes things for the allotment like a new polytunnel, turned up; I went outside to have a chat with him, and we had a good old moan about our landlord Colin White and his evil ways. Still no customers. I went to go and see John, who was in the polytunnel round the corner – the one Joe had built – selling tomato seedlings and the like and tried to have a chat with him, only I couldn't because he was too busy dealing with the long line of people who were queuing up to buy stuff from him.

By this time it would have been easy to start feeling bitter, but fortunately I didn't because suddenly a miracle happened: I had a customer. A chap came in and bought some manure. Then a woman came in and asked for some slug pellets and some Grow-more. From being on the brink of closure, things were now really taking off. A third customer appeared – three! In one morning! –

an Irishman in shorts and work boots who said: 'Have yer got anything for weeds?'

This was going to tax my knowledge of the retail gardening scene to the very limit. On the shelf there were some things called Weed Sticks, which looked a bit weird, and some packets labelled Weedol, which sounded a bit more familiar. I sold him one of those, and told him reassuringly: 'I think you'll find that that will be just the ticket.' He seemed quite satisfied with that, and I congratulated myself on a job well done. That's what the customers need, I thought – helpful, knowledgeable staff who can provide expert advice when it is needed.

I wasn't timing it, but I think that it was about three and a half minutes later that he walked back in, placed the packet back on the counter and announced: 'I have been advised that it's the other stuff I want for my problem.' He was the last customer I had all day.

I may only have sold £9 worth of gardening sundries that morning – and frankly I blame Kitty; if she had been devoting herself to marketing our products instead of reading her book in the sunshine, I believe it would have been a very different situation – but it was a far from wasted morning. Shortly before midday Eliza and Orlando turned up, and said they were going to have a look round the main site, taking Kitty with them. About twenty minutes later they reappeared with a dozen eggs and two large punnets of tayberries. The eggs had straw on them, just like in the country, except that we were in East Acton, which hadn't been countryside for about eighty years; Eliza and the children had bought them from Adis, who kept hens on his plot down the far end of the allotments. I had heard about Adis and his hens before, and knew that he occasionally sold his eggs, only I thought it was just to one or two of his select friends. It turned out that Adis will happily sell eggs to any allotment-holder who has the money.

Adis is very proud of his hens. It took him about two years to build their home; it has a feeding trough, and a water hopper, walkways and sleeping quarters, and I think that if I were a hen I would regard it as a pretty luxurious billet. There were twenty of them, Rhode Island Red crosses, and when we went to inspect them – well, you like to know where your eggs are coming from, don't you? – Adis was feeding them handfuls of spinach from his plot to add to the pellets they had already been given. 'All this in the centre of London!' he said with a big smile, and Mrs Low and I realised there and then that we didn't want to buy our eggs from anyone else again, ever.

As for the tayberries, we hadn't even paid for those. Eliza had fallen into conversation with one of the plot-holders, a man called John, and when she happened to say something about his tayberry crop he said, 'Help yourself. I've got boxes full – take as many as you like.' She did, and a few days later we had three pots of Tayberry and Citrus Fruit Jam (recipe courtesy of Marguerite Patten). Very delicious it was too; I think I shall have to do the shop more often.

18

Inheriting the Earth

Earth is here so kind, that just tickle her with a hoe and she laughs with a harvest.

Douglas Jerrold, *A Land of Plenty*

It is 28 May, a year to the day since we ate our first vegetables from the allotment – our first proper vegetables, that is, in the form of those never-to-be-forgotten broad beans, not the two rather lonely radishes we had a few weeks earlier, which were pretty exciting at the time – and in that time we have learned . . . well, what? I suppose we have managed to pick up a few rudimentary gardening techniques – how to grow things without killing them the moment they appear, how to keep assorted pests and predators at bay. We have also learned about the joy of growing your own vegetables, about how there is nothing quite so delicious as the crops you have grown and picked yourself, and how there is nothing wrong with a carrot that is a bit knobbly and gnarled as long as it tastes good.

We have learned, too, how to be at one with nature, how there are various bugs and beasties out there who are pretty intent on eating your crops, and always will be, and perhaps one should not blame them because those crops are rather tasty, and the trick is to try to keep the bug-and-beastie attacks down to a minimum without kidding yourself that you will ever have lasting victory over your enemies. As John said, they are all God's creatures. We are also beginning to learn the fundamental truth behind the gardener's lament, which is that every year some crops will do well, and others badly, and they are going to take it in turns to be the star performer, and there is nothing much you can do about that. It's life, or nature, or a complex interplay of climatic variables, or whatever you like to call it, and these are forces that are all bigger than you; that's the way it is, and that's the way it always will be.

The gardener's life is a little easier, however, if he takes steps to ensure that he does not behave like a total dimwit. I said it was 28 May, didn't I? Which, as the more observant might notice, is a little later than 15 May, let alone 25 April – and I still haven't planted my giant pumpkin. Numbskull. How can I have possibly forgotten? It was very simple. All I had to do was take a couple of seeds, pop them into a pot of compost, water them, put them somewhere warm and light and forget about them for a week or so. But could I manage that? It appears not. I am surprised I can remember my own name. In something of a panic, I resolved to get the pumpkin seeds in that day, and then smother them in so much love – special pumpkin love – that they would grow nice and big just out of sheer gratitude. It would be an uphill struggle, though; record-breaking giant pumpkin growers do not normally fail to get their pumpkins sown in time. I do not think that Terry Walton forgot to sow his pumpkin seeds, and as for Mr Giant Pumpkin himself, Ron Wallace of Greene, Rhode Island, I don't suppose he was so much as five minutes late with his pumpkin sowing. I am going to have a lot of catching up to do.

As well as being a chance to remind myself what a complete dunderhead I can be on occasion, the anniversary of our first crop is also a good time to assess just what having an allotment means.

As an allotment-holder, there are two questions that people tend to ask on discovering that one grows one's own vegetables. One, of course, is 'So what are you going to bring us, then?' which is usually followed by a long list of the vegetables of which the interlocutor is particularly fond. The other question is something along the lines of 'So, do you save loads of money, then?' To which the answer – depending on how grumpy I am feeling that day, and whether the allotment has been a burgeoning harvest of all things good, or whether the pigeons have just wreaked havoc with the cabbages again – is either 'No it bloody doesn't, it probably costs me money,' or, if I am feeling rather more honest, 'I have no idea.' Which is rather an unsatisfactory state of affairs, to be frank: it would be a singularly useful piece of information to know whether growing your own veg actually saves you a significant amount of money, or whether it is just an expensive indulgence. I have a cousin, Jane, who for some years has been the chairman of her local allotment society in north London. When she first got her allotment in the 1970s, she tried working out how much money she saved over the year by growing her own produce instead of buying it from the shops: the answer, from memory, was £43. It doesn't really sound very much now, but this was a very long time ago and no doubt you could have fed a family of miners on best steak for six months on that kind of money.

Any calculation of the allotment accounts necessarily has to be a fairly rough and ready exercise, because I do not keep accurate records of what we spend and what we eat. Some people do, though; this is what the tenant of a ten-rod plot in Croydon reported that he had produced over the year in 1915:

About 200 spring cabbages, 100 cauliflowers, 1 row of broad beans, 2 rows of runner beans, 1 bed of shallots, 1 bed of turnips, 1 bed of beet, 2 rows of parsnips, 1 bed of onions, 1 bed of shorthorn carrots, 3 rows of intermediate carrots, 1 bed of vegetable marrows, 3 beds of lettuces, several crops of radishes, 4lb of tomatoes, and 18 bushels of potatoes. The ground is now well cropped with winter things, such as Brussels sprouts, savoys, broccoli and curly kale. Enough vegetables have been grown on this plot to keep my wife and family throughout the winter.

I cannot pretend that Eliza and myself have kept our family going over the winter, but we haven't done badly, and this is a guesstimate – a pretty crude one at that – of what we did, how much it cost us and what we saved.

Outgoings fall into two categories – capital expenditure, on such things as tools which you buy once and then never again, or at least not for a long time; and current expenditure, on things like seed and fertiliser.

Capital

You need a good fork, spade, rake and hoe, and although they can cost the earth, let's say they are £25 each	£100
Hand tools: trowel, fork, knife, say £15 each	£45
Sundries, such as watering can, trug, gloves	£35
10 raspberry canes	£25
TOTAL	£205

Current expenditure per annum

Rent of plot	£25
Seeds	£35
Seed potatoes	£8
Sundries: you always have to buy things like netting, bamboo canes, dahlia stakes and tomato feed	£60
Allotment shop, for blood, fish & bone, slug pellets, chicken manure	£15
Horse manure – free, I am very pleased to say	£0
TOTAL	£143

Savings

This is all inspired guesswork. I have tried to be honest and given a fair assessment of what we produce in an average year, and what it might have cost us in the shops. Sometimes I have put in the price for organic, sometimes I haven't. If I am at all inaccurate – well, it's not all about the money.

Salad: maybe an average of three salads a week from
    mid-May to mid-September, or roughly 18 weeks,
    at £1.50 a salad   £27

Cucumbers – 20 over the season, at 75p each   £15

Tomatoes – eight punnets, at £1.50 a punnet   £12

Cabbages, Savoy – four at £1   £4

Curly kale – eight bagsful (we are being very
    scientific here . . .) at say £1.50 a bag   £12

Brussels sprouts – four meals' worth (see above . . .)
    at £1.50 a meal   £6

Purple sprouting broccoli – six meals' worth at £2
    each (it's expensive stuff . . .)   £12

Onions – enough to keep us going for about eight
    months, at say 75p a week, which is roughly . . .   £25

Spring onions – 12 bunches (probably more) at 50p
    each   £6

Garlic – 30 heads at 40p a head   £12

Chard – practically as much as we can eat, but call it
    eight meals at a bargain basement 75p   £6

Beetroot – 15 lb at say £1 a lb   £15

Runner beans – 8 lb at least – and they were £3 a lb
    in Waitrose the day I checked   £24

French beans – another 8 lb (probably nearer 10,
    but I will err on the side of modesty) at £3 a lb   £24

Borlotti beans – no idea, frankly, but a reasonable
    guess would be . . .   £6

Broad beans – 8 lb at £2 a lb   £16

Sweetcorn – £1 each for the organic ones, and we eat
    at least 12   £12

Courgettes – say 8 lb at £1.50 a lb   £12

Leeks – 6 lb at £1.50 a lb   £9

Potatoes – earlies, say 10 lb at £1 a lb	£10
Potatoes – maincrop, 20 lb or so at 40p a lb	£8
Potatoes – Pink Fir Apple, maybe 8 lb at £1 a lb	£8
Carrots – a measly 8 lb, at 50p a lb	£4
Squash – six, at £1.50 each	£9
Raspberries – 12 lb at £3.50 a lb	£42

Flowers – the biggest saving of all. For at least four
  months of the year we get our flowers from the
  allotment, saving at least £5 a week (it's probably
  nearer a tenner). Some of the arrangements Eliza
  comes up with are the sort of thing you pay £50
  for in the fancier florists, but we are not here to
  show off, so we will call it a reasonable . . .   £80

TOTAL   £416

So, there we have it: possibly the most unscientific survey ever undertaken, representing a new low in the use of suspect data, dubious methodology and special pleading. But even if no one else is fooled, it convinces me that we save more than we spend each year, by some £250 or so, and that it took us no more than a year to recoup the money we spent on our capital investment. (There is a caveat here, though: if we factored in the amount of work we put into the allotment, we would be running at a horrendous loss. Eliza informs me that her hourly rate is quite expensive, and that I should be expecting a bill any day now.)

There was, though, one opportunity on the horizon which would not only tell us exactly what our crops were worth, but actually give us an opportunity to sell them for real money. The school summer fair was coming, and it was going to put Plot 8 on the map. (Now that I come to mention it, that sounds like a good name for our produce when the brand goes global. I can easily imagine the yummy mummies of west London boasting about where they get their organic veg: 'Camilla, darling, are those divine zucchini from Plot 8? They are absolutely perfect!')

As the day of the summer fair approached, we were having mixed results on the productivity and planning front. The beetroot were going great guns, and so were the spuds, but the carrots – while undoubtedly a distinct improvement on last year – were not exactly what one would call a glut. We didn't really have as many lettuces as I would have liked, either. On the other hand we had plenty of flowers, and spring onions, and some jams and chutneys Eliza had made with our produce the previous year. Talking of planning, or to be more precise planning failures, the giant pumpkin was in the ground by now, and had already had its first dose of pumpkin love. After it germinated I had kept it in a pot for a week or two until it looked a healthy size, and then taken it to the allotment to plant out. It would not be going into just any old hole, however. I dug a large pit for it, much larger than might have seemed necessary, and then filled the pit with an entire wheelbarrow load of well-rotted manure, which I then mixed in with the soil before planting the pumpkin. The other little trick I had up my sleeve was to take an old 1.5 litre plastic water bottle, cut the bottom off, remove the top, and half-bury it (neck end down) in the ground next to the pumpkin. That way I would be able to water the plant by filling up the bottle, thereby ensuring that as much water as possible went straight to the roots. It might have been sown a little late, but if the pumpkin didn't manage to produce any monster-sized fruits it was going to have quite a lot of explaining to do.

The day of the summer fair, 30 June, dawned early. I know that, because Eliza and I were up at first light so that we could go to the allotment and harvest the produce on the actual morning of the fair. You don't get much fresher than that. Now I must admit that getting up at five in the morning is not my idea of fun, and judging by Eliza's reaction it was a form of torture which should have been banned by international convention a long time ago, but I had successfully argued the previous evening that it was a sacrifice worth making (all right, I had browbeaten her into submission), and after an intravenous tea injection at dawn we both felt almost human. By the time we got to the allotment some ten minutes later we were no longer the slothful workers who had clung so frantically to the duvet, desperate to stay in bed at all costs, but were feeling instead decidedly jolly. There is something intensely invigorating about being on the allotment at first light. I don't know whether it is the quality of the early morning light itself, or the dewy stillness, or just the knowledge that you are up and about while the rest of the world is still fast asleep, but I do know that just a few minutes on the plot at five or six in the morning is enough to put me in a hugely good mood. Who needs artificial stimulants when there's early morning carrot picking to be done?

Eliza got to work on the flowers while I started gathering the veg. She picked: roses, nasturtiums, carnations, cornflowers (the weird black ones which I fear we may never see the end of), poppies, love-in-the-mist, dahlias and some kind of thistle thingy, which the less sophisticated among you might confuse for a weed – OK, which I nearly confused for a weed – but is in fact a highly stylish addition to the modern flower arrangement. On the veg front, I gathered some chard, spring onions, lettuce, more beetroot than is decent – some fifteen roots or so, which I thought was probably enough although there was plenty more – and one plant's worth of Kestrel potatoes. There was about

2½ lb of them, and I can say with my hand on my heart that they were absolutely gorgeous; nicely oval-shaped, completely blemish-free, and with these beautiful eyes on them that look like purple eyebrows. They were also all exactly the same size, and in short were such an image of potato perfection that you could have taken their photograph and stuck it in *Potato Fanciers' Monthly* and no one would have been any the wiser. Most of the time I think that people who enter their veg for produce shows are a little bit weird, verging on the obsessive-compulsive, but when I looked at my lovely spuds I could, for a brief moment, see what they were on about. By the time we left we also had some spinach which Mr T the kind Moroccan had given us.

Back home, after a brief debate on what needed cleaning and what didn't – yes to the salad and spring onions, no to the beetroot and potatoes, on the grounds that a bit of earth on them gave them that authentic allotment touch – our kitchen was transformed into a horticultural production facility as we trimmed the flowers and arranged them into bunches, and washed and bagged the salad. Each bag of salad had the addition of four or five nasturtium flowers, carefully positioned so that they would be facing up when the bag was placed on the display table at the fair: I am not sure where I got the idea for that, but I feel Sarah Raven would have been proud of me. Meanwhile Kitty and Orlando sat at the breakfast table eating their cereals, and thought we were mad.

In addition to all that fresh produce, there was also some rhubarb and ginger jam (the rhubarb came from Michael's allotment, so I think that counted), some green tomato chutney made with last year's end-of-season tomatoes, and a couple of other chutneys of rather more mixed provenance, including a plum and apple one which Eliza had made with the fruit from her parents' garden in Wiltshire, and which I suppose could be criticised on the grounds that it had run up rather more food miles than anything else we had. Perhaps if we thought of them as chutney miles they wouldn't sound so bad.

When we got to the playing field where the summer fair is held every year, we were met by Mrs Low's friend and fellow parent Sophie, who grows vegetables in her garden near Wormwood Scrubs and was sharing the stall with us. Having two sets of people on the stall could only be a good thing, one might have thought. More flowers and vegetables to make the stall look good, more money raised for the school, everyone pulling together, isn't everything lovely? And indeed everything was lovely; Sophie arrived with – amongst other things – a massive bag of chard, far bigger than ours, some proper blue cornflowers, just like normal people grow, and some pots of herbs with delightful hand-decorated labels. The cow. I looked at her lettuces, which were a little undersized and the only thing among her offerings which looked at all unimpressive, and said, 'They're not very big.' She glowered back, and started arranging her cornflowers on the table in front of ours.

The fair opened at noon, and by 12.22 we had sold the last of the beetroot. Sophie bought some (she had reluctantly decided to forgive me for the remark about her lettuces), the woman from the borough education committee bought some, someone else bought some, and then that was it. For a while I wanted to jump into the car and go back to the allotment to pull up some more – here was a heaven-sent opportunity to get rid of our entire beetroot crop, and I was about to let it slip between my fingers – but Eliza said that that would be madness, and that I was needed on the stall. I tried not to sulk, which was hard when a succession of people came up to ask if there was any beetroot left, and what a shame it was it had all sold out because they had been so look-ing forward to it.

In a sense I was glad I didn't go, though, because ten minutes later it started raining; a steady, insistent kind of rain, not exactly monsoon conditions but the sort of rain you know isn't going to go away. The head teacher put on her special big smiley voice and announced over the PA system, 'We're not going to let a drop of rain spoil anything,' an expression of optimism which was slightly undermined by the sight of a crowd of parents and teachers rushing headlong towards the big tent to take cover. Although I was not able to move from my post, our stall was protected by a small gazebo and I remained more or less dry. Just to make sure though I slipped over to the next-door stall and bought myself a bottle of beer, on the grounds that I might not be able to stay dry all day, but if I drank enough beer at least I wouldn't mind so much.

I stayed dry; the display did not. The pretty tablecloth which had made our stall quite the most charming in the whole fair quickly became a sodden mess, and the ink on all the jam and chutney labels ran so that they became totally illegible. 'What's this?' said a prospective customer, holding up a jar of some inde-terminate product or other. 'It's jam,' I said. 'Or possibly chutney. It's very nice.' The rain continued to fall, and one of the older teachers came over and announced gloomily: 'This is the worst I've known, ever – and I've been here twenty-two years.' I walked over to the drinks stall and bought another beer.

Despite the horrendous conditions – like Glastonbury, but without the music, or the drugs – the parents did a great job of rising to the occasion, buying everything they could and cheer-fully ignoring the outrageous prices we were charging ('Cos lettuce, £2 a go! We're practically giving it away!'). One dad saw our tastefully arranged basket of Kestrel potatoes, seven for £2 – I think that even Waitrose would baulk at that one – and said that he would just take four, but still pay the £2. 'I'm flush with cash,' he said. 'I've just sold a house.' I wish he had told me before; I would have charged him even more.

There was, however, one exception. A couple of women – possibly of Middle Eastern extraction – wandered over and started inspecting Mr T's spinach (which was, as it happens, in pretty good nick). 'What's that?' one of them said.

'Spinach,' I said, with my helpful shopkeeper's smile.

'No it's not.'

I was rather taken aback by this. 'Yes it is,' I said.

'No it's not.'

'Yes it is, I picked it this morning.' I wasn't going to tell them that it wasn't strictly speaking ours; in fact I think the fact that they were insulting Mr T's spinach and not mine made the whole situation even worse.

'Well, how much is it?'

'A pound a bunch,' I said, doing my best to make nice. 'It's lovely stuff.'

'That's too much. You should be giving it away!' And with that they walked off. I bought another beer.

A short while later the rain stopped, and normal service resumed at the fair; Kitty disappeared to play football with her mates, while Orlando exercised his ingenuity by thinking up ever more imaginative ways to persuade his parents to give him money for sweets and fizzy drinks. There was an auction, for which I gave Mrs Low the strict instructions that she was not to buy anything at all, on the grounds that everything going under the hammer was either going to be far too expensive, or was totally superfluous to our lives. For some reason the Paul Smith silk kimono – 'worth more than £1,000' according to William, the irrepressible auctioneer – has stuck in my mind. She didn't buy the kimono, for which I am grateful; she did buy a whole ham, which as I write is still taking up half the space in our freezer.

Then the fire brigade turned up. They are good sports, the local crew, and every year they bring a fire engine to the fair and allow all the children to clamber all over it, pressing every button and pulling every lever they can find. It is all good, clean noisy fun. Unfortunately the driver thought that it was a good idea to park the fire engine about fifteen yards from where I was standing. It took the kids about three minutes to discover how the horn worked – Honk! Honk! HONK! HONK-HONK-HONK! – and another four minutes to discover how the siren worked – Woo-ooo-ooo! Woo-ooo-ooo-ooo! When they were feeling particularly ambitious, they sounded the horn and the siren at the same time, which I am sure must have been great fun. I bought another beer, and started selling the remaining vegetables at heavily discounted prices, before I lost my reason.

By the time Eliza put me in the car, patting my head and saying 'There, there,' we had sold the lot: our produce, Sophie's, and a few pots of plants which had been provided by some bene-factor or other. We made £209.79 and 10 Greek drachma, which made me feel very proud indeed.

Meanwhile back on the allotment there was a giant pumpkin doing its best to make me feel proud, too. It obviously liked the manure bed I had made for it and was rampaging all over the plot with a manic energy that verged on the scary. Every time I looked it seemed to have grown another couple of feet, twining itself between the stalks of sweetcorn growing nearby and wrapping its tendrils round anything and everything it could find –

plants, stakes, netting, small children. A pumpkin appeared, and then another, at which point I started giving it pumpkin love Version 2, in the form of organic tomato feed. This is supposed to deliver truckloads of potassium to help the fruits swell, not to mention phosphorus and nitrogen, and although I do not know the precise chemical make-up of the organic tomato feed Eliza bought for the purpose I do know that it was so expensive it must have been the equivalent of trying to fatten up the pumpkin on lobster and foie gras. Do pumpkins have any notion of the concept of gratitude? Probably not, but here's hoping.

As the weeks went by the pumpkin – pumpkins, actually; I kept a spare in case of disaster and cut off any others as soon as they appeared – got fatter and fatter. First it was the size of a grapefruit, then a football, then a beachball, except flatter, as though it had been sat on by a small elephant. Every week I dutifully gave it its tomato feed – 'Would sir like a little phosphorus with his potassium?' – and every time I visited the allotment I watered it, to make sure its roots never dried out. I do not think I am being overly boastful when I say that I gave that pumpkin every possible advantage in life. But there eventually comes a moment when you have to let a pumpkin do what it has to do, and some time in late summer it was clear that the pumpkin had decided to stop growing. It was ripening all right, changing colour from primrose yellow to mustard yellow to a burnt sienna, but when it came to changing size there was nothing doing. It was out of my hands now; the time for pumpkin love was over, and it was all down to nature.

We weighed the pumpkin one sunny Saturday afternoon at the end of September, one of those balmy days when summer seems to be mounting a brave but doomed last stand against the encroachments of autumn. Eliza, Kitty, Orlando and I trooped off to the allotment and, with as much ceremony as we could muster, cut the pumpkin from its vine, washed it, dried it, and loaded it into the car boot to take to our friends Polly and Charlie, the only people we could think of who had a set of bathroom scales. 'My God, that is a monster,' said Charlie admiringly as he opened the front door; and yes, we knew it was big. But how big? Kitty and Orlando could only hold it up for a few seconds without dropping it; that seemed to be a good sign. On the other hand it did not look quite as big as the photographs I had seen on the Internet of Terry Walton's 32-pounder. With some nervousness we took it up to the bathroom and placed it on the scales. For several agonising seconds the digital read-out was blank as the scales made up their mind. Finally a verdict came: 2 1¾.

Er, 2 1¾? What the hell does that mean, Charlie?

It means, he said, 2 stone and 1¾ pounds. Twenty-nine and three-quarter pounds: or, to put it another way, not enough. Terry Walton had beaten us by 2¼ pounds. I should have been dejected, but I wasn't really, because like all good gardeners I had my excuses lined up already. I had sown the pumpkin late, and who knows what it could have done with three more weeks' growing time? Also, mine had the virtue of having been a teetotal pumpkin; none of that Welsh beer for us. Anyway, I think it was a pretty good effort for our first pumpkin, and there was always next year. 'It's four pounds bigger than the biggest salmon I ever caught,' said Charlie reassuringly, 'and I thought that was big.' I felt better after that.

In the dying days of summer Michael sidled up to us one morning: he had something to say. He was getting on a bit, he said, and didn't feel like he could manage two plots any more. Would we like to take over half of one of his plots? Eliza and I were momentarily stunned. Here was this man who, only yesterday it seemed, had been laughing at us for our overenthusiastic digging exploits, a man who over the months had become something of a father figure on the allotment for us, guide and mentor and friend; and now he was offering us half of one of his precious allotments. It felt like a moment heavy with significance, as though he was making an important bequest. We had started as clueless no-hopers, and had ended up – well, possibly still fairly clueless, but sound enough to be trusted with Michael's land.

It was crazy, of course. I had a full-time job, and when Eliza was not working she had her hands more than full with the demands of the children, the house, and the assorted committees she finds herself sitting on. We struggled to find enough time to look after the one plot we had already, without taking on even more land.

Naturally we said yes. There were all sorts of exciting crops we have never tried, such as peas – how could we call ourselves gardeners and not grow peas? – and winter radishes and turnips, not to mention weird and wonderful things like scorzonera and Italian *cima di rapa*. If we had more land perhaps we could grow some more sweetcorn and freeze it for the winter, like John does, or plant a decent-sized strawberry patch. We might even have room for some comfrey, which real hard-core gardeners rot down and use to make their own liquid plant feed. There were so many possibilities out there that I felt almost dizzy with anticipation, but they all boiled down to one thing: more land meant more fun, and the great allotment adventure could continue apace. Who knows, if I ran out of ideas I could even grow some more beetroot. I'm quite coming round to it these days.

Bibliography

Lindsey Bareham, *A Celebration of Soup* (Michael Joseph 1993)

Antonio Carluccio, *Antonio Carluccio's Vegetables* (Headline 2000)

Sam and Sam Clark, *Moro East* (Ebury Press 2007)

David Crouch and Colin Ward, *The Allotment* (Faber and Faber 1988; my edition Five Leaves Publications 1997)

Liz Dobbs, *The Gardening Which? Guide to Growing Your Own Vegetables* (Which? Books 2001)

Fergus Henderson, *Nose to Tail Eating* (Macmillan 1999)

Dr D. G. Hessayon, *The Vegetable & Herb Expert* (Expert 2001)

Dick Kitto, *Planning the Organic Vegetable Garden* (Thorsons 1986)

Joy Larkcom, *The Organic Salad Garden* (Frances Lincoln 2001)

Felicity Lawrence, *Not on the Label* (Penguin 2004)

Chris Opperman, *Allotment Folk* (New Holland 2004)

Anna Pavord, *The New Kitchen Garden* (Dorling Kindersley 1996)

Michael Pollock (ed.), Royal Horticultural Society, *Fruit and Vegetable Gardening* (Dorling Kindersley 2002)

Steve Poole, *The Allotment Chronicles* (Silver Link 2006)

Michael Rand, *Close to the Veg* (Marlin Press 2005)

Sarah Raven, *The Great Vegetable Plot* (BBC Books 2005)

The Gardening Year (Reader's Digest 1968)

Michael Wale, *View from a Shed* (Allison & Busby 2006)